Chesapeake Bay

Nature of the Estuary

A FIELD GUIDE

By Christopher P. White

With drawings by Karen Teramura

Tidewater Publishers : Centreville, Maryland

Library of Congress Cataloging-in-Publication Data

White, Christopher P.
        Chesapeake Bay.

        Bibliography: p.
        Includes index.
                1. Natural history—Chesapeake Bay Region (Md.
and Va.)—Handbooks, manuals, etc. 2. Chesapeake
Bay Region (Md. and Va.)—Description and travel.
I. Teramura, Karen. II. Title.
QH104.5.C45W47 1987   508.3163'47   86-40602
ISBN 0-87033-351-8

Manufactured in the United States of America
First edition, 1989; fifth printing, 1997

COURTNEY
MARKES
BAY ECOLOGY
Chesapeake Bay
REID 214

By Christopher P. White

Endangered and Threatened Wildlife
of the Chesapeake Bay Region
Chesapeake Bay: Nature of the Estuary,
A Field Guide

Contents

To Thomas Gary Hardie III,
fellow traveler and friend,
whose humanity and vision
embraced the ecological ethic,
sharing it selflessly from the very beginning

Introduction

THIS field guide is for the Bay watcher—the fisherman, canoeist, sailor, sportsman, naturalist, beachcomber, and student—for anyone who is interested in the life of the Bay and what makes it tick. The book is designed as a "user friendly" introduction to the natural history of the Chesapeake Bay. Scientific jargon is kept to a minimum. Illustrations and text are paired to present an easy-to-use primer on the estuarine system.

Students and residents of the Bay area should not keep this book on a shelf; it is meant for the field. The classroom is the Chesapeake Bay, for, in the words of Rachel Carson, "to understand the shore, it is not enough to catalogue its life." Understanding each species will require more than simply naming the creature. You must view its surroundings, its relative abundance, its predators, and its prey—in a word, its *niche* in the estuarine world. Through exploring various species and their communities, you will come to understand the Bay itself. To this end, the book takes an ecological approach to life above and below the Chesapeake's surface. Wetland and aquatic communities are emphasized.

How to Use This Book: Nature of the Estuary comprises two sections. The introductory section consists of four chapters that describe the machinery of the Bay: first, a definition of the nation's premier and most productive estuary; second, a geological history of the Chesapeake basin; next, the all-important salinity gradients, tides, and circulation of the brackish milieu; and, finally, the ecological relationships of the Bay's flora and fauna to each other and to the ecosystem at large. The second part is the field guide section, the bulk of the book. Each of nine chapters looks at the community profile of a major habitat zone within the Bay. These chapters provide a "snapshot" of the plant and animal species that are typical, or representative, of each habitat. The short introductions to each chapter will help you identify which habitat is close at hand. In most cases, the logical first step is to identify dominant plants. In each chapter, the species descriptions and illustrations appear in the standard ascending order: plants, invertebrates, fishes, amphibians and reptiles, birds, mammals. Characteristics most useful for field identification are highlighted.

Geographical Focus: The book concentrates on the coastal province of the Chesapeake watershed—the tidewater region below the *fall line*. Salinity ranges and habitat preferences within this region are given for most species. Though Bay organisms congregate in these definable zones, the Chesapeake is by no means a static place. The wetland-estuarine system is a dynamic environment where changes in tides and salinity may transform one habitat into another in a few hours or from season to season. At all times, Bay habitats form a continuum, one habitat gently flowing into the next. Many species, particularly fishes and birds, migrate between these habitats or occupy several sites. Seasonal migrations are also frequent, and, therefore, you will find summer, migrant, and wintering species (e.g., birds) identified within each chapter. A glossary (explaining italicized words) and diagrams of migratory patterns of fishes and the blue crab are included as appendices.

Common and Scientific Names: A basic knowledge of taxonomy and scientific nomenclature will be helpful. Each organism has a Latin (or scientific) name composed of two parts: the genus name, followed by the species name. When appropriate, family, order, class, or phylum are listed parenthetically. All common and scientific names are accepted terms within the scientific community. Specifically, terminology follows these authoritative sources: Department of Agriculture 1982 (plants), Lippson and Lippson 1984 (invertebrates), Robins et al. 1980 (fishes), Collins et al. 1982 (amphibians and reptiles), American Ornithologists' Union 1983 (birds), and Jones et al. 1982 (mammals). Please note that plants and invertebrates do not have "official" common names; herein, we follow local convention. A selected bibliography lists these references and many other useful publications. An index to the illustrated species concludes the volume.

Scope of This Guide: There are certain limitations to the "habitat approach," mainly compromises resulting from space considerations. To be comprehensive of all species would, unfortunately, require nine volumes, one for each community type. Geographically, the Bay region marks the northern or southern limits of hundreds of coastal species. As an introductory text, however, this primer will supplement the more comprehensive field guides on your shelf that cover broader regions and supply background on anatomy and taxonomy. Always carry an authoritative field guide to North American birds in your daypack to be confident of positive identification of migratory species. Also remember that a species at hand may be a less common resident or visitor to the estuary, not included in this guide. In particular, invertebrates are discussed in only a cursory manner. The reader is referred to Lippson and Lippson for more thorough accounts of Chesapeake invertebrates and their many adaptations to life in the estuary—subjects and details that are outside the scope of this book.

As an introduction to the mechanics and wildlife of the estuary, however, this field guide may also function as a baseline inventory of the species common and abundant today—in the late 1980s. What was here 300 years ago—in the 1680s—is another story. And, if the present destruction of wetlands and deterioration of water quality continue, the species lineup for 2090 will require a book perhaps half this size. To be certain, the Chesapeake is in trouble. Watch your favorite marshes and creeks. In the years ahead, you—the Bay watcher—will become an important monitor of the estuarine environment.

Acknowledgments: A book of this type is built upon the work of hundreds of taxonomists, biologists, and ecologists who have spent a lifetime devoted to the study of plants and animals. To these unnamed pioneers I owe tremendous thanks. My appreciation also extends to the many individuals who reviewed species lists, text, and drawings over the past five years. For this help I am especially grateful to the following: Irvin Ailes, Chincoteague National Wildlife Refuge (NWR); Dan Boone and Arnold W. Norden, Maryland Natural Heritage Program; Mitchell A. Byrd, College of William and Mary; Virginia P. Carter and Nancy A. Rybicki, U.S. Geological Survey; Harold M. Cassell, Maryland Department of Natural Resources (DNR); Eugenie Clark, Bryan Dutton, James Reveal, Eugene B. Small, Cindy Smith, and Edward Terrell, University of Maryland College Park; L. Eugene Cronin; Steve Croy, Virginia Natural Heritage Program; Richard J. Dolesh, Maryland-National Capital Park and Planning Commission; George A. Feldhamer, Southern Illinois University; Carter R. Gilbert, Florida State Museum; Steve Goodbred, Sr., U.S. Fish and Wildlife Service (USFWS); Steve Goodbred, Jr.; John D. Groves, Philadelphia Zoological Society; William J. Hargis, Jr., John A. Musick, Gene M. Silberhorn, Willard A. Van Engel, and John A. Keinath, Virginia Institute of Marine Science; Robert E. Jenkins, Roanoke College; Stanley A. Kollar, Harford Community College; George Krantz, Cooperative Biological Laboratory, DNR and National Marine Fisheries Service, Oxford, Maryland; Norman E. Larsen, Virginia Marine Resources Commission; Joseph Mitchell, University of Richmond; Chandler S. Robbins and Daniel Bystrak, Patuxent Wildlife Research Center, USFWS; Robert K. Rose, Old Dominion University; Frederick R. Scott, Virginia Society of Ornithology; William S. Sipple, U.S. Environmental Protection Agency; J. Court Stevenson, Roger Newell, and Don Meritt, Center for Environmental and Estuarine Studies (CEES), University of Maryland, Horn Point; Elgin Dunnington and Martin L. Wiley, Chesapeake Biological Laboratory, University of Maryland, Solomons Island; Guy Willey, Blackwater NWR; Dwight Williams, Battle Creek Cypress Swamp Sanctuary; James D. Williams, National Fisheries Research Laboratory, USFWS; John Page Williams, Chesapeake Bay Foundation; and George R. Zug, Bruce Beehler, and Thomas E. Bowman, National Museum of Natural History (NMNH), Smithsonian Institution. Responsibility for any errors, however, lies solely with the author.

Karen Teramura and I would also like to thank those who helped locate specimens in the field or in museums. In particular, we acknowledge: Hollis G. Bedell, former curator of the Herbarium, University of Maryland College Park; Dave Bohaska, Calvert Marine Museum; Don Clark, Patuxent Wildlife Research Center; Roger Cressey and Marilyn Schotte, Division of Crustacea, NMNH; Richard Efrim, Naturalists' Center, NMNH; Joseph and Ilia Fehrer, Nassawango Creek Sanctuary; Janet Goman, Susan Jewett, and Edward O. Murdy, Division of Fishes, NMNH; Frank Groves, Baltimore Zoological Society; Harry G. Jones, West Chester University of Pennsylvania; Greg Lewis and Greg Kearns, Patuxent River Park; Heather Nicklas, Blackwater NWR; Harold C. Olson and Cathy Freeburger, Eastern Neck NWR; George Russel, curator of the Herbarium, NMNH; Kim Shank, Chincoteague NWR; Donna Stotts and Lorie Winchell, CEES, Horn Point; and Terry Thompson, Marine Science Consortium, Wallops Island, Virginia.

Finally, we thank Rose Broome, Chris Cusimano, Lenny Cusimano, Dorothy P. Dillon, Peggy Duke, Donna Grosvenor, Leksei Grosvenor, Lisa Kaufman, Terry Olenick, Brigid Robbins, and Alan H. Teramura for their help and encouragement.

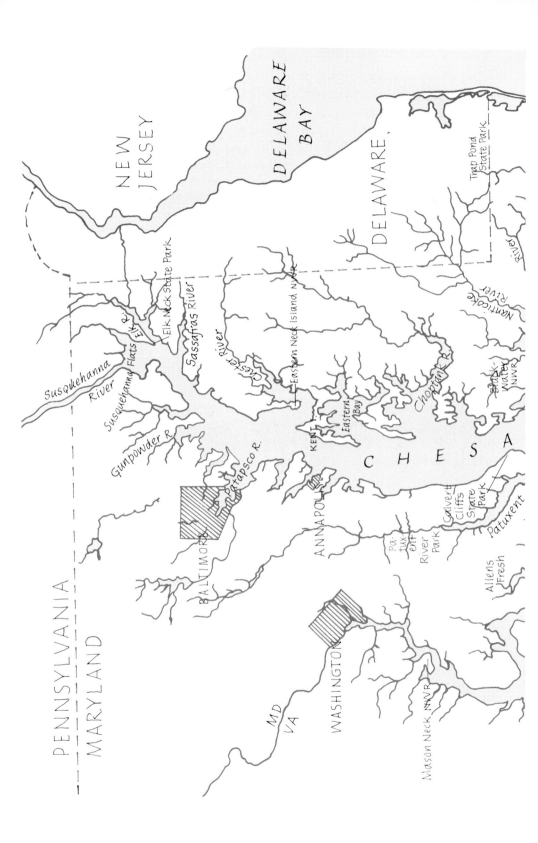

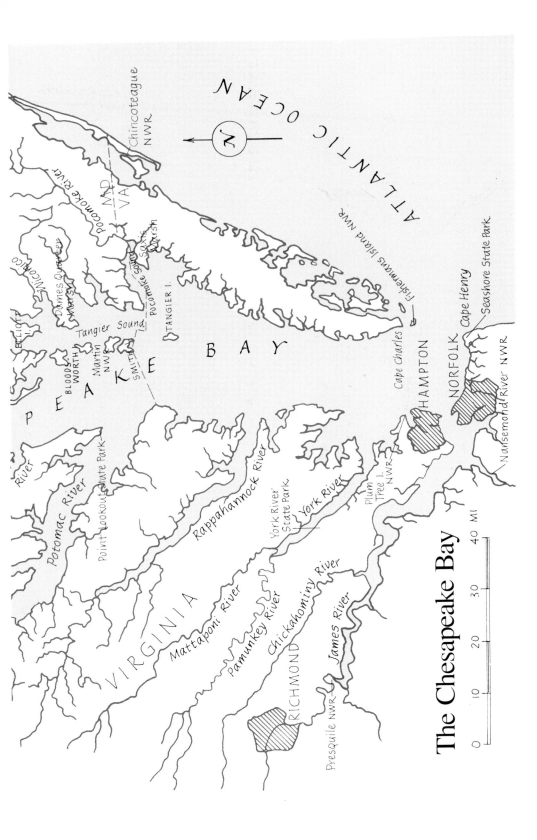

The Chesapeake Bay

Chesapeake Bay

The Nature of the Estuary

*The country is not mountainous nor yet low but such
pleasant plain hills and fertile valleys . . . rivers and brooks,
all running most pleasantly into a fair Bay. Of fish we were
best acquainted with herrings, rockfish, shad, crabs, oysters
. . . and mussels. In summer no place affordeth more plenty
of sturgeon, nor in winter more abundance of fowl.*

—Captain John Smith (1612)
A Description of Virginia

MANY years before John Smith rounded Cape Henry the Algonquin Indians named it "Chesepiooc" for "great shellfish bay." In hindsight, that was an understatement. Ever since the mapping of the continent by geographers, the Bay has been described with superlatives. It is the largest bay in the United States (2,500 square miles) and the longest (195 miles). It has the greatest number of tributaries (150) and more miles of shoreline (4,000 miles) than the entire West Coast.

Our Bay is also the most productive. During 1986 the Chesapeake harvest represented 20 percent of the oysters and over 50 percent of the blue crabs and soft-shelled clams caught in the entire United States. More than 200 million pounds of seafood are gleaned from its waters annually with a dockside value exceeding $100 million. No other coastal fishery rivals the Bay's harvest. In fact, only the Atlantic and Pacific oceans surpass the Chesapeake in U.S. seafood production each year.

H. L. Mencken once called the Chesapeake an "immense protein factory." Yet, it is not simply the size of the basin that makes its bounty great. Many other coastal regions (e.g., the Gulf Coast, the New England states, and Alaska) outrank the Bay in size. So what makes the Chesapeake so special? Why does this brackish basin outproduce other coastal regions?

An explanation of the Bay's remarkable productivity can be found in the chemistry and mechanics of the Atlantic Coast estuary. An *estuary* is a semi-enclosed coastal body of water that has a measurable *salinity gradient* from its freshwater drainage to its ocean entrance. Most estuaries are characterized by daily tides, seasonally variable flow and salinity, and a two-layer circulation pattern: a salty deepwater layer that flows landward and a fresher surface layer travelling seaward that produces a net flow downstream. Typically, mixing is promoted between the two layers by the action of wind, friction, and tides. These are minimum criteria. More than 850 such basins are found in the United States alone.

The Chesapeake qualifies as an estuary, as do Delaware Bay to the north and Pamlico Sound to the south. So do Cook Inlet in Alaska and Puget Sound, the port of Seattle. Thousands of estuaries are located worldwide. Most spectacular perhaps are Trondheimsfjord and Oslofjord in Norway, their steep granite walls and deep blue water echoing back to the last ice age. In Nova Scotia, the ice-carved Minas Basin off the Bay of Fundy is known for its record tides. Even along the Newfoundland coast, estuarine systems as rugged and splendid as the Gray River wander through majestic, 1,200-foot valleys where the northern ice sheet once roamed.

The beauty of the Chesapeake is more subtle. Its shores are modest, its tides reserved. Its history is bound in sand and clay and water, not granite and ice. In its moderation is found the key to its teeming productivity.

Differing from the glacier-cut fjords of Norway, Canada, and the Pacific Northwest, mid-Atlantic estuaries like the Chesapeake are less dramatic, more finely sloped, and shallower. This very shallowness allows sunlight to nurture rooted aquatic plants. The gentle slopes give marshlands a foothold along the shore. In turn, this plant life provides oxygen, detritus, and habitat for aquatic species. Lacking these wetland communities, rock-lined fjords are less productive. Many, due to their depth and poor circulation, are stagnant. For this reason, Canadian and Norwegian fishermen are observed more often on offshore banks than close to home like watermen on the Chesapeake Bay.

On the east coast of North America healthier estuaries, in general, have an open aperture to the sea. Tidal flushing is therefore more vigorous, and this promotes circulation of oxygen and nutrients within the brackish basin. A model estuary must also receive an influx of fresh water from one or several rivers, instead of simple rainwater runoff or contributions from intermittent streams. These rivers provide another source of *detritus*, dissolved gases, and nutrients, as well as an input of minerals, each important to plant growth and the dual food chain intrinsic to estuaries. Also, high river flow drives estuarine circulation—yielding a net discharge towards the ocean. Some coastal lagoons, such as Choctawhatchee Bay on the Florida Gulf Coast, lack either strong freshwater inflow or a wide ocean entrance and, therefore, are saltier, less productive, and more prone to overenrichment.

Along the Atlantic seaboard the rich networks of healthy estuaries share these assets in common: a number of freshwater tributaries, shallowness, low-lying wetlands, and a wide portal to the sea. Such protein factories play with an advantage. Abundant raw materials (oxygen, minerals, nutrients), energy (sunlight), and machinery (good circulation) are rarely in short supply. As the largest member of this coastal plain conglomerate, the Bay also earns superlatives as the most productive. Historically, the Chesapeake has been the *greatest* shell- and finfish bay in North America. Second to none.

A Stressful Environment

Ironically, the Bay's 21-foot (on average) depth—the trademark of its productivity—is a double-edged sword. While the shallow cut of the basin enhances aquatic growth, it exposes the entire estuary to the vacillations of temperature and wind. As a result, Chesapeake waters are colder in winter and warmer in summer than the adjacent open ocean and subject to the major influences of wind.

Not only temperature fluctuates within the Bay. A salinity gradient traverses the estuary—like a ladder spanning two worlds from marine to fresh. This span serves as a transition zone where both freshwater and marine species test their limits during their efforts to spawn or feed in the Bay's prodigious nursery. Many can traverse the estuary just so far. Indeed, throughout the earth's history, the estuarine zone has been a barrier, a no-man's-land of sorts. Estuaries have comparatively few residents, mostly visitors, and these appear only at certain times of the year.

Oscillations in temperature and salinity are only two of many reasons for this lack of hospitality. The estuary is characterized by a highly variable set of physical and chemical parameters (see chapters 3 and 4). These fluctuating conditions result in an unstable environment for most organisms, particularly visiting freshwater and marine animals and plants. For most species—even estuarine species—the Bay is a stressful place.

Fortunately, most of these perturbations coincide with the seasons. Accordingly, various organisms take advantage of the Bay's nutrients and temporary bounty during specific months of the year. One finds more than 265 fish species utilizing the estuary for food and reproduction in summer, while only 29 resident species (and a few visitors) endure the winter months. Across the board, one finds relatively few species of plants and animals that can persist in this rigorous environment, but those that can survive usually flourish here in greater abundance than anywhere else on earth.

Estuarine Productivity

The Bay is not only the standard-bearer for the estuarine community but also for coastal systems at large. Bay organisms either tolerant of the salinity range, such as the grass shrimp and blue crab, or adapted to a specific salinity zone, such as the soft-shelled clam, some killifishes, and certain copepods and polychaete worms, grow and multiply in enormous numbers in the Chesapeake, creating more biomass, acre for acre, than found in coastal waters or the open Atlantic.

In turn, these relatively few, prolific species are dependent on the plant community for food. More than anything else their abundance is tied to the organic yield of plant species within the basin. In every ecosystem, the plant kingdom and its crop make up the base of a food pyramid. The larger this base the greater the number of consumers (i.e., animals) that can be supported, or, in the case of the seafood industry, cultured and harvested for market. It is here—within the estuary—that basic plant, or primary, productivity reaches grand proportions (see fig. 1).

Each of the Bay's many plant communities (fresh, brackish, and saltwater wetlands; phytoplankton; benthic algae; epiphytic algae; and submersed aquatic vegetation [SAV]) is a powerhouse of photosynthetic activity. Salt marshes alone may produce nearly 10 tons of organic matter per acre each year. (By comparison, the average yield of domestic wheat, including stems and leaves, is only 1.5 tons per acre per year.) Most of this tonnage is devoured by wetland bacteria and higher animals, but nearly half of the crop is flushed by tidal action into shallow waters surrounding the marsh. Much of this detritus is consumed by aquatic organisms, and some is reclaimed by the marsh on the next turn of the tide. The high productivity of salt marshes and other Bay communities is promoted by the enormous quantities of nutrients flowing into the basin from land, riverine, wetland, and tidal sources.

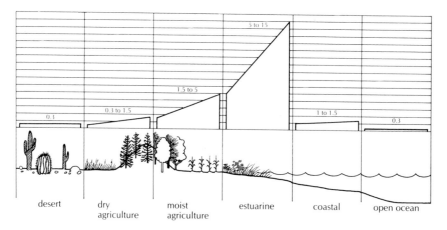

Figure 1. A comparison of primary productivity for representative ecosystems. Productivity in tons carbon/acre/year (adapted from Teal and Teal 1969).

It is important to remember that the deep, open ocean has just one plant community (phytoplankton), while estuaries have several, and offshore coastal areas have at least two if they are shallow enough to support benthic algae. These two plant communities also contribute significant caches to the Bay's organic supply. In fact, the estuary outproduces marine ecosystems on every front. To give just one example, the abundance of nutrients in the estuary readily enhances phytoplankton growth, which may yield up to 1.5 tons of organic matter per acre per year (125 to 295 gC [grams carbon]/m^2/yr). This phytoplankton yield is substantially greater than that of the nutrient-poor open ocean, which averages less than 0.25 tons per acre per year (50 gC/m^2/yr)—that is, one-sixth the level of an estuary.

Even when lacking bottom-dwelling plants, coastal regions are usually more productive than the open ocean since nutrient levels are moderately high on the inner continental shelf. One might say coastal waters are the breadbasket of the Atlantic, as productive as well-irrigated wheat. By comparison, the deep ocean is a desert, while inshore estuaries, supported by fertile soils and water and a variety of plant communities, are even richer—as rich as tropical forests.

Nursery Grounds

Lured by this oasis of plant growth at the edge of the sea, most commercial fish species along the Atlantic Coast utilize estuaries as juvenile feeding grounds. Here, when conditions are optimal, they find few competitors and plenty of food in the form of phytoplankton, marsh detritus, and invertebrates.

Hundreds of fish species use the Chesapeake in a variety of ways. Anadromous species such as herring and shad leave the ocean each spring and, traversing the estuary, swim up freshwater rivers to spawn. Afterwards, they return to the sea while their offspring mature and feed in the Bay. Semi-anadromous species such as striped bass spawn in brackish water along tributaries and the upper Bay. Meanwhile, estuarine species like white perch live out their entire life cycles within the basin. Others—marine species such as croaker and menhaden—spawn in the Atlantic, but their larvae are carried into the estuary by deepwater currents and there they mature into juveniles and adults. Attracted by these nursery stocks, adult bluefish and other marine carnivores enter the estuary to feed (see "Migratory Patterns and Life Cycles," pp. 201-203).

For the most part, the Bay's nursery grounds are found in the moderately brackish (i.e., low mesohaline) reaches of major tributaries and the Bay proper. These are the murky areas where fresh and salt water meet and where detritus, nutrients, and phytoplankton are at a maximum. Within this zone, submersed aquatic vegetation may serve as protective shelter for vulnerable fish stocks.

Wetlands and Wildlife

Surrounding the Chesapeake Bay (and integral to the estuarine system) are 498,000 acres of emergent wetlands. These range from shrub swamps and cattail marshes along secluded streams to the open salt marshes of the lower Bay. Acting like enormous sponges, they enhance water quality and provide hydrological benefits such as flood control and groundwater recharge. Wetlands are nature's purifiers. More than that, they are reservoirs of productivity and furnish valuable habitat for crustaceans, fishes, reptiles, birds, and mammals.

Most visible in both fresh and brackish marshes are the flocks of nesting birds that use the Bay's vast wetlands for shelter and food. In addition, Chesapeake wetlands supply a major stopover for migratory waterfowl along the Atlantic flyway. More than 500,000 Canada geese, 40,000 tundra swans, and 250,000 ducks (25 species) make the Chesapeake their winter home.

The diversity of wetland communities is an important feature of the estuary. Imagine canoeing down a Chesapeake river from its source to its mouth, first passing by stands of wild rice, then bulrush, finally cordgrass, and out into open water. Marsh ducks, bay ducks, and sea ducks each choose specific habitats along this estuarine gradient. So do fishes and aquatic reptiles and mammals. Like the plants and invertebrates they consume, each resident, each visitor, prefers its own piece of the Bay.

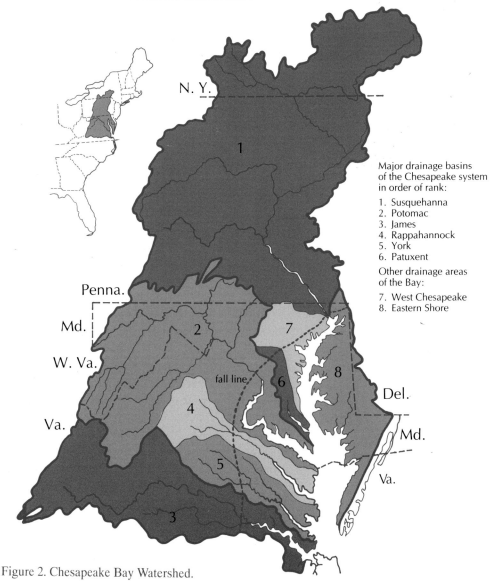

Major drainage basins of the Chesapeake system in order of rank:

1. Susquehanna
2. Potomac
3. James
4. Rappahannock
5. York
6. Patuxent

Other drainage areas of the Bay:

7. West Chesapeake
8. Eastern Shore

Figure 2. Chesapeake Bay Watershed.

PHYSICAL CHARACTERISTICS OF THE CHESAPEAKE BAY

Length	195 miles	Surface Area	
Width	4 to 30 miles	Bay proper	2,500 sq. miles
Average Depth	21 ft (6.4 m)	Bay and tributaries	4,400 sq. miles
Greatest Depth	174 ft (53 m)	Shoreline	
Drainage Area	64,000 sq. miles	Bay proper	4,000 miles
Wetlands	498,000 acres	Bay and tributaries	8,100 miles

Adapted from EPA 1982.

Geological History and Sediments

*Today ship captains running to Baltimore know the old
river well; it is the route of seagoing commerce.*

—William W. Warner
Beautiful Swimmers

THE origin of the estuary dates back 20,000 years to the last ice age, near the end of
the Pleistocene, when a colder climate ruled the earth. At that time, sea level was 325 feet
(100 m) lower than it is today. Mammoths roamed the exposed continental shelf. For the
previous 100,000 years, the Atlantic had steadily retreated into its main oceanic basin as
if someone had pulled a plug. But the water had not disappeared; it was simply locked up
in ice. Temperatures on the average were 20°F colder than today, still warm enough to
excite massive evaporation from the sea, but—in northern latitudes—the water rarely fell
as rain. Year by year, over those 100 millennia, the North American ice sheet had grown
and thickened with new-fallen snow. On warmer days some of the water returned to the
sea, but more often the snow remained frozen, adding weight and measure to the ice below.
The mile-thick glacial sheet stretched from the Arctic Circle across the Canadian Shield
into New York, stopping in Pennsylvania, just short of the present site of the Bay.

The tongue of this enormous glacier fed the headwaters of the Susquehanna—mother
river of the Chesapeake—with glacial melt. For centuries this "upstart" river had carved a
deep valley through Pennsylvania, Maryland, and Virginia, as well as 100 miles across the
dry, flat, continental shelf. Then, 18,000 years ago, the ice sheet began to melt. The climate
grew warmer: The end of the long Pleistocene winter was at last in sight. Now, the
Susquehanna raged. Centuries melted away as the torrential river flowed south, south past
the old Patapsco, south past Calvert Cliffs and the Patuxent towards her surging, deafening convergence with the Potomac, the Rappahannock, the York. From there with doubled
force she spilled toward the remote Atlantic with a power surpassing the Mississippi of
today.

The Atlantic overflowed. The long-dormant ocean crawled out of its basin, then
marched across the continental shelf at a rate of 50 feet per year. The river mouth retreated,
and its racing freshwater current flowed over the advancing salt-laden water, turning the
continental shelf into a brackish sea.

Around 10,000 years ago, the brackish waters reached the longitude of Virginia
Beach, Ocean City, and the current mouth of the Bay. At that moment the old river made
its last unimpeded journey to the Virginia Capes. For the last time in recent history the
Susquehanna held dominion over its streambed. But the Atlantic kept coming, flooding the
valley, backing up the river like a tidal dam. About 7,500 years ago the Bay front reached
the mouth of the Potomac—the Maryland-Virginia state line. In another 2,500 years the
expanding Bay passed Annapolis and the current site of the Bay Bridge. Within 2 more

millenia, that is, 3,000 years ago, the Bay head reached its present location. Then the rising sea essentially stopped. Temporary equilibrium was reached. The Bay as we know it was born.

Life and Death of the Estuary

Along the Atlantic Coast all bays, including the mouths of the Delaware, Hudson, and Narragansett, have shared a similar history. During the glacial retreat that marked the end of the Pleistocene epoch the rising sea level invaded these young coastal valleys so recently carved by water. As a result, the topography of the East Coast changed dramatically. One very large inland lake disappeared altogether; it became Long Island Sound. And the ancient Susquehanna, as we have seen, lost more than a third of its length to the encroaching sea.

The Chesapeake and most other coastal plain estuaries are thus termed *drowned river valleys*. Nevertheless, estuaries can be formed in at least three other ways. Just south of the Bay one finds an example of the *coastal embayment* or *lagoon*. Pamlico Sound, which occupies nearly half of the North Carolina coast, is located behind a series of barrier beaches, collectively known as the Outer Banks. These dune-covered sandbars have built up parallel to the coastline, cutting off Pamlico Sound from the sea. Incoming tides and runoff from the land keep the lagoon brackish, and, when this mix is expelled via one of several barrier beach inlets, one finds riptides—a dangerous hazard to swimmers. Similar embayments are found behind Ocean City, Maryland, and Assateague and along the Florida and Texas Gulf coasts.

At high latitudes, for example in Newfoundland, Alaska, and Norway in the northern hemisphere and Chile and New Zealand in the southern, glaciers (rather than meltwater) have carved coastal valleys, allowing invasion by the rising sea. These estuaries, known as *fjords,* are often impressive, but their deep waters prevent the growth of rooted aquatics, while marshes, too, are usually absent, having no purchase along the steep rock walls. Fjords may also suffer from oxygen depletion since good circulation is often thwarted by the glacial debris that typically obstructs each entrance.

The fourth type of estuary is a mirror image of the other three. Instead of the ocean rising to flood a valley or lagoon, in a *tectonic estuary* the land subsides to a point below the sea. Violent earthquakes and the shifting of continental plates have caused such sinking in areas of high seismic activity. An excellent example is San Francisco Bay.

Whatever the class of estuary, some mixing of fresh and salt water always exists. Another characteristic they share is their ephemeral nature. Geologically speaking, estuaries are short-lived.

A 30-foot (10 m) drop in sea level would make dry land of more than 75 percent of the Chesapeake Bay. Such a recession (i.e., another ice age) is possible in the near (or, rather, geologically near) future, unless the climate is altered by man.* At present, we are in the midst of the Holocene Interglacial, a period to date lasting nearly 20,000 years. An

---

*The excessive burning of fossil fuels may release abnormal levels of carbon dioxide into the atmosphere, thus causing a warming trend, popularly known as the "greenhouse effect."

interglacial period is a temporary time-out. The last several million years have seen alternating glacial and interglacial episodes as the world's ice budget has fluctuated, along with the level of the seas. Interglacials are usually brief, on average lasting 10,000 years. Glacial maximums last for, well, an ice age. The most recent one chilled the earth for 100,000 years.

The ebb and flow of the seas is continual. The Susquehanna will someday regain the valley only to lose it again to another estuary. Thus while "our" Chesapeake Bay is doomed to perish, it has the promise of rebirth. Ancestral bays have filled its basin and future Chesapeakes may reign in the valley as well. Only the timing is inexact in this perpetual tug-of-war between river and sea.

Erosion and Sedimentation

In the rivers and tributaries of the Atlantic Coast a natural pattern of erosion and deposition takes place. Chesapeake rivers and their feeder streams carry silt from the Appalachian and Piedmont provinces into the coastal plain where the rivers lose their speed and drop their sediment load. Consequently, in the Chesapeake system, as in most estuaries, deposition exceeds erosion; there is a net accumulation of silt.

The transitory nature of the estuary is enhanced by this condition. Huge quantities of mud and other sediments settle onto the floor of the Bay and at the mouths of major tributaries. Sandbars and mud flats can be seen at river junctions where deltalike alluvial plains are exposed at low tide. Often, these deposits are colonized by marsh grasses, thus beginning a succession of events that return the estuary to the land. The rapidity with which sediments can fill an estuary can be striking. Stone mooring posts are visible at Joppatown, Maryland, where a prosperous seaport operated in colonial times. Today, the town is more than 2 miles from navigable water. Deforestation and agricultural expansion are responsible for such accelerated siltation in the last 350 years.

In the upper Bay, the suspended sediments discharged by rivers are mostly fine-grained silts and light clays that remain suspended and can travel long distances. Tidal currents continually resuspend these particles, which finally drop into "sediment traps" such as Baltimore Harbor. Within the main section of the Bay, the cohesive particles accumulate (often after passing through the digestive tracts of zooplankton) as a combined clay-silt mud in the ancient river bed of the Susquehanna. This channel mud becomes progressively coarser—due to inputs of sand and gravel—as one proceeds south. Some of these coarse deposits result from shore erosion of the Bay proper, and, due to their weight, settle quickly to the bottom. Only a small amount ever reaches the ocean, as the ancient riverbed steadily fills in with silt. Surprisingly, ocean currents actually transport additional coarse sediments into the Bay. These various sources of sedimentation—along with an inevitable climate change—assure that the Chesapeake will someday disappear.

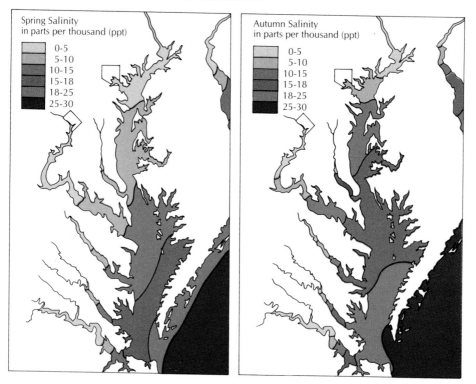

Figure 3. *Isohalines*, or salinity contours, on the maps above mark the salt content of waters at the surface of the Bay. The *salinity gradient* varies with freshwater inflow: fresher during spring rains, saltier during the drier months of autumn (adapted from EPA 1982).

SALINITY ZONES

ECOSYSTEM	ZONE [1]	VENICE SYSTEM [2]	SALINITY [3]
Riverine	Nontidal freshwater	Fresh	0 ppt
Estuarine			
Tidal limit	Tidal freshwater	Fresh	0-0.5 ppt
Upper Bay and upper tidal rivers	Low brackish (slightly brackish)	Oligohaline	0.5-5 ppt
Mid-Bay and lower tidal rivers	Brackish (moderately brackish)	Mesohaline[4]	5-18 ppt
Lower Bay	High brackish (highly brackish)	Polyhaline	18-30 ppt
Marine	Marine	Euhaline	above 30 ppt

[1] Terminology as used in this field guide.
[2] After Cowardin *et al.* 1979.
[3] Salinity expressed in parts per thousand (ppt).
[4] Lower mesohaline: 5 to 10 ppt; upper mesohaline: 10 to 18 ppt.

Salinity, Tides, and Circulation

Plucked up and kneaded by the sun and the moon, the
tides are systole and diastole of earth's veins.

—Henry Beston
The Outermost House

WATER is the lifeblood of the Bay. Within this liquid medium are carried *organic* (i.e., carbon-containing) and inorganic (e.g., mineral) compounds, dissolved gases, and nutrients—the building blocks of plants and higher life. This nurturing fluid also supports myriad planktonic forms, including the egg and larval stages of fishes, crustacea, molluscs, and worms (termed *meroplankton*). As if weightless, this meroplankton as well as jellyfish and thousands of minute phyto- and zooplankton species are transported effortlessly from point to point. The circulatory system in which these estuarine components float is governed by a dynamic interaction of freshwater input, the salinity structure, and tidal flow. Each parameter is highly variable and this variability leads to an unstable environment for estuarine organisms and visiting species. A familiarity with these fluctuating conditions is an important step in understanding the nature of the estuary itself.

Freshwater Input

The Chesapeake Bay holds some 18 trillion gallons of water. If the entire tidal system were drained and the ocean blocked off, more than a year would pass before all the rivers, streams, and annual storm runoff could fill the basin. On average, 70,000 cubic feet (2,000 cubic meters) of water flow into the Bay each second from all its tributary sources. In view of the size of the estuary (68 billion cubic meters) this seems small, and, in fact, this freshwater input is barely one-ninth the volume of seawater flowing into the Bay at any instant.

One might expect, therefore, that the freshwater flow, though obviously diluting the salt water somewhat, would have a negligible influence on the estuary since it is "outvoted" 9 to 1. For several reasons, this is not the case.

Storm pulses can send a surge of rainwater into the Bay like a transfusion of fresh blood. The ratio of fresh to salt water can thus change dramatically, and the net outflow to the ocean can also increase. In oceanographic terms, the extent to which floodwaters can alter the salinity structure of an estuary is determined by the size of its watershed relative to the volume of the brackish basin. In this, the Bay excels. The Chesapeake watershed spans 64,000 square miles stretching like a capillary network into the far reaches of 6 surrounding states (see fig. 2). Rainfall in Pennsylvania, even a snowstorm in southern New York, is sooner or later felt in the Chesapeake Bay. The volume of the Susquehanna River, which contributes around 50 percent of the Bay's freshwater drainage, can vary 15-fold during the course of a year.

A second reason the freshwater tributaries play an influential role is that some carry more weight than others. Out of the 150 rivers, creeks, and streams draining the watershed, only 46 are considered major tributaries and 8 of these provide 90 percent of the freshwater inflow. Six of these river systems (the Potomac, James, Rappahannock, York, Patuxent, and West Chesapeake Drainage) are located on the western side of the Bay. The primary freshwater source, the Susquehanna, of course, flows from the north, while the lone Choptank drains only part of the Eastern Shore. As far as fresh water is concerned, the Chesapeake is right-handed and top-heavy: These eight major tributaries (and the ocean) shape the circulation and salinity character of the Bay.

Salinity

The dominant feature of the estuary is its salinity regime. From the headwaters of the Susquehanna (and every other tributary) to the mouth of the Bay, the salinity varies from near absolute zero to almost marine.

Salinity is defined as the number of grams of dissolved salts in 1,000 grams of water. This concentration, though defined in grams, is usually expressed in *parts per thousand* (ppt). Thus, seawater, which averages 35 grams of dissolved salts per kilogram of water, is said to have a salinity of 35 ppt. In the upper reaches of tributaries, fresh water contains few salts (usually less than 0.5 ppt) while the highly brackish water at the Bay's mouth usually exceeds 25 ppt.

Since the presence of dissolved salts increases the density of water, fresh water exiting from rivers is lighter than salt water inbound from the Atlantic. In the estuary, this buoyancy difference retards immediate mixing between river discharge and saltwater influx since they occupy different layers. Consequently, at most points along the Bay, especially at its southern end, salinity at the surface is less than salinity at depth. This vertical structure, nevertheless, does not alter the basic surface salinity pattern found from the head of the Bay to its mouth or along any of the major tributaries. Salinity increases seaward as mixing slowly takes place.

This *salinity gradient* is basic to the estuary but varies in amplitude—especially over time—because of influence upon it by celestial forces: the sun, the moon, and the rotation of the earth. The sun's influence depends on the path and tilt of the earth about its star. In our temperate climate the most dramatic and noticeable effect of this orbit is the change in seasons. This seasonality, in turn, causes remarkable shifts in salinity (see fig. 3).

During the spring, rainfall and melting snow from Cooperstown, New York, to Richmond, Virginia, cause a freshwater pulse through the estuary, circulating huge quantities of fresh water down every tributary toward the main stem. The Bay itself flushes more rapidly, and salinity declines by 5 ppt or more along each stretch of the Bay. With each season, the salinity contours (or *isohalines*) shift, reflecting the variable freshwater input to the Bay. In April, the water beneath the Bay Bridge extending from Annapolis to Kent Island may be 7 ppt salinity thanks to rainfall; by October, it is nearly 13 ppt, after the lower rainfall of summer.

The salinity map also reveals the consequences of another driving mechanism for the salinity gradient—the *Coriolis force*. Due to the rotation of the earth, flowing water is deflected to the right in the northern hemisphere. Thus, in the Chesapeake Bay fresh water flowing down the estuary moves toward the western shore while salt water moving up the estuary is pulled toward the Eastern Shore. The considerable freshwater input of the Potomac and other western shore rivers tends to magnify the displacement below the Maryland-Virginia state line. In fact, the combined power of the western rivers and the Coriolis force causes a counterclockwise motion in the lower Bay. At the mouth more of the incoming salt water enters the Bay along Cape Charles to the northeast while more fresh water escapes along Cape Henry to the south.

Tides

The rotation of the earth and its yearly, seasonal orbit about the sun thus help to drive the circulation of the Bay. Meanwhile, the tides follow a timetable governed by the phases of the moon.

Tidal movement is a consequence of the gravitational attraction between the earth, its lunar satellite, and the sun. The close proximity of the moon makes it the prime mover of the seas, while the sun plays a subsidiary, though still important, role. In theory, tidal dynamics are simple, but in practice—especially in semi-enclosed basins such as estuaries—tidal forces can be complex. First, it is best to examine the simplest case: the intertidal zone of an Atlantic beach adjacent to the open sea.

On the coast, the cycle of tidal ebb and flow occurs twice each day. Why? One would expect a *high tide* when the moon is overhead, and this is so. But a second high tide occurs when the moon is nowhere in sight. A simple explanation is apparent to anyone who has been on a ferris wheel or merry-go-round, and felt an outward tug. The gravitational attraction between the moon and the earth (and its oceans) is balanced by an outward centrifugal force that results from the rotation of these two spheres about the earth-moon center of mass. For this reason, a second high tide is found when the moon is on the opposite side of the earth. In other words, a bulge of water rises toward the moon and away from the moon at any given instant. One high is caused by the moon's attraction, the other by centrifugal force. A simultaneous *low tide* is found at right angles to the earth-moon axis. Since the moon passes over the coast every 24 hours and 50 minutes, there are two high and two low tides observed each day. The sun's gravitational force can either amplify (spring tide) or reduce (neap tide) the effect of the moon. Spring tides occur every 2 weeks when the sun is in line with the earth and the full or new moon (see fig. 4).

Within bodies of water smaller than an ocean, the timing and height of the tides are dependent upon the size and depth of the basin. In an estuary, the length of time that a wave (i.e., a tidal high) takes to travel from one end of the basin to the other determines the tidal pattern. In the Chesapeake Bay the travel time is long but the periodicity is in synchronization with daily oceanic tides.

Twice each lunar day (i.e., each 24.8 hours) the Atlantic tide moves into the Bay from the ocean. Each tide travels up the Bay in a progressive, then standing, wave, reaching its

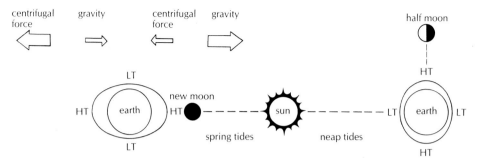

Figure 4. The tides represent a balance between centrifugal force and gravity. At any given moment a high tide rises toward the moon (due to gravity) and away from the moon (due to centrifugal force). Low tides are found at right angles to the earth-moon axis and, like high tides, are observed on the coast twice each lunar day (24.8 hours). *Spring* (or maximal) *tides* occur every two weeks at the new and full moons, while *neap* (or minimal) *tides* occur at the first and last quarters because of the gravitational influence of the sun (adapted from Nybakken 1982).

upper limit in 12.8 hours, just about the same time the next tidal high begins at the mouth. Halfway, or 6.4 hours into the cycle, there is a high tide at mid-Bay, while low tides are found at the headwaters, Capes Henry and Charles, and the Atlantic Coast. There are certain slack effects, but the Bay is just the right length so that a *semidiurnal tidal pattern* persists, instead of the mixed tide found in midsized estuaries such as San Francisco Bay.

In effect, this regular vertical flux sends a twice-daily ripple through the estuary, which, as we shall see, causes friction with the freshwater flow. Throughout the Bay, circulation is enhanced by this tidal pump.

Tidal currents are horizontal movements of water that accompany the rise and fall of the tide. Bay currents are moderate and average less than 0.5 knots (0.3 mph), except in narrows and bottlenecks where some reach 3 knots (1.8 mph) during the outgoing, ebb tide. High tides drive salt water farther up the estuary, temporarily shifting salinity contours farther upstream. A local shift of 5 ppt over a lunar day is not uncommon at some sites.

The vertical range of the tides is greatest (2.5 ft; 0.76 m) at the capes, intermediate through the main Bay where it averages 2 ft (0.61 m), and lowest along the upper reaches of tidal streams (1 to 2 ft; 0.3 to 0.61 m). Twice each day, the tides alternately expose and submerge the shoreline. Consequently, shoreline habitats are divided into zones based on the tidal range (see p. 152, fig. 11).

Circulation

Freshwater input, tides, and shifts in salinity are, one might say, the earthly manifestations of celestial forces that keep the Chesapeake in motion. Within the basin fresh and marine waters chart their paths across the estuary in a complex but predictable manner, slowly joining, while at the same time dispersing nutrients, transporting oxygen, and, in general, nurturing life. However, if one characteristic outweighs the others in determining this circulation pattern, it is not the lunar tides nor the deflecting *Coriolis effect*, but rather the inherent density difference between these two aquatic regimes.

As we have seen, fresh water is always lighter, that is, has a lower density, than brackish or marine. River drainage, therefore, tends to flow seaward along the surface of the estuary while heavier saline water from the ocean travels northward along the bottom, particularly within the deep, central channel that once served as the streambed for the lower Susquehanna. It is this lower density of fresh water relative to seawater that is responsible for a *two-layer estuarine flow*. In the lower Chesapeake, the southbound fresh water essentially floats over the underlying salt layer (see fig. 5).

All estuaries share this basic estuarine pattern; however, the isolation of these two layers varies with each basin depending on the amount of freshwater input and the degree of tidal mixing and friction. In the absence of friction, the deepwater layer, theoretically, would extend upstream to mean sea level, forming an isolated salt wedge. When river flow prevails over tidal motion, as in the Mississippi River, such a highly stratified estuary can persist. Yet in the face of moderate tidal motion and intermediate freshwater flow, frictional forces between the upper and lower layers cause mixing at all depths and, therefore, an exchange of water across the density barrier. This two-way exchange produces a *moderately stratified estuary* such as the Chesapeake Bay. It is most important to note, however, that more salt water reaches the upper layer during mixing than vice-versa. Consequently, the surface flow increases in volume *as well as salinity* as one proceeds seaward. Not surpris-

Figure 5. The two-layer circulation pattern of the estuary results in a zone of maximum turbidity where freshwater and marine fronts meet—typically near the head of the Bay and its major tributaries. Nutrients, as well as sediments, are mixed and resuspended in this zone, making it a highly productive nursery area (adapted from EPA 1982).

ingly, there is a compensating increase in the upstream flow within the deeper layer to replace seawater lost in this exchange. In fact, when it is measured, one finds the gross discharge to the ocean to be 10 times the average freshwater input (70,000 cu ft/sec) from all tributary sources. The remaining 630,000 cu ft/sec is called the *entrainment velocity,* and results, as one would guess, from the steady vertical flow of seawater into the freshwater layer that continually takes place throughout the estuary. Like a freight train that has picked up salt water and speed, the surface stream discharges nearly 700,000 cubic feet of brackish water into the ocean every second. This dynamic combination of seawater, rainfall, runoff, groundwater, and river flow makes up the waters of the Bay.

Retention Time

Continually, fresh water flows down the Bay's arteries only to mix with salt water inbound from the sea. The degree of brackishness at any point along the Bay is inverse to the seasonal freshwater flow—fresher in spring, saltier in autumn. Yet, at all times, the Bay is large in comparison with the daily freshwater pulse. On average a parcel of water takes about 2 to 3 weeks to cycle along the Bay's 195-mile length. On the way, some water evaporates, some is replaced from the saltwater wedge or by rain. But the turnover is slow, and thus plankton communities and the Bay's few "residents," including larval fish, oysters, and crabs, have a permanent, if stressful, home.

Ecology of the Bay

Each kind of wetland—whether . . . its water is fresh, salty,
or brackish—is a distinct community, a unique roster of
plant and animal life contributing to the ecosystem as a
whole.

—William A. Niering
The Life of the Marsh

IT is here, in the estuary, that fresh and salt water meet. The slow mixing of these waters creates distinct biological zones along the salinity gradient from headwater drainage to open sea. More than anything else, this gradient and the basin's topography—from deep-water channels to shoals to tidal shores—control the distribution of life and the number of species within the Bay.

The study of the distribution and abundance of organisms is called *ecology,* a relatively young science that seeks to understand the relationships between organisms and their environment. The word *ecology* stems from the Greek *oikos,* meaning "house," while *estuary* (Latin *aestuarium*) derives from the root *aestus,* meaning "tide." Thus, estuarine ecology—our task at hand—could be termed the study of the tidal house, and, in particular, where species are found among its many chambers and rooms.

For a moment visualize the network of 150 headwater streams that drain 6 states as they weave through various geophysical provinces, supplying the Chesapeake with a mixture of "fresh" waters with a broad geochemical range. In the Bay these diverse freshwater streams, loaded with nutrients and silt, ride up and over the salty water inbound from the Atlantic. The silts slowly settle, the waters slowly mix, while always fresher upstream and saltier toward the ocean. Every habitat along this gradient supports a unique community of plants and animals, each particularly suited to the water chemistry and bottom substrate of a given salinity zone.

Many of these communities have familiar names—cypress swamps, cattail marshes, brackish wetlands, salt meadows, tidal flats, eelgrass beds, oyster reefs—characterized by the plant canopy, species, or substrate that makes up its basic architecture. In theory, the greater the number of different habitats in an ecosystem, the greater the potential variety of life. Estuaries offer a large array of such ecological partitions, mainly due to the diversity in water chemistry, depths, and soils, and the variety of plant communities within the basin. However, as we have seen, many of the Bay's 2,700 species are transients, temporary visitors in the estuarine world. Compared to freshwater and marine systems, few organisms are physiologically adapted to reside permanently in this dynamic environment (see fig. 6).

The plant composition of Chesapeake wetlands illustrates the point. Freshwater swamps along small tributaries offer a broad catalogue of species: herbs, wildflowers, vines, shrubs, and trees. Even the cattail marshes of slightly brackish streams present a

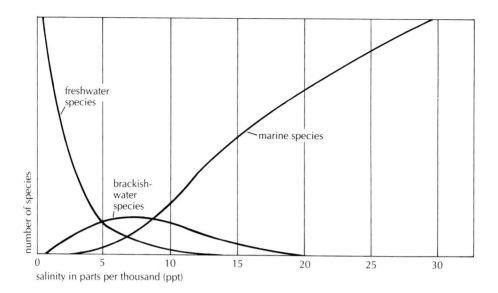

Figure 6. The number of species varies dramatically within an estuary and reaches a minimum between 5 and 8 ppt salinity. Below this zone freshwater species dominate. Above 10 ppt marine species dominate. Though the variety of estuarine species is never high, their populations are often enormous. Historically, blue crabs, oysters, and other prolific species—tolerant of estuarine conditions—have literally carpeted the Bay at certain times of the year (adapted from McLusky 1971).

wide variety of emergent plants. On the other hand, the salt meadows of the lower Bay are dominated by cordgrass—one (or two) species for miles and miles.

The Bay itself can also be inhospitable. The estuary's two-layer flow, for example, creates serious problems for zooplankton, which drift randomly or at the mercy of surface or deepwater currents. In order to cope with estuarine circulation, various species of copepods ride deepwater upstream currents during the day and then migrate to the surface at night where they are transported back downstream. The resulting circular motion keeps each species within an optimal salinity range. In the absence of this or similar behavioral mechanisms, many species would be carried out to sea or would perish, for parts of the Bay are as alien to some organisms as the surface of the moon is to man.

One such forbidding region is known as the *critical salinity* and ranges between 5 and 8 ppt along major tributaries and the upper Bay. Above this region a rich community of freshwater fishes, molluscs, and other invertebrates is found, but species diversity decreases dramatically toward this band. Similarly, marine bivalves and fishes are rare at this salinity but their species numbers increase readily as one proceeds down the Bay.

A *faunal break* appears at this salinity because of low physiological tolerance on the part of both freshwater and marine species. Above this region marine bivalves, for example, are incapable of maintaining necessary body salts, while freshwater species similarly cannot maintain cell volume in highly brackish water. Only a few transitional species, such as the anadromous herrings and shads, can easily cross this barrier.

Since only a few species are tolerant of estuarine conditions, and because of the wide selection of habitats, a remarkable phenomenon takes place. The decrease in species diversity is accompanied by *niche expansion* in those species able to survive the stress. The Baltic macoma clam, *Macoma balthica* (p. 155), for example, is strictly intertidal in the North Atlantic, but has large subtidal populations in the Chesapeake Bay. Due to this expanded niche breadth, a paucity of predators, and a ready supply of food, the Chesapeake Bay supports enormous populations of a relatively small number of resident species.

Limiting Factors

Invisible and transient though they may seem, the salinity contours limit and define the distribution of plant and animal species within the Bay. Meanwhile, a variety of other *limiting factors* keep populations in check within any given zone.

Water temperature fluctuates widely (32°-84°F; 0°-29°C) in the Bay because of freshwater input and the Bay's shallow depth. Since the rates of chemical and biochemical reactions increase dramatically with temperature (and sunlight), photosynthesis and other life processes are highest during summer and at low ebb during the cold winter months. In the spring and fall, vertical mixing of nutrients (and oxygen) is promoted by the creation and dissipation of vertical thermal gradients. Temperature also influences spawning and migratory behavior and is, therefore, responsible for seasonal changes in animal abundance.

The level of *dissolved oxygen* in water, an element essential to plant and animal life, decreases with increased temperature and salinity. Cold water can hold more oxygen than warm water; fresh water holds more oxygen than seawater. Thus, oxygen levels in the estuary vary seasonally and from place to place. Deep waters in mid-Bay or midriver channels, despite being colder than surface layers, may be *anoxic* (devoid of oxygen) during the summer because of poor mixing or organic decay. Fish require oxygen levels above 4 milligrams/liter (mg/l) for survival; 6-9 mg/l is optimal.

In the same way that fertilizers promote growth in agricultural crops, *nutrients*— particularly nitrogen and phosphorus—are vital to the growth and maintenance of plant life within the Bay. Nitrogen (N) is important in the production of plant and animal tissue, while phosphorus (P) is essential to cellular growth and reproduction. These nutrients are generally required in the ratio of 16 parts N to 1 part P. Whenever the availability of either nutrient drops below this ratio, that element typically becomes the limiting factor of plant growth.

Overloading of nutrients can spell the proverbial "too much of a good thing." When phosphate levels are too high, algal blooms result, creating turbid, or cloudy, conditions at the water surface. The first problem arising from increased *turbidity* is the blocking of light that normally penetrates into the water column. Photosynthesis declines within the phytoplanktonic, algal, and submersed-grass communities, lowering both primary productivity

Figure 7. A simplified food web for the Chesapeake Bay (*at right*) shows the various pathways along which nutrients and energy are transferred among trophic levels. The Bay nursery profits from a dual food chain: a direct pathway, in which living plants are consumed, and an indirect (*detrital*) pathway, in which dead organic matter from the uplands, marshes, algae, and SAV decomposes and is then reused. A typical direct chain may consist of five steps: diatoms, copepods, anchovies, rockfish, osprey. By comparison, a detrital pathway may be complex: marsh detritus, bacteria, protozoan, clam (*filter feeder*) or polychaete worm (*deposit feeder*), blue crab, black drum (benthic fish), man. Or it might be simple. A simple indirect pathway would be: detritus, oyster, man. The detrital chain is the most important pathway in marsh, SAV, and benthic communities, while the direct pathway often predominates in the water column.

marsh plants

PRIMARY

swamp trees
and shrubs

and oxygen levels. As the algal mass decays, microbial respiration depletes oxygen further, leading to anoxic (and odorous) conditions.

A variety of other factors may limit the abundance (and/or distribution) of plant and animal populations within the wetland-estuarine system. Chemical factors such as acidity/alkalinity (pH), carbon dioxide levels, and trace elements of seawater define the physiological limits of certain species. For example, cobalt (a minor element of seawater) is required in the production of vitamin B_{12}, a necessary ingredient in the growth of many organisms. Toxic chemicals, heavy metals, and other pollutants can also limit growth and exclude species from contaminated areas. Physical factors such as currents and substrate composition can affect growth and distribution patterns. Finally, species interactions—predation, parasitism, competition, and disease—regularly keep populations in check. The American oyster, *Crassostrea virginica,* has a physiological range from 7 ppt to full ocean salinity, but is most abundant in brackish water between 10 and 18 ppt because of parasites and predators (e.g., oyster drills and starfish) that live in high-salinity waters.

Bay Communities

The distribution of most aquatic and wetland species is coincident with certain community types within the Bay. Each of the five major communities discussed below can be further segregated into freshwater, low brackish, moderately brackish, and high brackish zones along the length of the Bay or its tributaries (see fig 3; p. 12). Within each, species com-

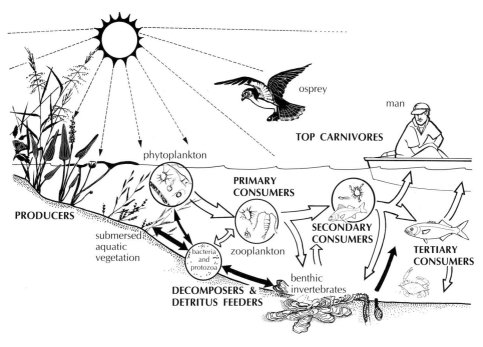

position varies depending on local shifts in salinity, elevation (or depth), sediments, and the topography of the substrate.

Wetlands. Nearly 500,000 acres of marshes and swamps border the Chesapeake and its tributaries. These areas are kept wet by runoff, groundwater seepage, adjacent stream flow, and tides. In addition to being among the most productive plant communities in the world, wetlands enhance water quality by trapping sediments and by recycling nutrients, and provide a host of hydrological benefits. Most furnish outstanding habitat for invertebrates, juvenile fishes, and higher vertebrates. At the base of this robust community are emergent and floating-leaved plants, which become less numerous (in terms of species) as one proceeds from the complex, freshwater wetlands along streams and creeks to the simple salt marshes of the lower Bay.

Submersed Grass Beds. Another major plant community consists of less than three dozen species that live in the shallow waters of rivers and streams and the Bay proper. Only 10 species are fairly common and are collectively known as submersed aquatic vegetation, or SAV (see pp. 163-166). By definition, these aquatic plants are fully submersed, living with their leaves at or below the surface of the water. Like marsh plants, different species are segregated according to salinity and depth and provide habitats for freshwater (p. 64), slightly to moderately brackish (p. 84), and highly brackish (p. 167) communities.

Plankton. Organisms that drift at the whim of currents and tides are known as plankton—the major food source of larger organisms in the estuary. This community includes phytoplankton (a third major plant group in the Bay), zooplankton, bacteria, and large jelly-fish (pp. 179-181). The tiny, floating larvae of benthic animals and fish, known as *meroplankton,* are, for a short time, part of this community as well.

Nekton. Larger aquatic organisms capable of swimming are collectively termed nekton. This group includes fish, crustaceans such as the grass shrimp and blue crab, and other in-vertebrates. Nearly 300 fish species can be found in the Bay. Permanent residents include anchovies, silversides, killifishes (pp. 171-172), and the white perch (p. 85). Freshwater species (pp. 65-68) and marine species (pp. 184-190) also visit the Bay, as do anadromous and catadromous species (see Migratory Patterns and Life Cycles, pp. 201-203).

Benthos. The array of organisms that inhabit bottom sediments are commonly called the benthos. Though often described in terms of animal groups (e.g., oyster beds), benthic com-munities usually include algae, bacteria, and ciliates as important components in both shal-low (pp. 161–170) and deepwater (pp. 177-183) habitats. Intertidal species (pp. 153-156) are a special class of bottom dwellers that can survive temporary exposure to air.

Energy Flow

Each species within the Bay is dependent upon its neighbors and habitat, its community, for shelter and food. These communities overlap and intertwine to form the Chesapeake *ecosystem.* Perhaps the most important relationship demonstrating this interdependency is the network of feeding links known as the *food web* (see fig. 7). Movement of energy through the food web is called the *energy flow.*

Nutrient cycles and other ecological processes characterize food web patterns. For example, elemental carbon is transferred at each step of a given food chain, as proteins, carbohydrates, and fats are created and broken down. Energy also flows through the sys-tem via the food web. Plants produce high-energy organic matter (e.g., sugars) through photosynthesis, fueled by energy from the sun. Next, herbivores (or *detritovores*) consume living (or dead) plants as materials and energy are deeded to the next *trophic* (food) *level.* Carnivores consume herbivores, and so on. Since about 90 percent of the energy is lost at each transfer, fewer animals are found at each successive link in the chain. It takes nearly 4 tons of plankton to produce 1 pound of rockfish.

Like a pyramid of stones, the animals at the top are dependent on the size of the plant base. Top carnivores such as crabs, bluefish, and ospreys are very abundant in the Chesapeake only because of the enormous plant productivity in the Bay. This high produc-tivity is supported by the estuary's unique circulation pattern that helps to accumulate and retain nutrients in the basin. The Bay's various plant communities are thus nurtured and sustain the nation's most prolific estuarine fisheries.

The Rivers and Tributaries

Freshwater Swamps

Freshwater Tributaries and
Adjoining Freshwater Marshes

Estuarine Rivers and
Associated Brackish Marshes

Freshwater Swamps

AT the headwaters of many Bay tributaries are small pockets of wet, soggy habitat known as freshwater swamps. If cypress knees, dark-stained water, dense thickets, and bullfrogs come to mind, then you are familiar with the swamp environment. Actually there are many types of swamps, both shrub and forested, but all are dominated by woody plants and are thick with undergrowth, vines, and the sounds of songbirds.

By definition, *swamps* are seasonally saturated or permanently flooded wetlands with greater than a 50 percent cover of woody vegetation—either trees, shrubs, or vines, or a mixture of these. Swamps should be distinguished from bottomland forests and wet woods, however. Swamps normally are saturated to the surface or flooded by up to a foot of water, while bottomland forests and wet woods conceal their water tables below the surface for most of the year.

In addition to headwater swamps, tree- and shrub-dominated wetlands are located along the borders of tidal creeks and streams and along the landward margins of freshwater and brackish marshes. These swamp bands represent a transition zone between the marsh environment and the drier woods of upland areas.

In the Bay region, *wooded swamps* are typically dominated by red maple and green ash, but some forested swamps, most notably those along the Pocomoke River of the Eastern Shore, are dominated by bald cypress. Some trees, such as Atlantic white cedar and loblolly pine, are even tolerant of brackish conditions, and you will find loblolly pine swamps adjacent to brackish marshes throughout the lower Bay.

At a certain point along the upper reaches of an estuarine river, such as the Pocomoke or the

Patuxent, the tidewater swamp forest changes almost imperceptibly into a nontidal, or inland, swamp forest. A discerning eye, however, can spot the tidal limit. Within tidal jurisdiction the trees are smaller and usually grow on pronounced hummocks. These trees show their autumn colors earlier than swamp trees above tidal influence.

Shrub-dominated wetlands, or *shrub swamps*, are most often found in linear thickets along creeks or adjacent to freshwater marshes. Most are dominated by red maple and green ash saplings, and thus represent an early stage of forest regrowth. There are three types of shrub swamps in the Chesapeake coastal plain. In Maryland, maple/ash shrub swamps outnumber the other two varieties (alder/willow *and* swamp rose) 3 to 1. Smooth alder and black willow grow along the flooded banks of tidewater creeks, especially in the upper Patuxent and Elk river watersheds. Examples of this shrub swamp category can be found along Black Walnut and Mattaponi creeks in Patuxent River Park (Prince George's County, Maryland) and within Thackery Swamp at Elk Neck State Park in Cecil County, Maryland. The third type of shrub swamp is characterized by swamp rose and is quite prevalent along rivers of the western shore.

The shrub swamp is an intermediate step in the slow succession of a wetland from marsh to tidewater forest. In freshwater areas red maple is the first pioneer. In brackish areas, the saltbush hummock may offer a foothold for the invading loblolly pine. In both cases, water-tolerant shrubs begin the process of succession, trapping detritus with their woody roots, thus inviting other woody species to follow. Underneath the growing swamp canopy you will find a few marsh plants remaining, surviving until the advancing shadow of the woods shuts out the last bit of light. (See list of transitional marsh plants, p. 39.)

Plants and animals native to the swamp have one thing in common: They are adapted to the aquatic environment. When the water disappears, most of the swamp's inhabitants depart, and those less mobile than birds and mammals usually perish. For this reason, draining of these wetlands by man can cause irreversible damage. Most of the vast acreage that constituted the Great Cypress Swamp in Delaware during the nineteenth century has disappeared, drained for farmland. Before its demise in the 1930s, this headwater swamp had the largest and most spectacular stand of bald cypress north of Virginia. Visit Trap Pond State Park near Laurel, Delaware, to see a vestige of this once-great swampland. This remnant and other smaller swamps are now being preserved: Nassawango Creek (tributary to the Pocomoke), Battle Creek Cypress Swamp (tributary to the Patuxent), Zekiah Swamp above Allens Fresh on the Wicomico (tributary to the Potomac), Cohoke Swamp on the Pamunkey (tributary to the York), Dragon Run Swamp at the head of the Piankatank, and the many swamp bands of the upper Chickahominy (tributary to the James) are especially worth seeing.

PLANTS of freshwater swamps

frequently consist of myriad herbs, vines, shrubs, and trees, entangled into a wetland jungle. Still, usually a few plants dominate, and 30 of the most common species are illustrated here. If an obvious canopy of trees is present, you are in a *wooded swamp*. Look in the overstory for red maple and green ash, which are indicative of the most common swamp type in the region. In all three types of wooded swamps (*maple/ash, bald cypress*, and *loblolly pine*), the understory may contain shrubs, woody vines, and broad-leaved herbs. Full-grown trees are found only in wooded swamps. If you find yourself in a shrubby, but unforested, wetland, you are in a *shrub swamp*, which lacks a tree canopy and is typified by *swamp rose, alder/willow*, or *maple/ash saplings*. Shrub swamps may contain some herbaceous species (e.g., grasses, sedges, and rushes) in the understory that are more typical of freshwater marshes (p. 57) than swamps.

HERBS, or herbaceous species, are fleshy, non-woody plants. They may be *perennial*, living for years (though dying back in winter to tubers or rhizomes), or *annual*, the entire plant dying after one season and propagating only by seeds.

Lizard's tail, *Saururus cernuus* (**a**), is a perennial herb found in scattered groups within open swamps. *Leaves* are dark green, thin, alternate, heart-shaped, and up to 6 in (15 cm) long. *Stems* are erect and jointed. *Flowers* are white and tiny, clustered onto a 4-6 in (10-15 cm) spike with a nodding tip, giving the terminus a "lizard's tail" appearance. Propagates by seeds and *rhizomes*, which are highly aromatic. *Size:* 2 to 3 ft (60 to 90 cm) tall. *Blooms* June-August.

Skunk cabbage, *Symplocarpus foetidus* (**b**), known for its aroma, grows in scattered groups in swamps and wet woods. *Leaves* are broad, ovate, up to 2 ft (60 cm) long, deeply veined, and have a *skunklike odor* when crushed. *Leaf stems* are grooved and resemble celery stalks. True stem is lacking; leaf clusters arise from a perennial rhizome hidden in the soil. The mottled green (or purplish) *spathe*, or flower sheath, appears in March-April—before the leaves. Inside this hoodlike structure a rounded flower head, or *spadix*, develops at the end of a short, elliptic stalk, in a fashion similar to jack-in-the-pulpit (*Arisaema triphyllum*).

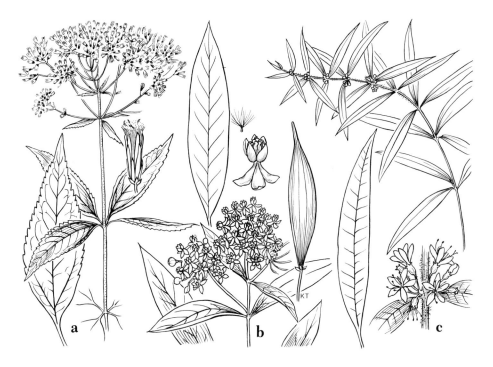

Eastern joe-pye-weed, *Eupatoriadelphus dubius* (**a**), is a tall perennial with a rough, *purple-spotted stem.* Grows in colonies in open swamps and freshwater marshes. *Leaves,* which radiate from the single stem in whorls of 3, 4, or 5 at even intervals, are toothed and ovate, having 3 prominent veins arising from the *petiole. Flower cluster* at summit is flat-topped and purple; *blooms* July-September. *Size:* 2 to 5 ft (0.6 to 1.5 cm). *Related species:* Trumpetweed (*E. fistulosus*) has hollow stem, domed cluster, and tapered leaves (1 vein only) in whorls of 6. Sweet joe-pye-weed (*E. purpureus*) has domed flower cluster, green stem, and tapered leaves (1 vein only) with a vanillalike odor when crushed.

Swamp milkweed, *Asclepias incarnata* (**b**), a perennial herb, grows in small groups or alone in wooded swamps, freshwater marshes, and along stream margins. *Leaves* are smooth, opposite, lance-shaped, and up to 5 in (12.5 cm) long. *Stem* is branched, hairy or completely smooth, and leafy to the top. Unlike other milk-weeds, stem has little milky juice. Several small, pink umbrellalike *flower clusters bloom* at the top of each stem during July-August. The *spindle-shaped seedpods* contain many seeds, each bearing a tuft of long silky hairs. *Size:* 2 to 4 ft (0.6 to 1.2 m). *Confusing species:* New York ironweed (*Vernonia noveboracensis*) has alternate, toothed leaves.

Swamp loosestrife, *Decodon verticillatus* (**c**), also known as water-willow, is an herbaceous, though somewhat shrubby, perennial that grows in open swamps and along edges of shallow pools in freshwater wetlands. The long, smooth or downy *stems,* which are often arched or reclining, root again at the tips, thus forming thickets. *Lance-shaped leaves,* 3 to 4 in (7.5 to 10 cm) long, occur in pairs or in whorls of 3. *Flower clusters* in the axils of the middle to upper leaves *bloom* with pinkish to purple inflorescence during July-August. *Size:* to 4 ft (1.2 m). *Seeds* eaten by wood ducks; leaves and stems by muskrats.

VINES are symptomatic of freshwater swamps, weaving through branches of shrubs and trees to form dense, relentless thickets. Certainly greenbrier and poison ivy are the most familiar, but other woody vines, such as summer grape (*Vitis aestivalis*), fox grape (*V. labrusca*), muscadine (*V. rotundifolia*), Virginia creeper (*Parthenocissus quinquefolia*), Japanese honeysuckle (*Lonicera japonica*), and American mistletoe (*Phoradendron flavescens*), are found here, too. Herbaceous vinelike plants include climbing hempweed (*Mikania scandens*, p. 61), and dodder (*Cuscuta gronovii*, p. 99), which grow in marshes and swamps.

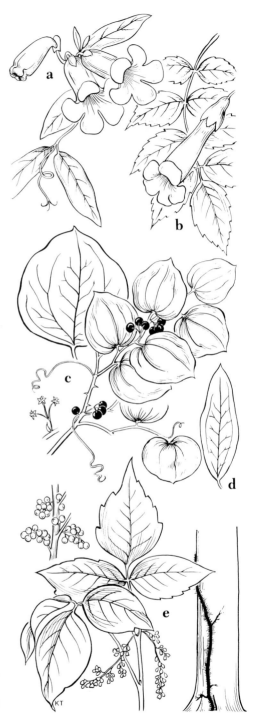

Crossvine, *Bignonia capreolata* (**a**), is a beautiful woody vine with bright *red trumpet-like flowers* found in swamps and wet woods. *Evergreen leaves* are compound, consisting of 2 paired, oval leaflets. When cut in half, *stem* reveals a cross. *Blooms* May-June. *Confusing species:* **Trumpet creeper,** *Campsis radicans* (**b**), also has 3 in (7.6 cm) tubular flowers but its nonevergreen compound leaves have 7 to 11 toothed leaflets; *blooms* July-September.

Common greenbrier, *Smilax rotundifolia* (**c**), a *green-stemmed vine* with short, stout prickles, climbs by means of tendrils attached to the bases of leafstalks. *Heart-shaped leaves* are 2 to 5 in (5 to 13 cm) long with prominent, parallel veins. *Green flowers bloom* May-August. Its *blue-black berries* have 2 seeds, and are a popular food of songbirds. Foliage eaten by deer and rabbits. *Related species:* **Laurel greenbrier,** *S. laurifolia* (**d**), has leathery, elliptic leaves, fewer thorns.

Poison ivy, *Toxicodendron radicans* (**e**), comes in two varieties: as a woody vine with numerous aerial rootlets, or as a bushy shrub. In both, foliage can be highly variable, but the *compound leaf* is always composed of 3 leaflets that are oval with pointed tips. Clustered *green flowers bloom* June-July; white ball-shaped *fruits,* in same clusters, ripen August-November. All parts—stems, leaves, roots, and berries—contain a heavy, toxic oil that causes inflammation of the skin and blisters in susceptible persons. Remember: "Leaflets three, let it be."

WILDFLOWERS are found on herbaceous, as well as woody, plants. Illustrated here are a flowering shrub, a perennial herb, and a common annual herbaceous species.

Swamp rose, *Rosa palustris* (**a**), has a distinctive flower, emblematic of certain shrub swamps. Growing in loose colonies, these tall shrubs create impenetrable thickets thanks to a multitude of conical, hooked *prickles*. The branching, *woody stem* has a pair of these prickles at the base of each *compound leaf*, which typically has 7 ovate (or elliptic) serrated leaflets up to 1½ in (4 cm) long. *Flowers* are pale pink, *blooming* with 5 showy petals during July-August. Red, pulpy fruits (hips) and buds attract songbirds and deer. *Size:* up to 6 ft (2 m).

Cardinal flower, *Lobelia cardinalis* (**b**), a well-known wetland perennial, *blooms* July-August in wooded swamps and along stream banks. The plant bears numerous lance-shaped, *toothed leaves* up to 6 in (15 cm) long, which grow alternately along the smooth, *unbranched stem.* The *bright scarlet flowers* arise from a slender spike up to 18 in (45 cm) long at the top of the stem. Flower has 2 lips: the upper divided into 2 lobes, the lower into 3. The *fruit* is a many-seeded pod. *Size:* 2 to 5 ft (0.6 to 1.5 m).

Jewelweed, *Impatiens capensis* (**c**), or spotted touch-me-not (so named because ripe seedpods burst when touched), is a bushy annual plant common in freshwater swamps. The *elliptic, toothed leaves,* up to 4 in (10 cm) long, are alternately arranged, with long petioles, on a smooth, *branching stem* that is hollow, translucent, and filled with sap (purported to be an antidote for poison ivy). The *funnel-shaped flowers* are characteristically orange with brown spots, and hang—like ladies' earrings—from slender stalks originating in the upper leaf axils; *bloom* July-September. Ruby-throated hummingbirds favor its nectar; birds and mice eat the seeds; and rabbits browse on the foliage. *Size:* Plants are usually 1½ to 5 ft (0.5 to 1.65 m) tall.

CERTAIN SHRUBS AND TREES often grow together and are thus characteristic of particular swamps. The following three shrubs are common in areas dominated by swamp rose (p. 32).

Sweet pepperbush, *Clethra alnifolia* (**a**), is a tall woody shrub. The twigs have minute gray hairs, while the *leaves* are hairless, alternate, oblong above a narrow base, and sharply toothed from midleaf to the tip; 2 to 4 in (5 to 10 cm) long. Leaves suggest elm or alder. *Cylindrical flower clusters,* approximately 6 in (15 cm) long, consist of small, white, *sweetly scented flowers blooming* at the tip of branches during July-August. The small *tan fruits* resemble peppercorns on a stalk and persist through winter. *Size:* up to 10 ft (3 m).

Buttonbush, *Cephalanthus occidentalis* (**b**), is a common wetland shrub. The woody stem branches frequently, ending either in dead tips or flower heads. The 3 to 4 in (7.5 to 10 cm)

long leaves are shiny green on top, veined, opposite (or in whorls of 3 or 4), and oblong. Leafstalks, or petioles, are often reddish brown. *Small, white flowers* are crowded into a ball-like flower head, or "button," 1 in (2.5 cm) in diameter; *blooms* July-September. In late fall the flower buttons turn into brown *spherical fruits,* consisting of clovelike nutlets which are eaten by wood ducks and other birds through December. *Size:* 3 to 10 ft (0.9 to 3 m) high.

Silky dogwood, *Cornus amomum* (**c**), also known as swamp dogwood, is an upright shrub with reddish brown or purple twigs, the youngest of which have silky brown hairs. *Leaves* are smooth, opposite, egg-shaped with a short tapered tip, moderately stalked, and dark green above, reddening in the fall; up to 4 in (10 cm) long and half as wide. Flattened clusters of *white flowers bloom* June-July. *Size:* up to 10 ft (3 m). The *porcelain-blue berries* are favored by wood ducks and songbirds.

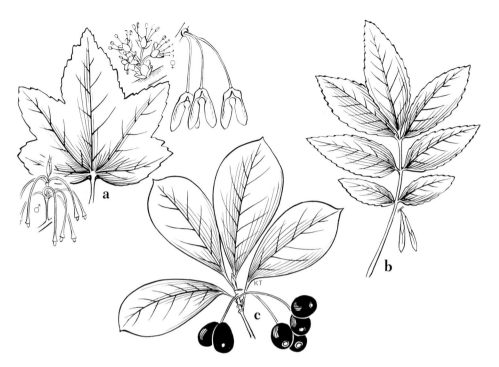

Red maple, *Acer rubrum* (**a**), is the most typical plant of both shrub and wooded swamps. Saplings and full-sized trees have red twigs and leafstalks. Bark of young trees is smooth and gray, becoming broken and darker with age. *Leaves* are opposite, 3- to 5-lobed, green above, whitish below, and up to 4 in (10 cm) long; scarlet (or yellow) in autumn. *Red flowers* appear before leaves; *bloom* in April. Also red, the *winged seeds,* or "keys" (food for birds and small mammals), float—like helicopters—to the ground in autumn. *Size:* 40 to 50 ft (10 to 15 m).

Green ash, *Fraxinus pennsylvanica* (**b**), along with red maple, is characteristic of our most prevalent shrub and wooded swamps. A large tree, this hardwood has dark, tight bark with deep furrows. Twigs are shiny and hairless. *Opposite leaves* are compound with 5-9 stalked,

toothed leaflets, 4 in (10 cm) long. *Flowers* are inconspicuous; *bloom* April-May. The *wedge-shaped fruits*—resembling the blades of canoe paddles—hang in drooping clusters until they drop off in late fall. *Size:* up to 60 ft (18 m).

Black gum, *Nyssa sylvatica* (**c**), or sour gum, a medium-sized tree, is found both in maple/ash and bald cypress swamps. Bark is dark brown with deep, irregular fissures. Submersed trunks are swollen at base. *Leaves* are alternate, obovate, and crowded toward the end of the brown twigs, never toothed, 2 to 5 in (7.5 to 13 cm) long, and scarlet in autumn. *Greenish flower clusters* appear with the leaves; *bloom* during April-May. *Blue berrylike fruits* droop in pairs or triplets like plums during August-September; eaten by raccoons, opossum, and birds. *Size:* up to 40 ft (12 m).

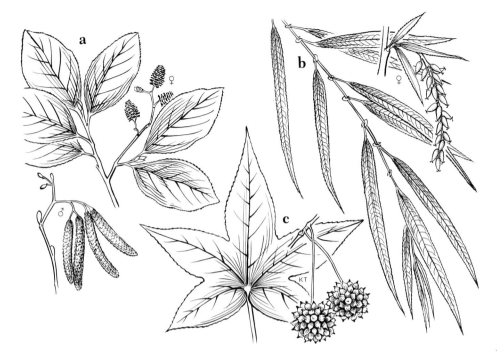

Common alder, *Alnus serrulata* (**a**), a branching shrub though sometimes a small tree, typifies certain dense shrub swamps in the region. Alder is easily identified by its alternate, oval, toothed, and often *wavy leaves,* 2 to 5 in (5 to 13 cm) long. *Stems* are smooth. Buds are reddish and stalked. *Flower spikes,* or catkins, of both sexes appear on same plant: male catkins drooping, female spikes erect; *bloom* April-May. *Fruits* are woody, barrel-shaped "cones," on short, erect stalks. *Size:* up to 25 ft (7.6 m). *Similar species:* Seaside alder, *A. maritima,* a species restricted to the Delaware-Maryland Eastern Shore, has glossy leaves; *blooms* in late summer or early fall.

Black willow, *Salix nigra* (**b**), like common alder, grows along streamlets that weave through shrub swamps in the Bay area. *Size:* As a tree it reaches 40 ft (12 m), but—like alder—it more often occurs as a branching shrub overhanging the borders of creeks and streams. *Stem* has dark, deeply furrowed bark. *Leaves* are narrow, sickle-shaped, alternate, and finely toothed, up to 5 in (13 cm) long but only ½ in (1.3 cm) wide. Leafstalks have 2 minute, winglike leaves at the base. Male and female *flowers* appear in long, thin, drooping spikes (catkins) on separate plants; *bloom* April-May. Beaver and deer browse on various parts of the plant. Wood used for boxes and baskets not requiring strength.

Sweetgum, *Liquidambar styraciflua* (**c**), is a tall tree of moist woodlands and wooded swamps. Bark is thick, gray, and grooved. The *star-shaped leaves* resemble those of maple but are alternate, toothed, 5- or 7-lobed, and fragrant when crushed. Twigs often have "wings." Distinctive *ball-like fruits* are prickly, hanging from *long stems* like those of sycamore (which are hairy, not thorny); mature September-November. *Seeds* eaten by songbirds and gray squirrels. Sap has a sweet flavor and hardens into a chewable gum. Foliage is a brilliant red-and-gold "liquid amber" in the fall. *Size:* up to 120 ft (36 m).

Spicebush, *Lindera benzoin* (**a**), is a common broadleaf shrub easily recognized by the spicy, aromatic odor of its twigs and leaves. *Leaves* are alternate, smooth, and ovate with pointed tips; up to 4 in (10 cm) long. *Small yellow flowers bloom* at axils before the appearance of leaves, during April-May. Male and female flowers are found on separate plants. *Red berries*—like the leaves—are spice-scented when crushed. Foliage, twigs, and fruits are consumed by deer, rabbits, opossum, and songbirds. *Size:* up to 10 ft (3 m) tall.

Redbay, *Persea borbonia* (**b**), an evergreen tree or shrub best known for its spicy "bay leaves," is most common in Virginia and south, particularly in maritime swamp forests. The bark is dark red, deeply furrowed, and has a spicy aroma. *Size:* Trees grow to 50 ft (15 m) tall. The *aromatic leaves,* used to season foods, are alternate, leathery, shiny green above, pale beneath, and 3 to 6 in (7.5 to 15 cm) long. *Small yellow flowers bloom* briefly May-June, while the *dark blue berries,* hanging plumlike from red stems, are conspicuous during late August-October. *Related species:* Bayberry, *Myrica pensylvanica* (p. 83), has waxy, bluish gray fruits (used for candle making) and deciduous, nonleathery leaves.

Sweetbay, *Magnolia virginiana* (**c**), also known as sweetbay magnolia or laurel-magnolia, is a swamp tree with the distinctive tropical look of the magnolia family (Magnoliaceae). *Alternate leaves* are thick, leathery, elliptic, dark green above, white underneath, and spicy when crushed; over 4 in (10 cm) long. Twigs are hairless with a chambered pith, but green like the hairy buds. *Large white ball-like flowers* are very fragrant; *bloom* June-July. In autumn the *seeds* of the fruiting cone hang from silklike threads when ripe. *Size:* to 50 ft (15 m).

Common winterberry, *Ilex verticillata* (**a**), also known as black alder, is a highly variable shrub common in swamps and wet thickets. The grayish, upright *stem* is multibranched. *Leaves* are dull green, alternate, coarsely toothed, and variable: elliptic to ovate. *Flowers* are white, the males clustered, females solitary, in leaf axils on separate plants; *bloom* June-July. *Berrylike fruits* (clustered at leaf axils) are red, lasting through winter. *Size:* to 15 ft (4.5 m). *Related species:* Smooth winterberry, *I. laevigata,* has shiny green leaves, more finely toothed.

American holly, *Ilex opaca* (**b**), the familiar tree with prickly leaves, grows in freshwater swamps and uplands. Bark is gray and smooth. The distinctive *leaves* are alternate, leathery, thorny, and evergreen; up to 3½ in (9 cm) long. Small, yellowish green male and female *flowers bloom* May-June on separate trees. *Bright red berries* appear on female trees in August on short stalks, and, if songbirds (e.g., catbirds) spare any, last through winter. *Size:* to over 50 ft (15 m). This is the familiar Christmas holly; lumber is ivory white, used for piano keys.

Southern arrowwood, *Viburnum dentatum* (**c**), a shrub with long, straight, hairy twigs, grows in freshwater swamps. *Leaves* are ovoid, opposite, and sharply toothed, up to 3½ in (8 cm) long, 3 in (7.5 cm) wide, on 1 in (2.5 cm) leafstalks; veins prominent and leaves sometimes velvety underneath. *Small white flowers,* on short stalks within clusters up to 4 in (10 cm) across, *bloom* during June-July. *Blue-black berries* contain a flattened, deeply grooved seed. Indians formerly used shoots for arrow shafts. *Size:* to 12 ft (4 m). *Related species:* Naked witherod, *V. nudum,* has glossy twigs and glossy leaves with smooth margins. Smooth blackhaw, *V. prunifolium,* has dull twigs and dull leaves with finely toothed margins.

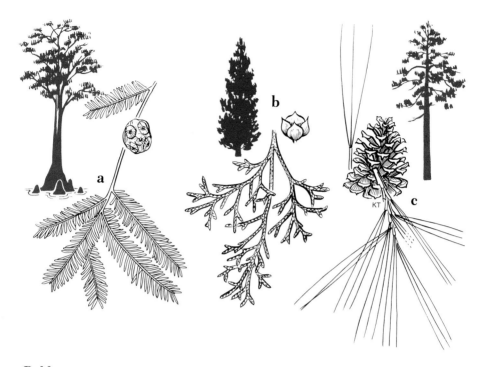

Bald cypress, *Taxodium distichum* (**a**), a southern swamp species, reaches its northern limit in the Chesapeake Bay watershed of Maryland and Delaware. The stringy, gray-brown bark, flanged lower trunk, and appearance of cypress "knees" at the water's surface are distinctive. *Size:* The towering trees regularly reach 120 ft (36 m) in height. Although a conifer, bald cypress is nonevergreen: the needles drop in winter, leaving the canopy bare, hence its name. The *needlelike leaves* are flat, somewhat 3-sided, ¼ to ⅞ in (0.6 to 2.2 cm) long, and green, turning brown in fall. *Ball-shaped cones* are 1 in (2.5 cm) in diameter; contain winged seeds that disperse in October. Bees, wood ducks, and barred owls nest in the hollow trunks of trees several hundred years old.

Atlantic white cedar, *Chamaecyparis thyoides* (**b**), is another conifer, like the loblolly pine, that invades fresh and brackish marshes, and is occasionally found in coastal swamps. *Size:* up to 50 ft (15 m) tall. Trunks and branches gradually taper to a point, giving the tree a characteristic profile. Bark is reddish brown and fibrous. Twigs form a moderately flattened, fan-shaped spray. *Leaves* are flat, scalelike, evergreen, aromatic, and completely cover the twigs. *Cones* are small (⅓ in; 1 cm), spherical, and light blue. Deer frequent cedar swamps in winter, feeding on foliage; songbirds consume the seeds.

Loblolly pine, *Pinus taeda* (**c**), is a colonizer, one of the first trees to invade fresh and brackish marshes, thus transforming them into wooded swamps. *Size:* The tree can grow to 90 ft (27 m), and is sparsely covered with evergreen needles. Bark is reddish brown and shaggy. The long, slender *needles* (5 to 10 in; 13 to 26 cm) appear in bundles of 3. *Cones* are stout, 3 to 5 in (7.5 to 13 cm) long, cylindrical with a broad base, and have short thorns painful to the touch. An important timber tree used for pulp. *Related species:* Pitch pine, *P. rigida*, has needles and cones only half as long as above.

OTHER EMERGENT PLANTS and trees of freshwater swamps and bottomland forests in the Chesapeake Bay region:

Sensitive fern, *Onoclea sensibilis*
Netted chain fern, *Woodwardia areolata*
Marsh shield fern, *Thelypteris thelypteroides*
Royal fern, *Osmunda regalis spectabilis*
Cinnamon fern, *Osmunda cinnamomea*
Woodreed, *Cinna arundinacea*
Tussock sedge, *Carex stricta*, p. 101
Jack-in-the-pulpit, *Arisaema triphyllum*
Golden club, *Orontium aquaticum*
Asian dayflower, *Murdannia keisak*
Turk's cap lily, *Lilium canadense michiganense*
Green woodland orchis, *Platanthera clavellata*
American elm, *Ulmus americana*
River birch, *Betula nigra*, p. 46
Sycamore, *Platanus occidentalis*
Swamp chestnut oak, *Quercus michauxii*
Water oak, *Quercus nigra*
Willow oak, *Quercus phellos*
Wood nettle, *Laportea canadensis*
False nettle, *Boehmeria cylindrica*
Swamp azalea, *Rhododendron viscosum*
American strawberry bush, *Euonymus americanus*
Bayberry, *Myrica pensylvanica*, p. 83
Swamp blackberry, *Rubus hispidus*
Virginia willow, *Itea virginica*
Swamp sweetbells, *Leucothoe racemosa*
Maleberry, *Lyonia ligustrina*
Fringetree, *Chionanthus virginicus*
Water horehound, *Lycopus americanus*
Virginia bugleweed, *Lycopus virginicus*
Water hemlock, *Cicuta maculata*
Water parsnip, *Sium suave*
Turtlehead, *Chelone glabra*
Hedge-hyssop, *Gratiola virginiana*
New York ironweed, *Vernonia noveboracensis*

TYPICAL HERBACEOUS PLANTS found in the transitional zone between shrub swamps and freshwater marshes:

Soft rush, *Juncus effusus*, p. 58
Broad-leaved cattail, *Typha latifolia*, p. 57
Halberd-leaved tearthumb, *Polygonum arifolium*, p. 61
Arrow-leaved tearthumb, *Polygonum sagittatum*, p. 104
Smartweeds, *Polygonum* spp., p. 61
Arrow arum, *Peltandra virginica*, p. 62
Pickerelweed, *Pontederia cordata*, p. 62
Bultongue, *Sagittaria falcata*, p. 86
Broad-leaved arrowhead, *Sagittaria latifolia*, p. 62
Tickseed sunflower, *Bidens coronata*, p. 63
Smooth bur marigold, *Bidens laevis*, p. 63

SWAMP INVERTEBRATES generally are aquatic during at least one

stage of their life cycle. Even the familiar, airborne mosquito (Culicidae; Diptera) begins its life as an egg floating on the surface of the water. Invertebrates found here include *carnivores* like the predaceous diving beetle (Dytiscidae; Coleoptera); *herbivores,* such as water boatmen (Corixidae; Hemiptera) and various pulmonate (i.e., air-breathing) snails (Basommatophora; Gastropoda), both of which feed on algae; *detritovores* (i.e., detritus feeders)—aquatic worms (Oligochaeta; Annelida) and isopods (Asellota; Isopoda; Crustacea), for example; and *filter-feeding* molluscs, such as fingernail clams (Sphaeriidae; Pelecypoda). To be certain, insects are the most visible among the swamp's many invertebrates, ranging from tiny midges (Chironomidae; Diptera) and punkies (Ceratopogonidae; Diptera) to the large dragonflies (Anisoptera; Odonata) that heighten the primordial appearance of the swamp.

Not to scale.

The **common skimmer** (Libellulidae; **1,** *at left*), a type of dragonfly, comes to rest on an arrow arum plant between flights in search of mosquitoes and midges, its most common prey. Meanwhile, a **skimmer nymph (1a)**, remains strictly aquatic until its metamorphosis the following spring. Gill-equipped larvae of dragonflies and other *amphibious insects*— those which spend their immature stages in water and adult life on land—are often found in the mud and debris of the swamp bottom.

At the water's surface, **water striders** (Gerridae; Hemiptera; **2**) skate along the dense and flexible surface film, feeding on emerging midges and other insects. **Whirligig beetles** (Gyrinidae; Coleoptera; **3**) spin about on the water's surface—like minispeedboats—in between dives for prey.

Just underneath the surface are **mosquito larvae (4)** and backswimmers (Notonectidae; Hemiptera), the former breathing with a snorkellike air tube, the latter swimming upside down, propelled with oarlike hind legs.

Other aquatic insects dominate the water column, most notably the **giant water bug** (Belostomatidae; Hemiptera; **5**), which can inflict a painful bite. The male shown *at left* carries eggs laid upon its back by a female. These voracious insects attack tadpoles and fish more than twice their size—about 1 to 2 in (2.5 to 5 cm).

These insects and other swamp invertebrates, such as the **fingernail clam** (*Sphaerium* sp.; **6**), serve as an important link in the food chain between plants and predatory fishes.

FISHES endemic to freshwater swamps are outnumbered by other freshwater species, typically found in rivers and streams, that are tolerant of the acidic and murky conditions of headwater swamps. The bluespotted sunfish, for example, is found in freshwater and slightly brackish streams (up to 12 ppt salinity), and is more common in swamp environments than the banded and blackbanded sunfishes, which are restricted to these environs. In fact, all 7 species illustrated here are also common in freshwater streams. Other freshwater species that enter swamps include the least brook lamprey (*Lampetra aepyptera*), redfin and chain pickerels (*Esox* spp.; p. 66), golden shiner (*Notemigonus crysoleucas*; p. 68), brown bullhead (*Ictalurus nebulosus*; p. 66), banded killifish (*Fundulus diaphanus*; p. 68), mosquitofish (*Gambusia affinis*; p. 68), redbreast sunfish (*Lepomis auritus*; p. 67), and pumpkinseed (*L. gibbosus*; p. 67).

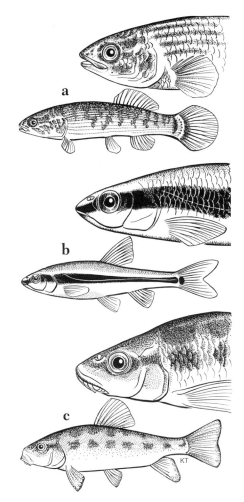

Eastern mudminnow, *Umbra pygmaea* (**a**), is the only member of its family (Umbridae) found in the Bay region. A resident of small sluggish streams and low brackish rivers, this species buries itself in silt or mud where its brown mottled body is well camouflaged. Characteristics include a dorsal fin situated far back on body, a rounded caudal (tail) fin, 10-14 stripes running along sides, and a dark bar at base of tail. *Size*: to 5 in (12.5 cm).

Ironcolor shiner, *Notropis chalybaeus* (**b**), is the smallest of the typical swamp-dwelling fishes. A member of the minnow family, this large-eyed shiner has an iridescent black lateral band extending from lower jaw, through eye, to base of caudal fin, ending in a dark spot. Usually dark above and pale yellow below, the male turns a bright rusty orange on lower half during breeding months. *Size:* no more than 2¼ in (5.5 cm).

Creek chubsucker, *Erimyzon oblongus* (**c**), is a member of the sucker family (Catostomidae), which includes the 2 ft white sucker (*Catostomus commersoni*) common in Maryland tributaries of the Chesapeake Bay. The chubsucker is smaller. A bottom-dwelling fish with a ventral, suckerlike mouth, this stocky species is recognized by the 5 to 8 black saddles across its olive-brown back; each ends in a dark, midlateral blotch or stripe (disappearing in older adults). *Size:* to 11 in (28 cm).

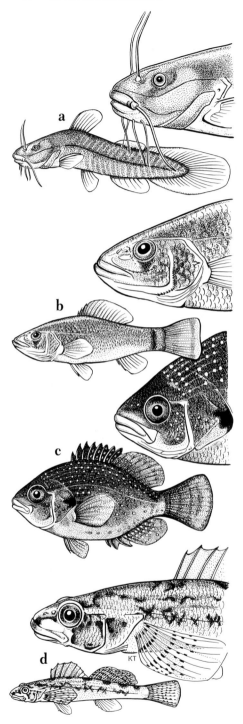

Tadpole madtom, *Noturus gyrinus* (**a**), a secretive inhabitant of slow, quiet streams and swamps, is a member of the catfish family (Ictaluridae). Brown above and yellowish underneath, this little madtom is shaped like a tadpole—broad up front yet narrow toward the rear. Note 4 pairs of *barbels* on head and long, olive-colored *adipose fin* behind dorsal fin that continues into a large, broad, fanlike tail. Pectoral fin has a single spine equipped with poison gland at base; can inflict a painful sting. *Size:* to 4½ in (11.5 cm).

Pirate perch, *Aphredoderus sayanus* (**b**), is the only living species of the pirate perch family (Aphredoderidae) that once included at least 6 species in North America. An oblong, olive-colored fish, heavy at front and compressed toward rear, the pirate perch has a mottled head and body, with eyes near top and directed upward. Dorsal fin has 2 to 3 sharp spines. In adults, anus is located in throat region, having migrated forward during maturation. *Size:* to 4½ in (11.5 cm). Backwaters of slow-moving streams are preferred.

Bluespotted sunfish, *Enneacanthus gloriosus* (**c**), is a colorful inhabitant of swamps and sluggish streams. Shading from nearly black above to light olive on belly, the greenish sides and fins are sprinkled with bright, sky-blue spots, as are fins. Caudal (tail) fin is rounded rather than forked, as in most sunfishes (Centrarchidae). *Size:* to 3 in (7.6 cm). *Related species:* Blackbanded sunfish, *E. chaetodon,* has 6 to 8 broad, black bands; lacks spots. Banded sunfish, *E. obesus,* has 5-8 dark bars and light blue spots on dorsal fin.

Tessellated darter, *Etheostoma olmstedi* (**d**), is a small (to 3¼ in; 8 cm) member of the perch family (Percidae) known for its habit of darting from place to place. Like other perches, this streamlined species has 2 separate dorsal fins, but tail is rounded rather than forked. The body is olive-brown above (yellowish below) and tessellated—bearing a checkered pattern of midlateral markings that resemble the letter W or X. *Related species:* Swamp darter, *E. fusiforme,* is smaller (2 in; 5 cm) and yellowish green with dark blotches on sides. Prefers flowing runs, not still swamps.

AMPHIBIANS AND REPTILES turn the swamp into a symphony of

color and sound. Beginning in spring, the tiny spring peeper (*Hyla crucifer),* as well as the small upland chorus frog (*Pseudacris triseriata* ssp.; p. 69), northern cricket frog (*Acris c. crepitans;* p. 69), and green treefrog (*Hyla cinerea;* p. 86), call resoundingly through the swamp. Below this high-pitched trill, larger frogs compete with their deeper mating calls. The swampland also harbors such quiet, hard-to-find amphibians as mole salamanders (*Ambystoma* spp.), dusky salamanders (*Desmognathus* spp.), brook salamanders (*Eurycea* spp.), and woodland salamanders (*Plethodon* spp.). Turtles and snakes are the most visible reptiles, with several species of freshwater turtles and three kinds of water snakes (p. 70) to be seen basking on stumps, rocks, and logs. The terrestrial eastern box turtle (*Terrapene carolina*), northern black racer (*Coluber c. constrictor;* below), and eastern garter snake (*Thamnophis s. sirtalis*) visit wooded areas on the swamp edge.

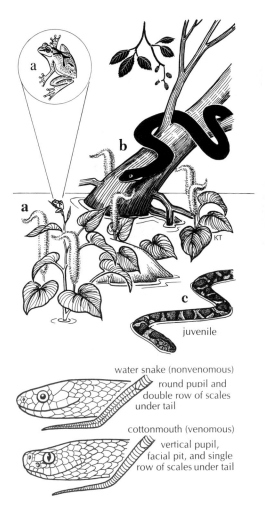

Northern spring peeper, *Hyla crucifer crucifer* (**a**), is the smallest (³/₄ to 1³/₈ in; 1.9 to 3.5 cm) treefrog (Hylidae) found in the Bay area and the best known. Though its coloring varies from grayish brown to olive, the dark diagonal crucifix on its back distinguishes it from all other frogs in the region. During March virtually every swamp and temporary pool resounds with the shrill, piping call of the males.

Northern black racer, *Coluber constrictor constrictor* (**b**), is a 30 to 60 in (76 to 152 cm) long, fast-moving snake, best described as a black streak in the grass. Racers frequent the edges of swamps, lured there by the abundant prey. This species does not constrict frogs and mice, however, as does a rat snake, but instead pins down a struggling victim with a loop or two of its cylindrical body. *Confusing species:* Black rat snake (*Elaphe o. obsoleta*) is shaped—in cross section—like a loaf of bread.

Northern water snake, *Nerodia sipedon sipedon* (**c**), is a *nonvenomous* resident of virtually every swamp, stream, river, and marsh in the Bay region. A medium-to-large (24 to 53 in; 61 to 134 cm) aquatic species with a highly variable pattern of markings. These and other water snakes (see p. 70) have a divided *anal plate* and a double row of scales under the tail. *Confusing species:* **Eastern cottonmouth,** *Agkistrodon p. piscivorus, bottom right,* has a deep pit between eye and nostril, a single *anal plate,* and a single row of scales under tail; *SE Virginia only*; VENOMOUS.

juvenile

water snake (nonvenomous)
round pupil and
double row of scales
under tail

cottonmouth (venomous)
vertical pupil,
facial pit, and single
row of scales under tail

TRUE FROGS (Ranidae) are long-legged, with fingers free and toes joined by webbing.

Bullfrog, *Rana catesbeiana* (**a**), the largest frog in North America, is best known for its deep, bass voice—resonating with a distinctive, thudding "br-rum." Unlike the other *Rana* species *above*, the bullfrog lacks a *dorsolateral ridge* along its body. Coloring is usually green to olive-brown above, with head normally solid green; pale below. On male, throat is mottled with yellow, and eardrum (*tympanum*) is larger than eye. Breeds from May to July. *Size:* to 8 in (20 cm).

Green frog, *Rana clamitans melanota* (**b**), is a typical frog of creeks, ponds, and small streams, but is often abundant in swamps. Typically half the size of a bullfrog, it has similar markings: bright green to greenish brown above and white underneath, yet highly variable (often more brown than green). Sexual differences similar to bullfrog above; however, *dorsolateral ridge* continues along body (though not reaching groin). Voice is a deep, twangy "p'tung"—like the low string on a banjo. Breeds mostly May to July. *Size:* to 4 in (10 cm).

Southern leopard frog, *Rana spheno-cephala* (**c**), the most common and widespread frog in the Bay region, is green to greenish brown above with 2 or 3 rows of irregular dark spots between prominent *dorsolateral ridges.* Ridges end at groin. Underbelly is white. Distinguishing marks include a long, pointed head and a white spot at center of tympanum. Mating call is a series of gutteral croaks followed by a few trill-like clicks—such as the sound made by rubbing a balloon. Breeds in early spring. *Size:* to 5 in (12.7 cm).

Pickerel frog, *Rana palustris* (**d**), occurs along shaded streams and swamps throughout the region, but populations are isolated (i.e., highly *local*). This species is distinguished from other *Rana* species by the 2 parallel rows of distinctly squarish (or rectangular) spots found between the conspicuous dorsolateral ridges that extend to the groin. White underbelly is mottled with brown, and inner surface of thigh is bright yellow or orange. Skin secretions are toxic to some animals; avoided by most snakes. Mating call is a low-pitched snore. Breeds March-May. *Size:* to 3 in (7.6 cm).

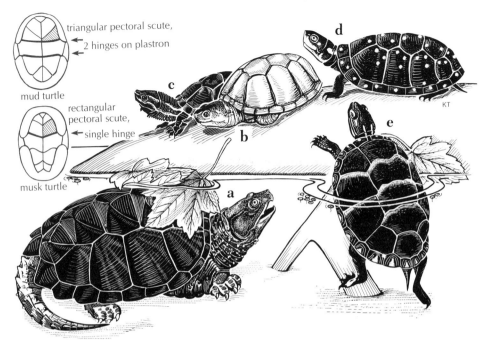

triangular pectoral scute,
2 hinges on plastron

mud turtle

rectangular
pectoral scute,
single hinge

musk turtle

TURTLES (Testudines) have an upper shell, the *carapace,* and a lower shell, the *plastron.*

Common snapping turtle, *Chelydra serpentina serpentina* (a), prefers slow-moving backwaters and muddy bottoms typified by Bay area swamps. The largest (8 to 18^1/$_2$ in; 20 to 47 cm) and most aggressive turtle in our area, this species is easily recognized by its large head, thick brown shell, and long, saw-toothed tail. The *carapace* has three prominent ridges, which become obscure with age. Snappers forage on plants, invertebrates, fish, and carrion.

Eastern mud turtle, *Kinosternon subrubrum subrubrum* (b), is a ubiquitous species that prefers shallow margins of ditches, swamps, and tidal marshes. This small (3 to 4 in; 7.5 to 10 cm), semiaquatic species is the *only* mud turtle in our region. *Carapace* is yellowish brown to black, with black margins at junction of each plate, or *scute. Plastron* is yellowish with 2 hinges, as seen at upper left. *Confusing species:* **Stinkpot,** *Sternotherus odoratus* (c), a musk turtle, has 2 light stripes on head and a small plastron with a single hinge.

Spotted turtle, *Clemmys guttata* (d), is best known for its many yellow spots sprinkled over the shell. A frequent basker, it is nonchalant and enters water leisurely if disturbed. *Carapace* is slate gray or black with a variable number of spots (1 to over 100); may disappear in older turtles. *Plastron* is yellow or orange with wide black smudges. Brown-eyed males pursue yellow-eyed females in wild courtship chase during March, April, or May, when they are most likely seen. *Size:* to 5 in (12.5 cm).

Eastern painted turtle, *Chrysemys picta picta* (e), is a colorful basking turtle, bearing a low, domed, black (or olive) *carapace* spectacularly trimmed in red. Neck stripes are red, turning into yellow on side of head and chin. Legs also marked with red. *Plastron* is yellow. On *carapace,* the larger *scutes* occur in straight rows across back. The smaller males have long, front fingernails that are used to stroke the necks of females during their face-to-face courtship ritual. *Size:* to 7 in (18 cm).

BIRDS abound in swamps and bottomland woods. Over the hammering of woodpeckers and above the hoots of owls can be heard a cacophony of chirps, whistles, and warbles, only finding rival perhaps in the forests of tropical realms. The abundant shelter and plentiful food—in the form of berries, seeds, and insects—attract many birds into these wet thickets during the breeding months. In fact most of the dozen or so *breeding birds* described below prefer to nest in swamps or floodplain forests. The prothonotary warbler, for example, is restricted to the habitat; that is, it nests only in wooded swamps or wet woods. During the fall many *migratory species* stop off in Chesapeake swamps; for example, the blue-winged warbler, *Vermivora pinus*, may visit on its way to Central America. Other transients are listed on p. 50. In winter only a few birds remain and the swamp is quiet. Staying behind, the barred owl patrols at dusk on silent wings.

Barred owl, *Strix varia* (**a**), is the largest and most common owl (Strigidae; Strigiformes) of swamps and bottomland woods. *Field marks:* Barred owl is the only eastern owl besides common barn owl (*Tyto alba*) that has dark brown eyes. Note barred markings across chest contrasting with vertical brown streaks on belly. *Size:* length to 24 in (60 cm); wingspan averages 44 in (110 cm). *Call:* Hoots 8 times, in 2 groups of 4—"who-cooks-for-you . . . who-cooks-for-y'all." *Food*: A nocturnal bird of prey, this swamp owl feeds on small rodents, rabbits, birds, and frogs. *Season:* All year; nests in natural cavities within river birch (*at left*) and other trees of wooded swamps.

Wood duck, *Aix sponsa* (**b**), is the waterfowl species (Anatidae; Anseriformes) most likely to be seen in wooded swamps. *Field marks:* Often seen perched in trees, the colorful wood duck is best known for the large head and swept-back crest of the male. Female is dull-colored with a dark crest and white ring around eye. *Flight*: Look for long squared-off tail and white belly (p. 73). *Size:* length to 20 in (50 cm); wingspan averages 28 in (70 cm). *Call*: A rising whistle. *Food*: Seeds of wetland and woodland plants, including acorns (oak), smartweed, wild rice, pondweed (SAV), and duckweed. *Season:* All year but uncommon in winter; nests in tree cavities, sometimes old pileated woodpecker holes.

WOODPECKERS (Picidae; Piciformes) are colorful year-round residents of wooded swamps. Diet is mainly wood-boring insects. Woodpeckers nest in holes excavated from live or dead trees. *Season:* All year.

Red-bellied woodpecker, *Melanerpes carolinus* (**a**), is the commonest woodpecker of forested swamps. *Field marks:* Though similar in size to the related red-headed woodpecker (*M. erythrocephalus*), the red-bellied has a red cap and nape (not head) and a black-and-white, ladderlike back. Female has red nape only; cap gray. Face and breast are light colored and rump is white. Red belly patch is difficult to see. *In flight*, note small white wing patch, hidden while perched. Tail is barred and stiff; used for support. *Call:* often a "chiv-chiv." *Size:* to 9 in (23 cm).

Downy woodpecker, *Picoides pubescens* (**b**), is another common permanent resident of bottomland forests and wooded swamps. *Field marks:* A small black-and-white species with a short slender bill, the downy is recognized by the vertical white stripe on back. A red patch marks the back of male's head, whereas female has continuous black cap. Note downy white nasal tufts. Wings are checkered with white. Outer tail feathers have a few black spots. *Call* is a series of "piks," softer than the hairy woodpecker's louder, sharper "peek." *Size:* to 6 in (15 cm). *Related species:* Hairy woodpecker, *P. villosus*, is larger (9 in; 23 cm); has a longer bill; lacks spots on tail.

Pileated woodpecker, *Dryocopus pileatus* (**c**), is a spectacular, large black woodpecker easily identified by its great *size:* 16 to 19 in (40 to 48 cm). *Field marks:* Look for white underwings, and brilliant red crest. Male has a red mustache and a full red crest while female has a blackish forehead topped with a red crown and a solid black mustache. In both, chin is white. Loud hammering on mature trees such as this loblolly pine (*at right*) resounds through the swamp and repetitive chipping at bark and trunk produces distinctive oval or oblong holes. *Call* is a loud, irregular series: "Kicka-kicka . . ." or "kick-kick-kick."

OTHER BIRDS of freshwater swamps include hummingbirds (Trochilidae; Apodiformes) and perching birds (Passeriformes). Also see p. 50.

Ruby-throated hummingbird, *Archilochus colubris* (**a**), is the smallest bird in the Bay area and the only hummingbird found in the mid-Atlantic region. *Field marks:* The iridescent ruby throat of the male, green back, and needlelike bill (used to sip nectar) are distinctive. Female lacks red throat and has a blunt tail, whereas male's tail is forked. *Flight:* Hovering with a rapid, humming wingbeat, they frequent the tubular flowers so common in swamps, preferring red flowers such as the crossvine (*above*). *Season:* Late spring-early fall; tiny 2 in (5 cm) nest in trees near swamp edges. *Size:* 3 to 3³/4 in (8 to 9 cm).

Acadian flycatcher, *Empidonax virescens* (**b**), is a small, short-tailed flycatcher that commonly nests in forested swamps and wet woods. *Field marks:* The Acadian has 2 white wing bars. Male and female are similar. Note white throat, greenish back, and distinct yellowish eye ring. *Call:* A sharp, rising "pit-see!" *Size:* 4¹/2 to 5¹/2 in (11.5 to 14 cm). *Season:* Late spring-

early fall; has a unique nest shaped like a shallow basket with long streamers of dried grass.

Great crested flycatcher, *Myiarchus crinitus* (**c**), has 2 light wing bars similar to the Acadian, but is much larger. *Field marks:* Olive crest, gray breast, yellow belly, and a long rust-colored tail. *In flight, primaries* are cinnamon as well. At rest, posture is erect; long tail is held still, does not bob like Acadian's. Like other flycatchers, this species catches insects on the wing with a loud snap of its broad bill. *Call* is a loud "wheep." *Size:* 7 to 9 in (18 to 23 cm). *Season:* Late spring-early fall; nests in tree cavity or abandoned woodpecker hole.

Tufted titmouse, *Parus bicolor* (**d**), is another crested bird but one that feeds in trees, with considerable acrobatics, sometimes upside down—like a chickadee. *Field marks:* In wooded swamps, titmice will associate with Carolina chickadees (*P. carolinensis*), but can be distinguished by their larger size, tufted gray crest, and missing cap and bib. *Call* is a clear "peter, peter, peter." *Size:* 5¹/2 to 6 in (13.75 to 15 cm). *Season:* All year; nests in tree cavity.

Gray catbird, *Dumetella carolinensis* (**a**), is a member of the mimic thrush family (Mimidae), which includes the brown thrasher and mockingbird; however, the catbird is a poor imitator and better known for its catlike mewing and musical songs. *Field marks:* A slender species, its body is slate gray with the exception of rusty undertail coverts. Often flicks long, thrasherlike tail while mewing. The black cap and tail are distinctive. *Size:* to 8 in (20 cm). *Season:* Spring-fall; uncommon in winter; nests in dense undergrowth of swamps and thickets.

Red-eyed vireo, *Vireo olivaceus* (**b**), is slightly larger than a warbler and less active. *Field marks:* Though red iris is not noticeable at a distance, it is distinctive, as are the black-and-white eyebrow stripes and blue-gray cap. This olive-backed vireo lacks the wing bars and eye rings of the yellow-throated vireo (*V. flavifrons*). *Call* includes a nasal "chway" and other notes, repeated 35 to 70 times a minute, sometimes all day long. *Size:* to 6 in (15 cm). *Season:* Spring-fall; cuplike nest is suspended in branch fork of sapling or tree.

Prothonotary warbler, *Protonotaria citrea* (**c**), is the most common of the many warblers that frequent wooded swamps. *Field marks:* The golden yellow head and breast and plain, bluish gray wings distinguish it from the blue-winged warbler (*Vermivora pinus*) which visits swamp edges (bears wing bars). Prothonotary has a long bill and a short tail streaked with white. *Call* is a series of 6 to 8 emphatic notes: "zweet, zweet, zweet," etc. *Size:* to 5 in (12.5 cm). *Season:* Spring-early fall; nests in tree cavity or old woodpecker hole.

Louisiana waterthrush, *Seiurus motacilla* (**d**), is a transient and summer resident of bottomland forests and wooded swamps. *Field marks* include a longish bill, white throat, brown back, and white breast stippled with brown. Note white eyebrow stripe. Walks along water's edge bobbing its tail like spotted sandpiper. *Size:* to 6 in (15 cm). *Call* consists of 3 whistles ("see-you, see-you, see-you"), followed by descending notes. *Season:* Spring-early fall; nest built in shallow hole near stream. *Related species:* Northern waterthrush, *S. noveboracensis,* a transient, has spotted throat and buff eyebrow stripe.

OTHER COMMON BIRDS of freshwater swamps in the Chesapeake Bay region:

Green-backed heron, *Butorides striatus* (common breeder), p. 88
Red-shouldered hawk, *Buteo lineatus*
Yellow-billed cuckoo, *Coccyzus americanus*
Eastern screech-owl, *Otus asio*
Northern flicker, *Colaptes auratus*
Eastern wood-pewee, *Contopus virens*
Blue jay, *Cyanocitta cristata*
American crow, *Corvus brachyrhynchos*
Carolina wren, *Thryothorus ludovicianus*
Blue-gray gnatcatcher, *Polioptila caerulea*
Northern parula, *Parula americana*
Yellow-rumped warbler, *Dendroica coronata* (winter)
American redstart, *Setophaga ruticilla*
Hooded warbler, *Wilsonia citrina*
Northern cardinal, *Cardinalis cardinalis*
White-throated sparrow, *Zonotrichia albicollis* (winter)
Purple finch, *Carpodacus purpureus* (winter)

LOCAL OR FAIRLY COMMON BIRDS of freshwater swamps in the Bay area:

Great blue heron, *Ardea herodias* (local nester), p. 71
Hooded merganser, *Lophodytes cucullatus* (local nester), p. 92
Yellow-bellied sapsucker, *Sphyrapicus varius* (winter)
Hairy woodpecker, *Picoides villosus*
Carolina chickadee, *Parus carolinensis*
White-breasted nuthatch, *Sitta carolinensis*
Brown creeper, *Certhia americana* (mostly winter)
Winter wren, *Troglodytes troglodytes* (winter)
Ruby-crowned kinglet, *Regulus calendula* (winter)
Swainson's thrush, *Catharus ustulatus* (transient)
Hermit thrush, *Catharus guttatus* (winter)
Wood thrush, *Hylocichla mustelina*
Yellow-throated vireo, *Vireo flavifrons*
Blue-winged warbler, *Vermivora pinus* (transient)
Yellow-throated warbler, *Dendroica dominica*
Northern waterthrush, *Seiurus noveboracensis* (transient)
Kentucky warbler, *Oporornis formosus*
Scarlet tanager, *Piranga olivacea*
Rusty blackbird, *Euphagus carolinus* (transient)

MAMMALS endemic to freshwater swamps are few, but many wide-spread furbearers are found within the confines of Bay area swamps. In shrub swamps, medium-sized mammals are the most commonly encountered, particularly the opossum, muskrat, eastern cottontail (*Sylvilagus floridanus*), and, in Virginia, the marsh rabbit (*below*). A greater diversity of mammals is found in wooded swamps. Here, cottontail, red fox, white-tailed deer, and other *upland species* frequently visit the swamp floor, while the *aquatic* muskrat, beaver, and river otter are spotted swimming on the surface of streams and pools. Overhead, the opossum, raccoon, gray squirrel (*Sciurus carolinensis*), and noc-turnal southern flying squirrel (*Glaucomys volans*) are seen in the mature trees of older swamps. Insectivores of shrub and wooded swamps include the northern short-tailed shrew (*Blarina brevicauda*), least shrew (*Cryptotis parva*), and star-nosed mole (*Condylura cristata*). Most abundant, however, are the many small rodents, including the white-footed mouse (*Peromyscus leucopus*), house mouse (*Mus musculus*), and Norway rat (*Rattus norvegicus*).

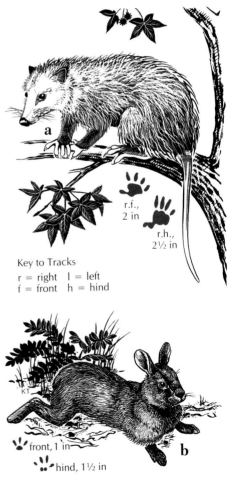

r.f., 2 in

r.h., 2½ in

Key to Tracks
r = right   l = left
f = front   h = hind

front, 1 in

hind, 1½ in

Virginia opossum, *Didelphis virginiana* (**a**), the only native North American marsupial, is nocturnal, omnivorous, and for the most part arboreal, found in trees such as the sweetgum (*at right*) in our local swamps and bottomland forests. *Field marks:* Grayish body is 15 to 20 in (38 to 51 cm) long, about the size of a domestic cat, but with short legs and a naked, ratlike prehensile (grasping) tail. Face is white with a pointed nose and black, paper-thin ears. *Breeding:* In swamps opossum typically den in hollow trees where up to 14 tiny young are born in spring and remain in pouch for 2 months; afterwards, 7 to 9 survivors travel on mother's back. *Food:* Omnivorous; fruits, nuts, insects, eggs, and carrion are eaten. *Note:* Adults may "play possum," feigning death when cornered.

Marsh rabbit, *Sylvilagus palustris* (**b**), is the only Chesapeake Bay area mammal restricted to swamps and marshes. *Field marks:* A southern species about the size of an eastern cottontail, this dark brown, small-footed rabbit with a small grayish tail reaches the northern limit of its distribution in southeastern Virginia below the James River. *Not found in Maryland. Size:* to 16 in (41 cm). *Food:* This nocturnal species feeds on herbaceous plants and grasses. *Breeding:* Typically 2-4 young are born in nest on ground. *Related species:* Eastern cottontail, *S. floridanus,* found on wetland edges, is recognized by large white feet, larger ears, and conspicuous white "cottonball" tail.

front, 3 in

hind,
6 in

Muskrat, *Ondatra zibethicus* (**a**), is a widespread, aquatic rodent found in ponds, streams, swamps, and marshes—wherever there is water. Individuals are often seen swimming on the surface of the water, only to disappear (via an underwater entrance) into a den in the stream bank or into a muskrat house, made of mud and soft-stem grasses. *Field marks:* Muskrats are recognized by their rich brown to blackish fur which covers the 10 to 14 in (25 to 36 cm) head and body and by their 10 in (25 cm) long, black, scaly, naked tail which is flattened from side to side. *Food:* Mostly wetland plants, although clams, frogs, and fish are eaten.

Beaver, *Castor canadensis* (**b**), were once extirpated from the Chesapeake Bay region due to trapping pressure, but have now been reintroduced with remarkable success. Their preference for alder, maple, willow, and river birch makes swamps and small streams prime beaver habitat. Gnawed limbs, dams, and stick-and-mud lodge indicate the presence of beaver. *Field marks:* Head and body are up to 30 in (76 cm) long, with a 10 in (25 cm) tail. Fur is dark brown; tail is flat, naked, and shaped like a pad-dle. The large, chestnut-colored front teeth are often visible on beavers when seen at midday, though for the most part the species is nocturnal. *Breeding:* Two-six young (kits) are born in one-room lodge in spring. *Food:* The vegetarian beaver lives chiefly on the inner bark and wood of twigs and trees as well as grasses (in summer). *Note:* Long-standing dams can create a swamp environment.

River otter, *Lutra canadensis* (**c**), is a secretive but playful member of the weasel family (Mustelidae). *Field marks:* Head and body measure 26 to 30 in (66 to 76 cm) long and are covered with dense brown fur, slightly silvery below. Tail is up to 19 in (48 cm) long, thick at base, and tapering at tip; used as a rudder while swimming. Males are larger than females. Feet are webbed; eyes amber. Highly aquatic, otters make dens in stream banks—like some muskrats—with an underwater entrance. *Food:* Fish, frogs, aquatic invertebrates, even small birds and mammals are eaten. *Similar species:* Mink, *Mustela vison,* is half as large, has a white chin patch, and does not have webbed feet.

Raccoon, *Procyon lotor* (**a**), is one of our most ubiquitous mammals. Because of a preference for frogs, crustaceans, and aquatic insects in a diet that also includes wild fruits and nuts, the familiar bandit often feeds in swamps and at the edges of streams. *Field marks:* The distinctive black mask and foot-long ringed tail are sufficient to identify this 28 in (70 cm) long carnivore. *Breeding:* Mostly nocturnal, they den in old hawks' nests or in hollow trees, such as this red maple *at right,* where 3 to 6 young are born in spring. A low twittering sound from the mother keeps her offspring close by and at ease.

Red fox, *Vulpes vulpes* (**b**), is the more common of two foxes that may be found in our local forests, farmlands, and swamps. *Field marks:* About the size of a small dog—head and body 25 in (63 cm), tail 15 in (38 cm)—the red fox is rust-red above and white below, with a bushy red-and-black tail tipped with white. Lower legs and feet are black. Several color variations are known. Mostly nocturnal, though seen at dawn and dusk. *Food* includes insects, berries, rabbits, and mice. *Breeding:* Male (dog) and female (vixen) raise and feed pups together in den. *Similar species:* Gray fox, *Urocyon cinereoargenteus,* has a salt-and-pepper coat and a tail striped and tipped with black; prefers upland forest.

White-tailed deer, *Odocoileus virginianus* (**c**), is best known for its large white tail, upright and flagging back and forth as it disappears into the brush. At rest, tail is brown above. Frequenting woods and edges of wetlands, whitetails often migrate to the seclusion of swamps in winter. *Field marks:* Antlered bucks are 5 ft long and stand up to $3^1/2$ ft (105 cm) high at shoulder, weighing 75-250 lbs. Female (doe) is one-third smaller. *Breeding:* Doe has 1 or 2 young in spring. Fawns remain spotted for 5 months, and travel with mother for 12 to 18 months. *Food:* Whitetails are browsers, feeding in swamps on greenbrier, jewelweed, and leaves and twigs of woody plants. *Note:* Though an upland species, deer (and their tracks) can be seen in most wetlands and along streams; they are good swimmers.

hind foot,

± 3 in

Freshwater Tributaries and Adjoining Freshwater Marshes

MORE than 150 tributaries contribute fresh water to the Chesapeake Bay. Of these, nearly half are tidal and run either full-length into the estuary or converge with large estuarine rivers before entering the Bay. In the present chapter, the freshwater reaches of coastal plain tributaries are the focus, with a particular emphasis on marshes bordering tidal streams.

The stream and marsh are linked together, symbionts in a watery world. And since tidal fluctuations are sometimes pronounced in the upper sections of tidal tributaries, the demarcation between creek and marsh is not always clear. For example, at high tide, spatterdock (*at left*) may show only leaves and flowers above the water, while at low tide the stems may be high and (nearly) dry on an exposed mud flat.

In this chapter we look at freshwater stream and marsh together as an integrated habitat. In the stream, *aquatic species* dominate, and, in the marsh, *wetland species* reign. There is much overlap, however, with many species of frogs, snakes, birds, and mammals utilizing both areas. (Only fish are tied to just one, though at high tide minnows may invade temporary shallows in the marsh.) Both environments are subjected to similar stresses: Stream and marsh contend with daily fluctuations in tide and seasonal variations in salinity.

Tidal fresh water is defined as the narrow region of the salinity gradient between 0 ppt (parts per thousand) salinity and 0.5 ppt (see fig. 3; p. 12). However, as we have seen, salinity zones are mutable; that is, they fluctuate over time. A tidal section that is normally freshwater may become slightly brackish (0.5 to 5 ppt) during a summer drought. Aquatic species (e.g., freshwater fishes) may migrate upstream at these times. The marsh community along this stretch will nonetheless remain a *freshwater* wetland, tolerating the temporary influx of brackish water, unless the salinity change is prolonged.

Thus, because of the indefinite boundary between fresh and brackish regions of a given river, we rely on plant composition to define the wetland habitat. The marsh plants described in this chapter may tolerate slightly brackish (i.e., oligohaline) conditions for a period of time but are *typical* freshwater species. Similarly, freshwater invertebrates and fishes may migrate into the oligohaline, but this downstream habitat is marginal.

Marshes are typically covered with a few inches of water at mean high tide, though the community may extend to the spring or storm tide limit. The plants are generally herbaceous (i.e., nonwoody) species. Emergent plants far outnumber both floating-leaved plants and the handful of submersed aquatic species (SAV) in the stream channel (see p. 163). While shrubs and trees may grow at the upland (or swamp) margin, they are not typical of the marsh community. The shading canopy of trees limits the growth of herbaceous species at these margins, and, when overhanging a creek, may prevent sunlight from reaching and nurturing SAV.

To verify that you are viewing a freshwater marsh, look for indicator plants. Important species include broad-leaved cattail, which grows in stable shallow-water areas; river bulrush, which typically grows in bands at the river edge; tall grasses, particularly wild rice and Walter's millet; smartweeds and tearthumbs; and, in shallow open water, spatterdock, arrow arum, and pickerelweed. In elevated areas of the marsh, look for swamp type shrubs, such as buttonbush, sweet pepperbush, or silky dogwood (p. 33). In addition to these shrubs, red maple (p. 34) and common alder (p. 35) may colonize the marsh edge, representing the transition (and succession) of marsh into woody swamp.

Herbaceous plants are distributed in small colonies (or larger tracts) within the wetland, typically in a zonation pattern that is influenced by water depth, soil type, and elevation (see fig. 8; p. 98). However, compared to salt and brackish marshes, generally there is a more heterogeneous mixture of plants.

The value of unpolluted streams and healthy adjoining marshes to the Bay, to wildlife, and to the public cannot be overestimated. Marshes provide a variety of benefits. They function as a buffer to shoreline erosion, recycle nutrients, improve water quality, recharge groundwater, and generate detritus for aquatic species, particularly zooplankton and invertebrates. Marshes also furnish habitat for wildlife, while clean streams and SAV supply spawning areas for anadromous fishes such as shad and herring.

A few freshwater marshes are now under protection as national wildlife refuges (NWR), state wildlife management areas (WMA), or local government natural areas and parks. Visit Merkle Wildlife Sanctuary and Jug Bay in Patuxent River Park (Prince George's County, Maryland), Jug Bay Wetlands Sanctuary (Anne Arundel County, Maryland), Dyke Marsh and Mason Neck NWR on the Potomac, the wild rice marshes of the Pamunkey off the York River, or Presquile NWR (near Hopewell) and the Chickahominy off the James River to see fine examples of pristine freshwater wetlands.

THE PLANT COMMUNITY of fresh river marshes can be nearly as diverse as the swamp profile upstream but differs strongly in the types of flora found. Marsh plants are typically herbaceous, whereas swamps by definition contain mostly woody plants. In the marsh environment woody "associated shrubs," such as buttonbush (*Cephalanthus occidentalis*, p. 103) only grow along upland margins or on elevated hummocks within the marsh. The emergent, herbaceous species also reside in certain zones relative to mean high tide (see fig. 8; p. 98). In a typical *mixed freshwater community*, no single herbaceous species covers more than half of the marshland. Notwithstanding this generalization, almost pure stands of cattail, common reed, or arrow arum and pickerelweed are sometimes found. Submersed even at mean low tide are a variety of underwater plants (p. 64 and pp. 163-165) that are able to grow in marsh-bordered streams where sunlight is not obscured, as it is along wooded streams and swamps.

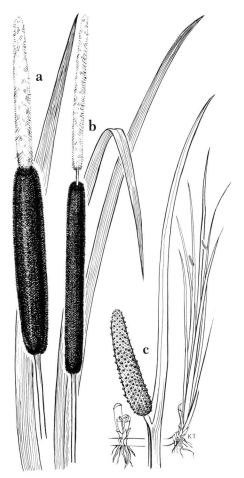

EMERGENT PLANTS of fresh marshes feature the cattails (Typhaceae) and arums (Araceae) with their distinctive flowering spikes *(at right)*. Grasses, sedges, rushes, and other herbaceous species follow. Most are *perennial* plants.

Broad-leaved cattail, *Typha latifolia* (**a**), grows in colonies in shallow water at stream or upland borders. *Leaves* are of two types: *basal leaves*, which arise from the stem base, are up to 6 ft (2 m) long; and *stem leaves*, which are alternate, up to 2½ ft (76 cm) long; both up to 1 in (25 mm) wide. *Stems* are stout and upright; grow from *rhizomes*. *Flowers* are inconspicuous, densely crowded on two terminal spikes; male flowers on the upper spike, female on lower spike (1 in; 25 mm thick); spikes touch. *Seedlike achene* has silky bristles attached to base. *Size*: up to 9 ft (2.7 m). *Related species*: **Narrow-leaved cattail,** *T. angustifolia* (**b**), has narrower leaves (up to ½ in; 12.7 mm wide); flower spikes are separate.

Sweet flag, *Acorus calamus* (**c**), grows in loose colonies in shallow water. *Basal leaves* are long and tapering, up to 5 ft (1.5 m) long; midvein is off-center; leaves up to 1 in (25 mm) wide, fanning out at plant base and ending in a sharp point. *Stems* are lacking; aromatic leaves arise from creeping rhizomes in mud. *Flowers* are small and yellowish on spikelike *spadix* up to 4 in (10 cm) long. *Size*: up to 5 ft (1.5 m).

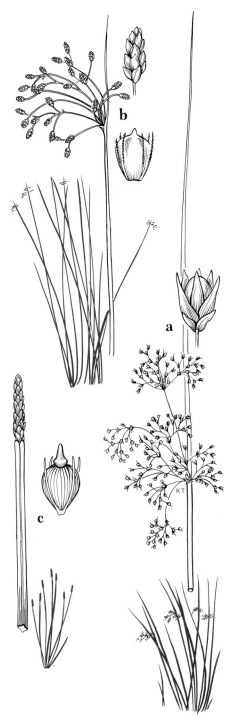

RUSHES (Juncaceae) typically have round, solid stems and fruit capsules that contain many tiny seeds.

Soft rush, *Juncus effusus* (**a**), a grasslike, apparently leafless plant, grows in dense clumps (tussocks) in freshwater marshes. *Leaves* lack blades; reduced to sheaths at stem base. *Stem* is round, soft, and green; tapers to a point; grows from stout rhizome. *Flowers* are borne at the tips of branching clusters arising from a single point on upper half of stem; greenish brown with 3 pointed sepals and 3 similar petals; *blooms* July-August. *Numerous seeds* are contained inside brownish capsule (shown) on spikelets. *Size*: up to 3^1/$_2$ ft (1 m).

SEDGES (Cyperaceae) include the familiar bulrushes and spikerushes. Sedges generally have triangular or round, solid stems. Fruits are single nutlets (*achenes*).

Great bulrush, *Scirpus validus* (**b**), or soft-stemmed bulrush, is a tall colonial species of tidal fresh and brackish marshes. *Leaves* lack blades (as in soft rush). *Stems*, either arching or upright, are round, soft, and grayish green; taper to a point; grow from stout red *rhizome*. *Flowers* are borne in budlike oval spikelets, arising from tip of stem; *bloom* July-August. *Achene* (shown) is brownish with 4-6 bristles attached to base; grouped in drooping clusters near top of stem. *Size*: up to 8 ft (2.4 m).

Spikerushes (*Eleocharis* spp.) are leafless, grasslike plants with terminal flowering heads. Typical species in Chesapeake tidal wetlands include blunt spikerush, *E. obtusa*, and common spikerush, *E. palustris*. Dwarf spikerush, *E. parvula*, invades brackish wetlands, forming low mats (see p. 100).

Square-stem spikerush, *Eleocharis quadrangulata* (**c**), is a tall freshwater species. *Leaves* are reduced to stem sheaths. *Stem* is distinctly 4-sided. *Flowers* inconspicuous on single, terminal spikelet. *Achenes* (shown) are grouped in terminal spikelet barely thicker than stem. *Size:* up to 4 ft (1.2 m).

River bulrush, *Scirpus fluviatilis* (**a**), grows in freshwater wetlands, often in bands at the river edge. *Leaves* are long and grasslike, arising from stem; typically less than ½ in (12.7 mm) wide. *Stem* is stout and triangular; grows from thick rhizome; ends in *sessile* (i.e., nonstalked) flower or seed spikelet. Drooping leaflike *bracts* radiate below flower clusters. *Flowers* are borne in brown budlike spikelets up to 1 in (2.5 cm) long; center flowers *sessile,* but many other spikelets typically drooping (or erect) on long stalks (*peduncles*); bloom July-September. *Achene* (shown) is a 3-sided nutlet, grouped in sessile and (mostly) drooping clusters. *Size*: up to 5 ft (1.5 m). *Related species*: Saltmarsh bulrush, *S. robustus* (p. 81), a resident of brackish and salt marshes, has one or more erect bracts, extending above flower spikelets, which are mostly *sessile*.

Sedges of the genus *Carex* are common in freshwater marshes; however, most do not have common names. In all, the achene is enclosed in a sac—the *perigynium*.

Sedge, *Carex lurida* (**b**), grows in dense clumps or meadows in freshwater wetlands. *Leaves* are narrow and grasslike; up to 10 in (25 cm) long and ¼ in (6.4 mm) wide. *Stem* is 3-angled. *Flowers* are grouped in spikes; the male spike erect at top of stem, female spikes (2-4) are thick, short-stalked, and densely flowered; *bloom* June-July. *Perigynium* has needlelike appendage. *Size*: up to 3 ft (90 cm). *Related species*: Tussock sedge, *C. stricta*, see p. 101.

GRASSES (Gramineae) have round, jointed, hollow stems. Fruits are single, grainlike seeds.

Common reed, *Phragmites australis* (**c**), an *introduced species,* grows in fresh and brackish wetlands, sometimes displacing native species. *Leaves* are flat; up to 2 ft (61 cm) long and 2 in (5 cm) wide. *Stem* is erect. Distinctive *flower head* (panicle) is purplish at first, white or brown (and feathery) when mature; up to 12 in. (30 cm) long. *Size*: up to 12 ft (3.6 m). *Confusing species:* Giant beard grass, *Erianthus giganteus*, has a feathery *panicle* with a silver tint; stem often purplish; up to 14 ft (4.2 m).

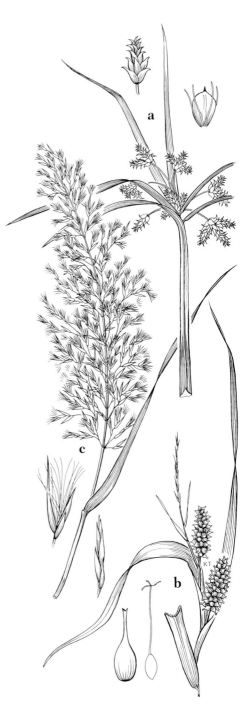

Wild rice, *Zizania aquatica* (**a**), a valuable plant to wildlife and waterfowl, grows only in freshwater marshes. *Leaves* are of 2 types: ribbonlike *underwater leaves* of immature plants, which are up to 4 ft (1.2 m) long; and *stem leaves* of mature plants, which have flat blades with rough edges, up to 16 in (40 cm) long and 2 in (5 cm) wide. *Stem* is upright. *Flower head* (panicle) has 2 sections: The upper branches bear the erect female flowers; the lower branches, spreading horizontally, bear the dangling male flowers; *blooms* June-August; panicle up to 2 ft (60 cm) long. *Rice grain* (shown) develops from the upper (pistillate) flowers; edible; important food for red-winged blackbirds, bobolinks, and waterfowl. *Size:* up to 10 ft (3 m). Annual; propagates by seeds only.

Rice cutgrass, *Leersia oryzoides* (**b**), grows in colonies, often forming dense thickets in fresh marshes. *Leaves* are flat blades with minute teeth at margins that easily cut skin or cloth; up to 10 in (25 cm) long and 1/2 in (12.7

mm) wide. *Stem* is slender and weak, often entangled with other plants. *Flower head* (panicle) blooms late (August-October); the terminal, yellowish green panicle (up to 10 in; 25 cm long) is enclosed by the uppermost leaf sheath. *Seed* (shown) is a dark red grain, borne in compact spikelets; eaten by birds. Perennial; propagates by rhizomes and seeds. *Size:* up to 4 ft (1.2 m).

Walter's millet, *Echinochloa walteri* (**c**), is a wild millet important to waterfowl and wildlife; it is often planted in refuges. *Leaves* are long and not as rough-edged as wild rice and cutgrass; up to 20 in (50 cm) long and 1 in (25 mm) wide. *Stem* is erect. *Flower cluster* (panicle) bears many reddish brown spikelets, each flower (floret) sporting an elongated bristle, or awn, up to 1 1/4 in (3 cm) long. Panicle, which may be 4-12 in (10-30 cm) long, may become weighted down with seeds, nearly touching ground. Annual; propagates only by seeds. *Size:* up to 7 ft (2.1 m).

BROADLEAF HERBS of fresh marshes include members of various plant families. Also see other *"associated species,"* pp. 103-105.

Tearthumbs and Smartweeds are members of the buckwheat family (Polygonaceae).

Halberd-leaved tearthumb, *Polygonum arifolium* (a)

grows in freshwater marshes in shallow water or muddy (intertidal) soils. *Leaves* are typically heart-shaped with lateral basal lobes; alternate; up to 6 in (15 cm) long; however, upper, generally smaller leaves may be unlobed or arrow-shaped. *Stems* are 4-sided, weak, and usually reclining (or climbing) on other plants. Stems, branches, and leaf midribs have recurved prickles. *Pink or white flowers* are loosely clustered at end of long stalks; *bloom* July-August. *Seed* is a lens-shaped nutlet. *Size:* up to 3 ft (1 m). *Related species:* Arrow-leaved tearthumb, *P. sagittatum,* see p. 104.

Dotted smartweed, *Polygonum punctatum* (b)

grows in wet soil or in shallow water. *Leaves* are alternately arranged and lance-shaped with short stalks enclosed in a sheath; covered with tiny dots; up to 6 in (15 cm) long and 1 1/2 in (3.8 cm) wide. *Stem* is typically erect. *Flowers* are white and tiny, loosely clustered on spikes; *bloom* August-October. *Seed* is a 3-sided or lens-shaped nutlet. *Size:* up to 3 ft (1 m).

Climbing hempweed, *Mikania scandens* (c)

a member of the aster family (Compositae), is an herbaceous vine that climbs over marsh plants and shrubs in fresh (and slightly brackish) wetlands. *Leaves* are opposite and heart-shaped, tapering to a narrow tip; up to 5 in (12.7 cm) long and 3 in (7.6 cm) wide. *Stem* is smooth, slender, and sprawling; over 15 ft (4.5 m) long. *Flower head* (shown) appears in a stalked cluster arising from leaf axil; each contains 4 flowers, which are white (or pink) and tubular, bearing 5 lobes at the summit; *blooms* August-September. *Seed* is a 5-angled nutlet.

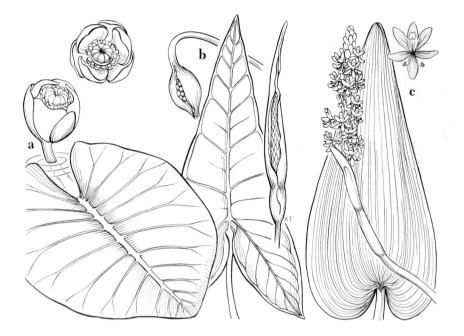

Spatterdock, *Nuphar luteum* (**a**), grows in open freshwater marshes and streams in shallow water. *Leaves* are rounded and fleshy with a notch at each base where erect, rounded leaf-stalks are attached; up to 10 in (25 cm) long. *Rootstalk* is a thick fleshy rhizome embedded horizontally in the mud. *Flower* is a yellow globe with 5-6 petals borne singly on a long stalk (peduncle) arising from leaf axis; up to 2 in (5 cm) wide; typically appears just above the water at high tide; blooms June-September. *Family:* Water lily (Nymphaeaceae).

Arrow arum, *Peltandra virginica* (**b**), grows in shallow water at the edges of fresh and slightly brackish streams. *Leaves* are thick and shaped like arrowheads; up to 18 in (46 cm) long; attached to long stalks arising from base of flower stalk; each basal lobe and main segment has a prominent midvein. *Stem* is lacking; leaf and flower stalks arise from thick rootstalk embedded in mud. *Flowers* cover a fleshy spike (*spadix*), concealed within green sheath (*spathe*); *bloom* May-July. *Fruits* are greenish berries borne on drooping spike. *Family:* Arum (Araceae).

Pickerelweed, *Pontederia cordata* (**c**), grows in colonies or alongside arrow arum in shallow water at the edge of freshwater marshes. *Leaves* are heart-shaped, borne on leafstalks (*petioles*): either *basal* (long-stalked) or *stem* (short-stalked and alternate); up to 15 in (38 cm) long. *Stem* is stout, typically with one basal leaf. *Flowers* are violet-blue; borne on terminal spike up to 4 in (10 cm) long. *Fruit* is a small sac with toothed ridges bearing a single seed. *Size:* up to 3 ft (1 m). *Family:* Pickerelweed (Pontederiaceae).

Broad-leaved arrowhead, *Sagittaria latifolia* (**d**; *opposite page*), grows at the borders of freshwater marshes and streams. *Leaves* are arrowhead-shaped, on long stalks; lobes triangular or elliptic, without distinctive midveins; up to 12 in (30 cm) long. *Stem* is lacking; leaf and flower stalks arise from fibrous root base. *Flower* has 3 white petals; yellow center; females on lower whorls and males on short stalks at top. *Fruits* are green nutlets (achenes) in flattened cluster. *Size:* up to 4 ft (1.2 m). *Related species:* Bultongue, *S. falcata* (p. 86), has lance-shaped leaves. *Family:* Water plantain (Alismaceae).

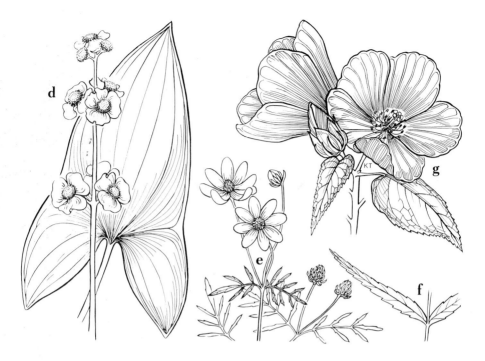

Bur marigolds (*Bidens* spp.) are members of the composite, or aster, family (Compositae).

Tickseed sunflower, *Bidens coronata* (e),

is a common wildflower of tidal freshwater marshes. *Leaves* are *opposite* and *compound* (or divided). *Stem* is smooth and slender. *Flower* is yellow and daisylike with 7-8 petal-like rays; blooms late (August-September). *Fruits* are barbed nutlets (achenes) that stick to clothing. *Size:* up to 4 ft (1.2 m). *Related species:* **Smooth bur marigold,** *B. laevis* (**f**), has simple (i.e., noncompound), opposite leaves.

Marsh hibiscus, *Hibiscus moscheutos* (g),

is a ubiquitous species, colonizing fresh and brackish wetlands. *Leaves* are wedge- or heart-shaped, tapering to a tip; alternate; smooth above and velvety below; up to 8 in (20 cm) long. *Stems* are round and finely haired. *Flower* is a distinctive large white or yellow blossom with a red center; up to 6 in (15.2 cm) wide; *blooms* late July-August. *Seed pod* (p. 122) is a rounded capsule. *Size:* up to 7 ft (2.1 m).

OTHER PLANTS of freshwater marshes and streams:

A. Emergent Species (tidal and nontidal)

Marsh fern, *Thelypteris thelypteroides*
Sensitive fern, *Onoclea sensibilis*
Royal fern, *Osmunda regalis spectabilis*
Umbrella sedge, *Cyperus esculentus*, p. 101
American three-square, *Scirpus pungens*, p. 101
Golden club, *Orontium aquaticum*
Asian dayflower, *Murdannia keisak*
Blue flag, *Iris versicolor*
Water dock, *Rumex verticillatus*, p. 103
American lotus, *Nelumbo lutea*
Sneezeweed, *Helenium autumnale*

B. Floating-leaved species (nontidal waters)

Little duckweed, *Lemna minor*
Big duckweed, *Spirodela polyrhiza*
Fragrant waterlily, *Nymphaea odorata*, p. 105

C. Submersed aquatic vegetation (SAV)

See pp. 163-165 for freshwater species

THE INVERTEBRATE COMMUNITY within freshwater

tributaries is most diverse along healthy, unsilted streams that are able to support luxuriant aquatic growth. Within the submersed grass beds of these freshwater runs are found grass shrimp (Decapoda) and other crustaceans, molluscs—both snails (Gastropoda) and clams (Pelecypoda)—and freshwater worms (Oligochaeta; Annelida). Many of the aquatic insects common to freshwater swamps (p. 40) also inhabit the water column of more open creeks and streams. The young (nymphs) of amphibious insects and various freshwater mussels dominate the sand or pebbled bottom. The typical submersed grasses of these areas are wild celery (*Vallisneria americana*), coontail (*Ceratophyllum demersum*), and common water-weed (*Elodea canadensis*), described on pp. 163-164. In wetland areas along the shore one finds marsh invertebrates typical of cattail communities and other emergent freshwater wet-lands (see p. 106).

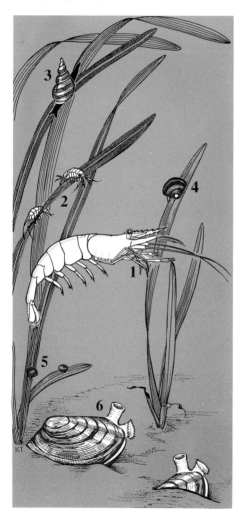

Amidst wild celery *at left*, the **freshwater grass shrimp** (*Palaemonetes paludosus;* **1**) may go unnoticed, since it is pale and nearly trans-parent, though it reaches 2 in (5 cm) in length. The species is an important prey item for juvenile fishes. Another common crustacean is the 1/2 in (1.25 cm) **banded amphipod,** *Gam-marus fasciatus* (**2**), which searches over plants for algae and other food at night when they are less easily seen by predators. Marine crus-taceans, such as barnacles and crabs, are rarely seen here, being restricted to higher salinities downstream.

Molluscs can be plentiful, however, par-ticularly the **river snail** (*Goniobasis virginica;* **3**) which grazes over plants. These 1 in (2.5 cm) river snails have long, turreted shells, usually olive-brown in color and marked with reddish bands. Unlike the tadpole snail (*Physa gyrina;* p. 106)—also found here—which can breathe air with a saclike "lung," the river snail is strictly aquatic and respires by means of a gill.

The bottom is inhabited by various fresh-water bivalves. A young **fingernail clam** (*Mus-culium* sp.; **4**), named for its diminutive size—1/2 in (12.7 mm) long—wanders about on an aquatic plant, while tiny **pill clams** (*Pisidium* sp.; **5**), up to 1/8 in (0.3 cm) long, may remain on plants throughout their adult lives. Large **freshwater mussels** such as *Anodonta* sp. (**6**, *at left*) and *Lampsilis* spp. may grow to 5 in (12.5 cm) or more in the bottom sand of healthy, fresh-water streams. Typically, these mussels are en-tirely hidden with only their siphons appearing above mud or sand (*lower near left*).

FRESHWATER FISHES of the coastal plain typically inhabit freshwater

streams but range downstream into brackish areas depending on their tolerance of salinity. Many species reach their limit at either 5-8 ppt or 18-20 ppt, the lower and upper limits of the mesohaline (see fig. 3, p. 12). In addition to *freshwater species* such as the yellow perch (below), tidal tributaries also provide habitat for transient *anadromous* and *catadromous species*, such as the shad (p. 185) and river herrings and eel (below; also see p. 201). Some *estuarine species* such as the temperate basses (Percichthyidae; p. 85) and anchovies (Engraulidae), killifishes (Cyprinodontidae), and silversides (Atherinidae), pp. 171-172, typical to brackish waters, also invade freshwater regions. Most plentiful are freshwater forms, including mudminnows (Umbridae; p. 41), suckers (Catostomidae; p. 41), and darters (Percidae; p. 42), as well as the catfishes, minnows, and sunfishes below. In all, 46 freshwater species typically inhabit the coastal plain; another 32 species sometimes stray from above the *fall line* or invade the Chesapeake watershed through Dismal Swamp.

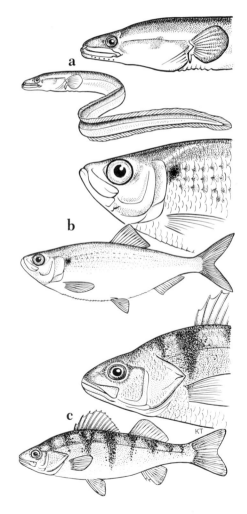

American eel, *Anguilla rostrata* (**a**), is the only catadromous species found in the Chesapeake Bay. Elvers (young eels) migrate into freshwater rivers and streams, departing as adults (after several years) to spawn and die in the Sargasso Sea. Eels are snakelike and smooth, as the scales are minute and embedded. Dorsal fin begins far back and is continuous with caudal (tail) and anal fins. Body is yellowish brown. *Size:* Females can exceed 3 ft (1 m); males are smaller.

Alewife, *Alosa pseudoharengus* (**b**), is 1 of 4 anadromous "river herrings" that spawn in the tributaries of the Chesapeake Bay. Alewives are silvery, narrow-bodied fishes with greenish backs; dorsal profile less rounded than belly. The eye is large, the width greater than length of snout. Silvery patch on cheek is longer than deep. *Size:* to 15 in (40 cm). *Related species:* Blueback herring, *A. aestivalis,* has a blue-green back; smaller eye, equal in size to snout.

Yellow perch, *Perca flavescens* (**c**), is a freshwater species that has partially adapted to estuarine life, invading moderately brackish waters (up to 13 ppt). A member of the perch family (Percidae) with 2 separate dorsal fins (like the tessellated darter, p. 42, also found here), this river species is bright yellow and marked with 5-8 dark vertical bands; tail forked. *Size:* to 12 in (30 cm). Feeds in shallow water at dawn and dusk.

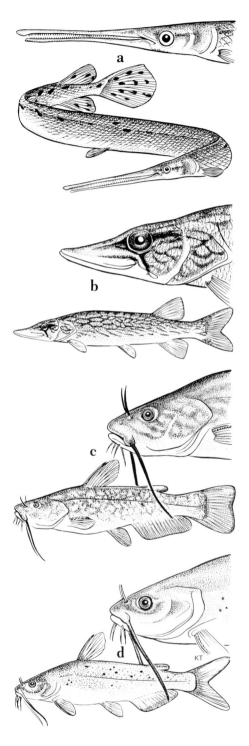

Longnose gar, *Lepisosteus osseus* (**a**), is a common resident of the fresh and brackish reaches of Bay tributaries (up to 23 ppt). Gars are primitive, retaining much cartilage in their skeletons and bearing diamond-shaped (ganoid) scales. Body is cylindrical. Olive-brown above and whitish below, adult is marked with spots on rear of body and *median* (i.e., dorsal, caudal, and anal) *fins.* The long, slender snout exceeds twice the length of head; armed with sharp teeth. Short dorsal fin is near rounded tail. *Size:* to 5 ft (1.5 m).

Chain pickerel, *Esox niger* (**b**), is a common predator of sluggish streams, swamps, and weed beds of most tributaries into brackish waters (up to 22 ppt). Yellowish brown above, the distinctive sides are marked with a chainlike network of dark lines; belly whitish; tail forked. Long head is flat above, with a concave snout; dark bar appears under eye. *Size:* to 2 ft (60 cm). *Related species:* Redfin pickerel, *E. americanus,* has vertical bars, shorter snout; to 14 in (36 cm). Up to 8 ppt.

Brown bullhead, *Ictalurus nebulosus* (**c**), is a resident of slow backwaters along fresh and slightly brackish streams (up to 8 ppt). Like other catfishes (Ictaluridae), it has a broad, flat head and dark brown *barbels* above and below the mouth. Body is brown and often mottled; whitish below. *Adipose fin* present between dorsal fin and rounded tail. Sharp spines present on dorsal and pectoral fins. *Size:* to 20 in (50 cm). *Related species:* Yellow bullhead, *I. natalis,* has yellowish body; pale (yellow or white) chin barbels. Fresh water only.

Channel catfish, *Ictalurus punctatus* (**d**), an introduced species, prefers channels at midstream, up to moderately brackish salinity (15 ppt). Like the bullhead, spines are present; *barbels* arranged in same pattern but lighter in tone. Bluish gray above and white below, the sides are marked with small, random spots. Tail is deeply forked. *Size:* to 4 ft (1.2 m). *Related species:* White catfish, *I. catus,* lacks spots; tail moderately forked; same habitat. Blue catfish, *I. furcatus, introduced,* has bluish body; eyes below midline of head; tail more deeply forked; *anal fin* has straight (not rounded) edge.

Common carp, *Cyprinus carpio* (**a**), is an introduced species, originally from Asia (like the goldfish, *Carassius auratus*), that has invaded all major tributaries. Unlike other minnows (Cyprinidae), these exotics have more than 10 dorsal rays as well as spines on dorsal and anal fins. Carp differ in having 2 barbels on each side of upper jaw. Body is robust, dark olive above and yellowish below. *Size:* to 3 ft (90 cm). *Range:* Fresh water to moderately brackish (up to 17 ppt).

Pumpkinseed, *Lepomis gibbosus* (**b**), a sunfish (Centrarchidae) like the next 2 species, is common along all tributaries into brackish waters (up to 18 ppt). Dorsal fins are joined and tail is forked. Body is compressed; color varies; sides are spotted; belly yellowish orange; orange cheeks striped with blue. Spot on gill flap is black at front, red behind, and bordered with white. *Size:* to 10 in (25 cm). *Related species:* Redbreast sunfish, *L. auritus*, has a reddish belly; gill flap long and black, without light border; fresh water only. Bluegill, *L. macrochirus*, has vertical bars on body; gill flap short and solid black; *introduced;* up to 18 ppt.

Black crappie, *Pomoxis nigromaculatus* (**c**), an introduced species, is restricted to nontidal and tidal fresh water. Distinctive head is concave above the eye; snout is long; large mouth extends past middle of eye. Dorsal fin is far back and has 7-8 spines. Body is compressed. *Median fins* and body are spotted. *Size:* to 16 in (42 cm). *Related species:* White crappie, *P. annularis, introduced,* is less common; dorsal fin even farther back; only 6 dorsal spines; body spots form 7-10 vague vertical bars.

Largemouth bass, *Micropterus salmoides* (**d**), resides in fresh and low brackish streams (up to 12 ppt). Field marks include a dark lateral band (absent in older fish) and a large mouth that extends past rear margin of eye. Differs from other sunfishes above in that a deep notch almost separates dorsal fins. Body is elongate and yellowish green. *Size:* to 30 in (76 cm). Introduced. *Related species:* Smallmouth bass, *M. dolomieui*, has mouth extending to eye but not beyond; *introduced;* up to 7 ppt.

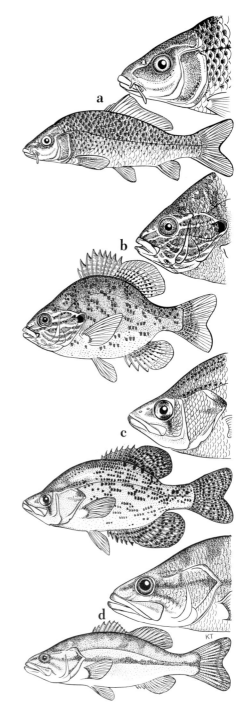

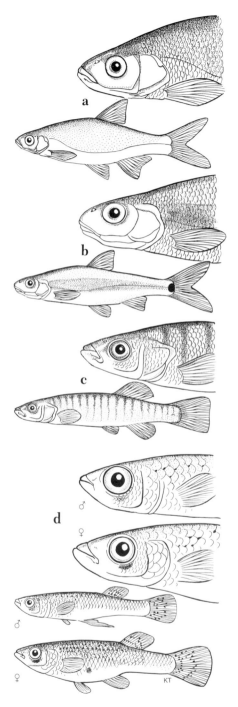

Golden shiner, *Notemigonus crysoleucas* (**a**), inhabits swamps and fresh and low brackish streams (up to 5 ppt). A member of the minnow family (Cyprinidae) like the small shiners below, this common baitfish has only soft rays in its dorsal fin. Usually yellow to green above and silvery below, the deep, robust body turns golden during the breeding season. Lateral line is strongly *decurved*. A fleshy keel is situated on belly between pelvic and anal fins. *Size:* to 12 in (30 cm).

Spottail shiner, *Notropis hudsonius* (**b**), is common along the main stem of major rivers (up to 10 ppt) as well as fresher streams. Body is silvery with a dusky lateral band, ending in black *caudal* spot at tail base. *Size:* to 5 in (13 cm). *Confusing species:* Eastern silvery minnow, *Hybognathus regius*, has a faint band only on rear half of body; no caudal spot. Satinfin shiner, *N. analostanus*, has dark band on rear half of body; no caudal spot; dorsal fin pigmented on rear edge. Bridle shiner, *N. bifrenatus*, has black band from upper lip to base of tail.

Banded killifish, *Fundulus diaphanus* (**c**), is a freshwater killifish (Cyprinodontidae) that invades brackish waters of most tributaries (up to 20 ppt). More robust than minnows and shiners, killifishes have protruding lower jaws and rounded tails. Greenish above and whitish below, this species has 16-20 narrow dark bands. *Size:* to 3 in (7.5 cm). *Related estuarine species:* Mummichog, *F. heteroclitus*, and striped killifish, *F. majalis*, are typical bull minnows of brackish waters; more chunky, with wider bands (see p. 172).

Mosquitofish, *Gambusia affinis* (**d**), a livebearer (Poeciliidae), inhabits fresh and brackish streams (up to 18 ppt). This topminnow feeds on mosquito larvae; resembles a killifish but is equipped for internal fertilization: anal fin of male is modified into a copulatory organ. Light brown to olive above and pale below, silver sides are marked by spots on scale edges, forming a diamondlike pattern. *Size:* Females 2$^{1}/_{3}$ in (59 mm); males smaller.

AMPHIBIANS AND REPTILES inhabit freshwater wetlands in

surprising numbers though most are rarely seen. In summer a splash in the water or a slither through the reeds may be the only sign that frogs or snakes are about. However, many *amphibians* betray their secrecy with mating calls in the spring. Male spring peepers and chorus frogs are the first to be heard—the former vocalizing from wetland plants, the latter calling from open places at the water's edge. Small treefrogs and allies (Hylidae) vary in their ability to climb, based on the presence or absence of adhesive discs at the ends of their toes (see below). After the short spring breeding season, treefrogs are mostly silent. The more visible (and larger) true frogs (Ranidae) breed into the summer and their loud croaking continues into July (sometimes September). True frogs can be spotted at the shoreline, often partially submersed. *Reptiles*, mainly freshwater turtles and snakes, can be seen sunning on banks or logs.

TREEFROGS AND ALLIES (Hylidae). Also see green treefrog, *Hyla cinerea*, p. 86.

Northern spring peeper, *Hyla crucifer crucifer* (**a**), is variable in color and markings but always has X-shaped mark on back. A good climber due to large toe pads on each webbed foot. Males emit a shrill peep in March. *Size:* to $1^3/_8$ in (35 mm).

Upland chorus frog, *Pseudacris triseriata* ssp. (**b**), is named for its "creeking" call, which sounds as if a thumb were dragged across teeth of a comb. A ground dweller, it has small toe pads and webbing, rarely climbs low shrubs. Note 3 stripes along its back. Another stripe runs from snout to groin, passing through eye. A light line marks the upper lip. *Size:* to $1^1/_2$ in (38 mm). Upland subspecies, *P. t. feriarum* (shown), has broken stripes; western shore only. New Jersey subspecies, *P. t. kalmi*, has broad stripes; Eastern Shore only.

Northern cricket frog, *Acris crepitans crepitans* (**c**), is a nonclimber; lacks pads on toes. Highly variable in color, this warted frog is distinguished by a dark triangular spot atop its head. Each hind leg has a dark stripe on rear of thigh. April mating call is a "gick-gick-gick," as if two stones were clicked together. *Size:* to $1^3/_8$ in (35 mm). *Related species:* Southern cricket frog, *A. g. gryllus*, has less webbing on feet; SE Virginia only.

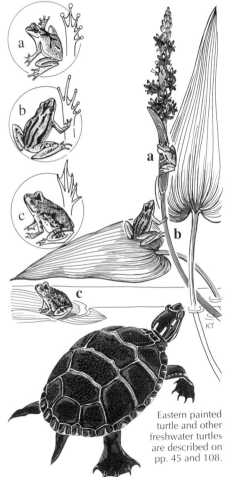

Eastern painted turtle and other freshwater turtles are described on pp. 45 and 108.

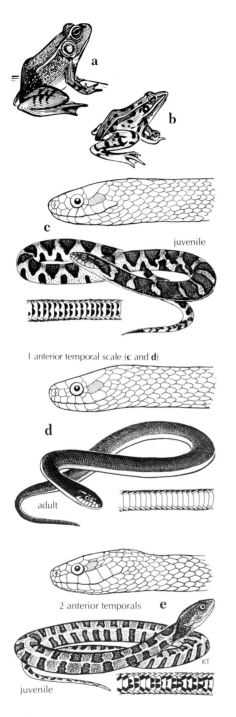

a

b

c

juvenile

1 anterior temporal scale (**c** and **d**)

d

adult

2 anterior temporals   e

KT

juvenile

TRUE FROGS (Ranidae). *Note:* Also see bullfrog, *Rana catesbeiana*, p. 44.

Green frog, *Rana clamitans melanota* (**a**), is a common resident of freshwater streams. Varying in color from green to brown above, body has distinct *dorsolateral ridges* extending two-thirds of body. Like the bullfrog (p. 44), adult male has a bright yellow throat and a large eardrum (*tympanum*). Call suggests banjo string plucked once loudly or 3 (or 4) times in a row. Breeds May through July. *Size:* to 4 in (10 cm).

Southern leopard frog, *Rana sphenocephala* (**b**), is a ubiquitous species, its habitat ranging from swamps to brackish streams. Leopard frogs are marked by 2 or 3 rows of oval spots between *dorsolateral ridges* that extend to groin. A white spot marks center of eardrum (*tympanum*); a white line marks the upper jaw. Mating call is a short guttural trill. Breeds March to May. *Related species:* Pickerel frog, *R. palustris* (p. 44), has rectangular spots; yellow on back of thigh.

WATER SNAKES (*Nerodia* spp.; Serpentes) are maligned creatures, largely due to their resemblance to the *venomous* water moccasin, or cottonmouth, *Agkistrodon piscivorus*, which finds its northern limit in southeastern Virginia. Cottonmouth is distinguished by deep facial pit on each side of head; pupil is vertically elliptic. Water snakes also differ in having a double row of scales under tail (see p. 43). They eat frogs and fish but are nonvenomous.

Northern water snake, *Nerodia sipedon sipedon* (**c**), has alternating dorsal and lateral bands with markings wider than spaces between (obscure in adults). Underbelly variable: spots (half-moons) usually present. *Size:* to 53 in (134 cm). *Related species:* **Redbelly water snake**, *N. e. erythrogaster* (**d**), restricted to SE Virginia and lower Eastern Shore, has red underbelly; plain brown above; to 62 in (157 cm). **Brown water snake**, *N. taxispilota* (**e**), has squarish blotches on back and alternating rows on sides; belly spotted; 2 *anterior temporal* scales (shown); to 69 in (175 cm); SE Virginia only.

MARSH BIRDS AND OTHER RESIDENTS of freshwater creeks

and streams are often visible at the water's edge, foraging amidst spatterdock, or flying above alder shrubs and cattail where woods and wetland meet. The birdlife changes with the plant profile of each stream. Wooded creeks, just downstream from headwater thickets, continue to host many *swamp species* including catbirds, vireos, warblers, and waterthrushes (p. 49). As the stream opens up, slows down, and levels out into vegetated wetlands, *marsh birds* appear. Featured here are bitterns and herons (Ardeidae; Ciconiiformes), waterfowl (Anatidae; Anseriformes), rails and coots (Rallidae; Gruiformes), shorebirds (Charadriformes), and a variety of perching birds (Passeriformes), including marsh-nesting wrens and blackbirds (for others, see p. 113). Species that forage over wooded and wetland streams include kingfishers (Alcedinidae; Coraciiformes), flycatchers (e.g., the Eastern kingbird, *Tyrannus tyrannus*), and swallows. Migrating bobolinks (*Dolichonyx oryzivorus*) and swamp sparrows (*Melospiza georgiana*) are frequent visitors in spring and fall.

HERONS AND EGRETS (Ardeidae) are wading birds with long necks and legs and spearlike bills. Also see green-backed heron, *Butorides striatus*, p. 88.

Great blue heron, *Ardea herodias* (**a**), is a local permanent resident of rivers, tidewater wetlands, and shallow-water bays. *Field marks:* A large bluish gray heron with a whitish head bearing black plumes. Underparts are dark. Note black "shoulder." *Flight:* Flies with neck folded in (see p. 109); legs hang down on takeoff (p. 88). *Size:* Length to 52 in (130 cm); wingspan averages 72 in (183 cm). *Call:* When alarmed, emits 3-4 hoarse croaks, "graahnk," etc. *Food:* Fish, insects, crustaceans, and frogs are hunted by slow stalking in shallows. *Season:* All year; nests colonially in wooded swamps and on isolated islands.

Great egret, *Casmerodius albus* (**b**), is a local transient and summer resident of tidewater wetlands, rivers, and bays. *Field marks:* Body is entirely white with contrasting long yellow bill and black legs and feet. Breeding plumage includes straight plumes on back extending beyond tail. *Flight:* Like heron above but neck held in more open curve (see p. 142). *Size:* Length to 39 in (99 cm); wingspan averages 55 in (140 cm). *Call:* a low harsh croak. *Food:* Similar to heron's diet of fish and other aquatic species. *Season:* Spring-fall; nests in trees or shrubs near water.

Marsh ducks
spring up.

MARSH DUCKS (Tribe Anatini; Anatidae), or dabbling ducks, feed at the surface on seeds, grasses, and submersed plants (SAV). Females are harder to identify but usually found with distinctive mate; both have bright patch (*speculum*) on rear of wing. Also see pp. 90 and 110.

Mallard, *Anas platyrhynchos* (**a**), is mostly a migrant (*transient*) and winter resident of fresh marshes, rivers, and bays. *Field marks:* Male has bright green head and rusty chest, separated by white ring on neck; yellow bill. Female is mottled brown with orangish bill. *Flight:* Look for green head (male) and blue speculum (with white borders) on wing. *Size:* Length to 28 in (70 cm); wingspan averages 36 in (91 cm). *Call:* Female (hen) has loud quack; male (drake) emits a low "kwek-kwek." *Season:* All year (though less common in summer); uncommon (though widespread) breeder; nests on dry ground near water.

Blue-winged teal, *Anas discors* (**b**), is a transient and local to uncommon summer resi-

dent of rivers and tidewater wetlands. *Field marks:* Male has white crescent on face. Female is brown and mottled. Both have blue patch on forewing and green speculum. *Flight:* Look for blue shoulder patch on front of wing. *Size:* Length to 16 in (40 cm); wingspan averages 24 in (61 cm). *Call:* Drake has a whistlelike peep; hen has a low quack. *Season:* Mostly spring and fall; rare in winter; uncommon and local summer breeder in marshes.

Northern pintail, *Anas acuta* (**c**) is a transient and winter resident of rivers and bays. *Field marks:* Male has a long, white neck stripe and pointed, needlelike tail; white neck and breast contrast with gray body. Female is brown and mottled. *Flight:* Look for long neck and brown *speculum* with white border; on male, white neck stripe and "pin" tail apparent at close range. *Size:* Length (male) to 30 in (75 cm); wingspan averages 35 in (89 cm). *Call:* Drake whistles; hen quacks. *Season:* Mostly spring and fall; less common in winter. Non-breeder.

PERCHING DUCKS (Tribe Cairinini; Anatidae)

Wood duck, *Aix sponsa* (**a**), is mostly a summer resident and transient in freshwater marshes. *Field marks:* Male has distinctive face pattern and swept-back crest. Dull female has white eye patch. *Flight:* Note crest, white underbelly, and long square tail. *Size:* Length to 20 in (50 cm); wingspan averages 28 in (70 cm). *Call:* Male (drake) calls "hoo-w-et"; hen emits a "crr-ek." *Season:* All year, but uncommon in winter; nests in tree cavities and nest boxes.

RAILS AND COOTS (Rallidae)

Sora, *Porzana carolina* (**b**), is a small, shy, transient rail of freshwater marshes. *Field marks:* Note the short, chickenlike bill. Black face mask (adults only) and white rump are also distinctive. *Flight:* Short flutters. *Size:* to 9³/₄ in (24 cm). *Call:* A descending whinny. *Season:* Spring and fall; rarely summer and winter; former breeder in the region. *Related species:* King rail, *Rallus elegans* (p. 112), and Virginia rail, *R. limicola* (p. 128), have long slender bills.

American coot, *Fulica americana* (**c**), is a transient and winter resident (uncommon in summer) along rivers, marshes, and bays. *Field marks:* A grayish black, ducklike rail with a white bill. *Size:* to 16 in (40 cm). *Call:* Short croaks ("kuk-kuk-kuk") and cackles ("ka-ka-ka-ka"). *Season:* All year, but mostly spring and fall; less common in winter; highly local (and sporadic) breeder; status uncertain.

SANDPIPERS AND ALLIES (Scolopacidae). Also see other migrant sandpipers (p. 112).

Spotted sandpiper, *Actitis macularia* (**d**), is a common transient and local summer resident of stream shores. *Field marks:* In summer, breast and belly spotted (absent in winter). Note white wedge at front of wing. Look for distinctive tail-bobbing. *Size:* to 7¹/₂ in (19 cm). *Call:* A shrill "pee-weet," or "pee-weet-weet." *Season:* Mostly spring and fall; nests in open fields or near streams (few records).

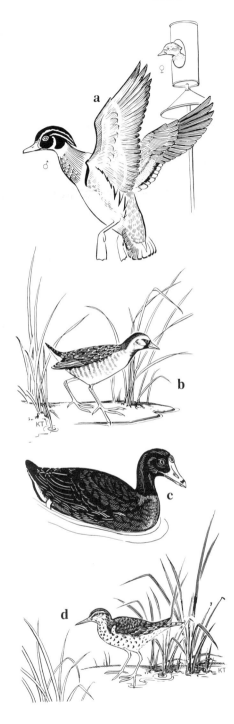

OTHER BIRDS of freshwater tributaries and wetlands include kingfishers (Alcedinidae) and perching birds (Passeriformes) illustrated here and on p. 113.

Belted kingfisher, *Ceryle alcyon* (**a**), is a permanent resident of rivers and bays. *Field marks:* Note large crested head and daggerlike bill. Bluish gray above; the male (shown) has a gray breast band; female has second rusty band below first band. *Flight:* Hovers before diving headfirst for fish. *Size:* to 13 in (33 cm). *Call:* A loud rattle when flying over water. *Season:* All year; uncommon breeder; nests in burrow excavated in riverbank.

Bank swallow, *Riparia riparia* (**b**), is a transient and local summer resident of rivers and bays. *Field marks:* A small brown-backed swallow distinguished by a dark breastband on white chest. Note long pointed wings. *Flight:* Swallows are elegant fliers, catching insects on the wing. *Size:* to 5½ in (14 cm). *Call:* A buzzing or rattling "trit-trit-trit," etc. *Season:* Spring, summer, and fall; uncommon colonial nester in steep banks near water.

Marsh wren, *Cistothorus palustris* (**c**), is a common summer resident and transient in tidewater wetlands. *Field marks:* Note distinctive white eyebrow stripe and brown back streaked with white. Belly is whitish. The slim bill is slightly curved. Tail bobs up and down when vocalizing. *Size:* to 5 in (13 cm). *Call:* A low "tsuk-tsuk" or a reedy, rattling "cut-cut-trrrrrrrr-ur," sometimes heard at night. *Season:* Common in summer; frequent visitor in spring and fall; uncommon in winter. Oval (globular) nest is lashed to cattail or other plants.

Red-winged blackbird, *Agelaius phoeniceus* (**d**), is a common permanent resident of tidewater wetlands. *Field marks:* Male is black with red shoulder patches bordered below with yellow. Female is dull brown with dark streaks; light eyebrow stripe. *Size:* to 9½ in (24 cm). *Call:* Male call is a guttural "konk-ka-ree." *Season:* All year; nests in loose colonies near water in cattail, reeds, or bushes.

MAMMALS seen along freshwater tributaries fall into two categories:

upland species, which visit the stream bank to feed, and true *wetland species*. Among the visitors are the red and gray foxes (p. 53), long-tailed weasel (*Mustela frenata*), striped skunk (*Mephitis mephitis*), opossum (p. 51), and raccoon (p. 53). White-tailed deer (p. 53) and rabbits—both the *upland* eastern cottontail and the *wetland* marsh rabbit (p. 51)—venture to the water's edge to forage upon plants, such as smartweeds. Aquatic mammals include the muskrat, beaver, and river otter (p. 52), as well as the nutria (*Myocastor coypus;* p. 115), an introduced species, and the mink (*Mustela vison*). Beavers, recently reestablished in the Bay area, feed mostly on woody plants, however, and are not typical of open marshes. Surprisingly, the star-nosed mole (*Condylura cristata*), a ground dweller, may be seen along marsh banks above ground or in the water; it is a good swimmer and feeds voraciously on aquatic insects. The eastern mole (*Scalopus aquaticus*) is even more at home in the water.

At dawn or dusk, one may find a **raccoon** (*Procyon lotor;* **a**) combing the stream bank for mussels, grass shrimp, or amphibians like the green frog caught *at right*. The well-known raccoon is omnivorous, varying its diet with nuts, insects, and grains, which it may wash off before eating. Though chiefly nocturnal, some adults (and young) may be seen along streams or in the marshes throughout the day.

Small herbivorous rodents are the most abundant mammals of freshwater marshes. At the river's edge (*far right*), the **meadow vole** (*Microtus pennsylvanicus;* **b**), is by far the most common species and is active both day and night. This small vole, up to 6 in (15 cm) long, ranges throughout northern North America and is distinguished by its dark brown fur, small ears, and short, 2 in (5 cm) tail. Meadow voles nest among marsh grasses or below ground in burrows, which are dug at intervals along their maze of surface runways that weave through the marsh. Often territorial, they feed on sedges, seeds, and grasses. Marsh rice rats (*Oryzomys palustris*; p. 94), common inhabitants of brackish marshes, reside in freshwater wetlands but generally are not as abundant as voles.

A larger rodent and one more visible is the **muskrat** (*Ondatra zibethicus;* **c**; *below right*), whose long, scaly, and laterally flattened tail is a sufficient field mark. Along streams it burrows in banks (through an underwater entrance) instead of building the usual conical house (p. 131).

Estuarine Rivers and Associated Brackish Marshes

OVER 45 major rivers flow directly into the Chesapeake Bay. With the exception in spring-time of a few large freshwater tributaries at the head of the Bay (e.g., the Elk and the Susquehanna), each Chesapeake river is an estuary in minia-ture—a subestuary to the main Bay. Along each river a *salinity gradient* runs from headwaters to mouth, where each subestuary discharges a brack-ish mixture of fresh and estuarine waters into the Bay proper.

These rivers and their associated brackish marshes are important breeding and nursery grounds for fishes and birds. In summer, marsh hibiscus blooms (*at left*) along the banks amidst stands of big cordgrass and narrow-leaved cattail. Here, marsh wrens and other birds lash their nests to the tall grasses. In the shallows, a great blue heron feeds on juvenile fish and grass shrimp, which depend on the close interaction of wetland and river. The twice-daily tides flush detritus and other food from the marsh soil, thus furnishing a rich source of nutrients for aquatic life.

Brackish waters are broadly defined as the middle range of the salinity gradient between tidal fresh water and marine. There is a lot of territory in the Bay (or any estuary) that falls in this range; in fact, during autumn the entire Chesapeake (and some of its shorter rivers) may be brackish, that is, between 0.5 and 30 ppt (see fig. 3; p. 12). There-fore, scientists have developed a scale to divide these waters into 3 brackish zones: oligohaline (0.5-5 ppt), mesohaline (5-18 ppt), and polyhaline (18-30 ppt), which one can term low (or slightly) brackish, moderately brackish, and highly brack-ish, respectively.

As discussed in the last chapter, freshwater marshes usually fall in the area defined by tidal freshwater (0-0.5 ppt) but range into slightly brackish (i.e., oligohaline) regions. Similarly, the lower sections of major tributaries (and their brackish marshes and SAV) are typically mesohaline. However, major rivers in the upper Bay may become oligohaline in spring while those in the lower Bay may become polyhaline in autumn. Throughout the year, these subestuaries are often inhospitable to both freshwater and marine species. In summer many marine fishes cannot invade the river mouths into the mesohaline, while most freshwater species remain sequestered upstream in tidal fresh and slightly brackish waters.

Estuarine river vegetation is, obviously, less mobile than fishes. To survive the seasonal variability in the brackishness of local floodwaters, wetland plants must be tolerant of wide swings in salinity. The most characteristic brackish-wetland species, Olney three-square, can grow in waters ranging from 1 to 18 ppt, but the middle of this range is optimal. Most brackish wetlands occur in the lower mesohaline (5-10 ppt; *spring salinity*). Above 10 ppt, saltmarsh species dominate and continue to thrive through the upper mesohaline (10-18 ppt) into highly brackish (i.e., polyhaline) waters.

To make certain you have come upon a brackish river marsh, it is important to identify a number of indicator plants. These include big cordgrass, growing along the river edge; narrow-leaved cattail, which grows in similar bands or in colonies in seepage areas at the upland interface; Olney three-square, either interspersed among big cordgrass or growing in pure stands; and tall grasses such as switchgrass and common reed. Associated species include marsh hibiscus, tidemarsh waterhemp, and saltbushes. If *extensive* low cordgrass meadows are present, you're in a salt marsh (p. 133); salt marshes occur along the mouths of major rivers south of the Patuxent and Choptank. If broad-leaved cattail, wild rice, swamp type shrubs, or pickerelweed and spatterdock are about, you're in a freshwater marsh (p. 55). Turn back a chapter or head downstream.

Emergent brackish-water plants are distributed in the marsh in distinct bands. Within a given salinity regime, this zonation is mostly influenced by the elevation of the marsh floor relative to tidal inundation (see fig. 9; p. 118).

Just as wetlands along major estuarine tributaries are a mixed bag of freshwater and saltmarsh species, the aquatic inventory in the river channel is an amalgam of freshwater and marine forms. The *few* true estuarine species, such as the blue crab and white perch, thrive here. The low mesohaline region (5-10 ppt) is also the most important nursery area for marine species, such as members of the drum family (pp. 186-187).

To explore brackish river wetlands, you may need a boat or canoe. Plan a trip to the mouths and bays of the major northern rivers such as the Chester, Magothy, and Miles. See the brackish marshes of the middle Choptank and Patuxent. By car or on foot, you can visit Patuxent Vista Natural Resource Management Area (NRMA) (near Benedict, Maryland) or the Nanticoke marshes (near Vienna) at the Route 50 bridge. In Virginia, visit York River State Park, Hog Island WMA on the James, and Nansemond River NWR.

WETLAND PLANTS growing along brackish estuarine rivers are

fewer in number than the freshwater species growing upstream. As in other marshes, these salt-tolerant plants grow in definite zones according to preferences for soil type and water depth (see fig. 9; p. 118). Only in a *mixed brackish-water community* is there a heterogeneous mixture of plants (mostly in wetter areas). Marsh communities dominated by a single species are common, however. In addition to the cattail and common reed communities found also in fresher areas (p. 57), these include *big cordgrass communities*, usually pure stands of *Spartina cynosuroides* at mean high tide (MHT) along the river edge; *three-square communities*, dominated by Olney three-square; and *black needlerush communities*. On hummocks in the brackish marsh, the *saltbush community* (p. 83) replaces the "associated shrubs" of freshwater marshes. For submersed aquatic vegetation (SAV) of estuarine rivers, see p. 84 and pp. 164-166.

Narrow-leaved cattail, *Typha angustifolia* (**a**), our only cattail (Typhaceae) tolerant of brackish conditions, is typically found in colonies in standing water at the marsh-upland margin. *Leaves* are narrow and of two types: *basal leaves* are up to 6 ft (1.8 m) long; and *stem leaves,* which are two-ranked and alternate, up to 3 ft (90 cm) long; both only up to $1/2$ in (12.7 mm) wide. *Stems* grow upright. *Flower spike* (when mature) has a gap between male (staminate) upper section and female (pistillate) lower section. *Seeds* are tiny *achenes* with numerous silky bristles attached to base. *Size:* up to 6 ft (1.8 m).

TALL GRASSES (Gramineae) of brackish wetlands are typically one of the next 3 species. All grow over 6 ft (1.8 m) tall.

Big cordgrass, *Spartina cynosuroides* (**b**), is a common resident of brackish wetlands, colonizing seepage areas at the upland edge as well as muddy soils at riverside. *Leaves* are rough saberlike blades, arranged along the stem in overlapping sheaths; up to 28 in (71 cm) long and 1 in (25 mm) wide. *Stem* is robust, round, and hollow. *Flower head* (panicle) is an open green cluster consisting of 20-50 erect spikes up to $2^{1}/2$ in (6.5 cm) long, each with dozens of densely packed spikelets. Entire panicle is up to 12 in (30 cm) long. *Seeds* are grainlike, one to each spikelet (*flowering scale*). *Size:* up to 10 ft (3 m).

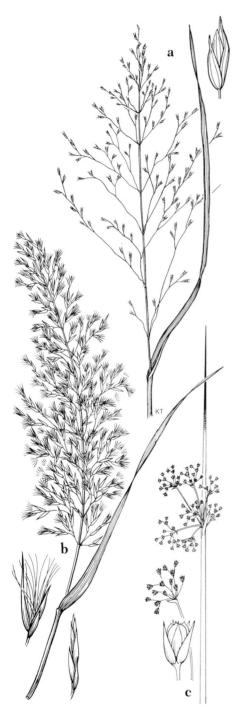

Switchgrass, *Panicum virgatum* (**a**), colonizes sandy soils at the marsh-upland interface of salt and brackish marshes. *Leaves* are tapered and smooth; up to 20 in (51 cm) long; some in basal clumps and usually one enclosing the flower head at summit. *Stems* are erect. *Flower head* (panicle) is an open delicate cluster of tiny florets at the tips of various branches; wiry in appearance and typically triangular (pyramidal) at top. *Seeds* are tiny grains. *Size:* up to 6¹/₂ ft (2 m).

Common reed, *Phragmites australis* (**b**), is a weedy species, growing in marshes and disturbed areas, often outcompeting native, more valuable plants such as big cordgrass. *Leaves* are flat and tapering; up to 24 in (61 cm) long and 2 in (5 cm) wide; arranged in 2 ranks on stem. *Stem* is round, hollow, and erect. *Flower head* (panicle) is distinctive: a feathery, multibranched plume. *Blooms* July-August. *Fruits* are tiny grains. Once established by seeds, common reed spreads via long, creeping rhizomes. *Size:* up to 12 ft (3.6 m). *Note:* Valuable only as cover; not an important food for waterfowl.

RUSHES (Juncaceae) differ from grasses in having solid (rather than hollow) round stems. Fruits are multiseed capsules, whereas grasses (and sedges) bear only one seed per *flowering scale.*

Black needlerush, *Juncus roemerianus* (**c**), typically grows in dense stands of uniform height in brackish and *upper mesohaline* salt marshes, often in sandier soils. *Leaves* are cylindrical, rigid, and resemble a stem, the uppermost leaf ending in a sharp point (often black compared to dark green lower leaf); each up to 8 in (20 cm) long. *Stem* is round and stiff. *Flowers* appear in branched cluster extending laterally about three-quarters of the way along stem; *bloom* June-August. *Seeds* are contained in capsules (shown) in cluster at upper leaf base. *Size:* up to 4 ft (1.2 m).

BRACKISH-WATER SEDGES (Cyperaceae) include the dwarf spikerush (*Eleocharis parvula*; p. 100) and the bulrushes and three-squares (*Scirpus* spp.) below. Solid stems are typically triangular on end.

Saltmarsh bulrush, *Scirpus robustus* (a),

is a common three-square of brackish and upper *mesohaline* salt marshes; however, it differs from other *Scirpus* species in having prominent leaves. *Leaves* are long, narrow, and grasslike, tapering to a long point; up to $\frac{1}{2}$ in (12.7 mm) wide. *Stem* is robust; triangular in cross section; grows from thick rhizome. *Flowers* are small and inconspicuous, borne in (mostly) sessile spikelets; few are stalked. Spikelets are surrounded by 2-4 erect leaflike bracts; *bloom* July-October. *Fruit* (achene) is a dark nutlet. *Size:* up to 4 ft (1.2 m).

Olney three-square, *Scirpus americanus*

(b), grows only in brackish wetlands, where it colonizes peaty soils. *Leaves* are lacking; reduced at base. *Stem* is stout, triangular, and deeply concave in cross section. *Flowers* are borne in 5-12 sessile (nonstalked) spikelets, located near top of stem (only $\frac{1}{2}$-2 in; 12.7-50 mm below apex); *bloom* June-August. *Seed clusters* extend laterally near apex of stem; *dark fruit* (achene) is rounded (as shown) with obtuse apex. *Size:* up to 5 ft (1.5 m). *Note:* Formerly named *S. olneyi*.

SHORTER GRASSES (Gramineae). Also see saltgrass, *Distichlis spicata* (p. 121), and salt-meadow cordgrass, *Spartina patens* (p. 120).

Saltmarsh cordgrass, *Spartina alterniflora* (c),

in brackish marshes may grow at creekside (intermediate form) behind big cordgrass. *Leaves* taper to a long point (and turn inward); up to 16 in (41 cm) long and $\frac{1}{2}$ in (12.7 mm) wide. *Stem* is stout, round, and hollow. *Flower cluster* (panicle) is narrow; composed of 5-30 spikes, each up to 4 in (10 cm) long; alternately arranged close to main axis; each spike consisting of 10-50 sessile spikelets. *Seeds* are small grains. *Size:* Short form up to 2 ft (61 cm) in high marsh; intermediate form (shown) up to 4 ft (1.2 m). *Note:* Also see pp. 120 and 135 for description of tall form.

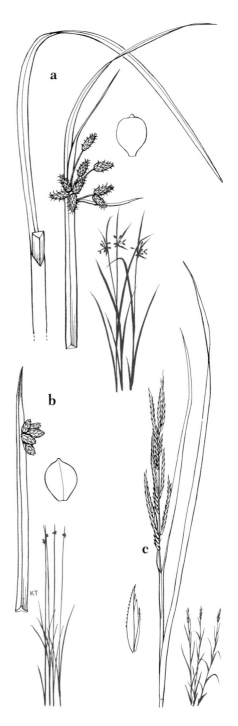

HERBACEOUS PLANTS other than grasses, sedges, and rushes, may have colorful flowers. Those tolerant of brackish waters are illustrated here and on p. 122. These marsh plants are termed *"associated species,"* never dominant but often common. Also see saltmarsh species (p. 137).

Marsh hibiscus, *Hibiscus moscheutos* (**a**), a *perennial* plant, grows along the upland margins of brackish wetlands. *Leaves* are alternate, serrated; smooth above and hairy below; typically wedge-shaped, up to 8 in (20 cm) long and 3 in (7.6 cm) wide. Lower leaves may have three lobes. *Stem* is round, smooth, and velvety. *Flower* is pink or white with characteristic red center; 5 petals; up to 6 in (15.2 cm) wide; *blooms* late July-August. *Seed pod* (p. 122) has 5 cells; rounded; persists in winter. *Size:* up to 7 ft (2.1 m). *Related species:* **Seashore mallow,** *Kosteletzkya virginica* (**b**), may be distinguished by its smaller, 2 in (5 cm) wide, pink flowers and triangular leaves; brackish wetlands only.

Saltmarsh loosestrife, *Lythrum lineare* (**c**), a *perennial* herb, resides in salt and brackish marshes, often colonizing the high meadows or the upper intertidal zone. *Leaves* are narrow and opposite; up to 2 in (5 cm) long and 1/8 in (3 mm) wide. *Stem* is smooth and angular with numerous branches. *Flowers* are small, purple or white blossoms borne in leaf axils; usually 5-6 petals; *bloom* July-August. *Size:* up to 3 ft (1 m).

Tidemarsh waterhemp, *Amaranthus cannabinus* (**d**), an *annual* herb, is a common willowlike plant of brackish marshes. *Leaves* are lance-shaped or, on the uppermost stem, linear; appearing on long stalks (*petioles*); alternately arranged on stem; up to 6 in (15.2 cm) long. *Stem* is smooth and erect. *Flowers* are small and yellow or green, borne on slender spikes; the males at top of the stem and the females at leaf axils. *Seeds* are produced in great quantities in late summer; eaten by waterfowl, marsh birds, and small mammals. *Size:* up to 8 ft (2.4 m).

SHRUBS (woody plants) of brackish wetlands include the saltbush community made up of *Baccharis* and *Iva* species and upland "edge species" found between woods and marsh such as wax myrtle and bayberry (*Myrica* spp.).

Groundsel tree, *Baccharis halimifolia* (**a**), is an unusual shrub in that it can grow to the size of a small tree. *Alternate leaves* are of 2 types: *lower leaves* are wedge-shaped and coarsely toothed; 1½ to 2½ in (3 to 6.25 cm) long; *upper leaves* have fewer teeth, and are smaller, more narrow or lanceolate. *Stem* is woody and branches into distinctive green angled twigs. *Flowers* on male and female plants *bloom* during September-October, forming yellow-white clusters. *Fruits* are tiny nutlets at the end of white silky hairs, which remain in *cottony clusters* throughout the autumn. *Size:* up to 15 ft (4.5 m).

Wax myrtle, *Myrica cerifera* (**b**), an evergreen shrub, is sometimes associated with the saltbush community. *Leaves* are alternate, wedge-shaped or lanceolate, and toothed like *Baccharis*; however, the wax myrtle's resin-dotted leaves are darker green, leathery, and highly aromatic, up to 3 in (7.5 cm) long and less than ½ in (12.7 mm) wide. *Twigs* are hairy and brown, with resin dots. *Male and female flowers* are borne in catkins; *bloom* April-June. *Fruits* are small, waxy, blue-gray berrylike drupes; up to ⅛ in (3 mm) wide; highly scented and conspicuous on branches below leafy tips. *Size:* Up to 30 ft (9 m), though often a 6 ft (1.8 m) shrub. *Related species:* **Bayberry,** *M. pensylvanica* (**c**), has thin, deciduous leaves more than ½ in (12.7 mm) wide; larger fruits.

Marsh elder, *Iva frutescens* (**d**), is similar in appearance to groundsel tree—both are members of the composite family; however, the family resemblance fades upon close scrutiny. *Leaves* are thick (fleshy), opposite, with regular serrated margins; up to 4 in (10 cm) long. *Twigs* branch from stem and show fine lines running lengthwise. *Small flowers* (greenish white) *bloom* in terminal clusters August-October. *Size:* Typically 3 ft (90 cm); up to 10 ft (3 m).

INVERTEBRATES of brackish-water SAV beds differ from their fresh-

water relatives in their greater tolerance of salinity. Freshwater worms (Oligochaeta), for instance, found upstream are replaced by marine and estuarine bristle worms (Polychaeta)—the capitellid thread worm (*Heteromastus filiformis*), for example. In a similar fashion, the river snail, *Goniobasis virginica,* an inhabitant of wild celery beds in freshwater streams (p. 64), is replaced in estuarine rivers by seaweed snails of the genus *Hydrobia,* which graze on the surface of salt-tolerant plants. Typically, the weed beds of moderately brackish waters are dominated by redhead pondweed (*Potamogeton perfoliatus*), sago pondweed (*P. pectinatus*), or horned pondweed (*Zannichellia palustris*), described on p. 165. Bordering the estuarine rivers are *Scirpus* marshes and big cordgrass (*Spartina cynosuroides*) stands that support fiddler crabs (*Uca* spp.), periwinkles (*Littorina* sp.), bent mussels (*Ischadium recurvum*), and the saltmarsh snail, *Melampus bidentatus* (see pp. 124 and 140).

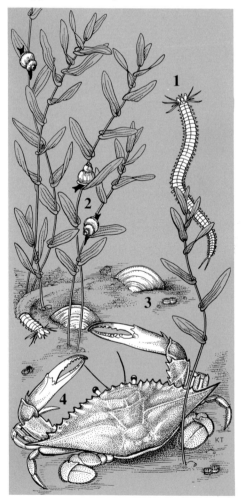

Swimming among the leaf blades of redhead pondweed is a **common clam worm** (*Nereis succinea*; **1**), the most ubiquitous bristle worm in the Chesapeake Bay. Though these and other bristle worms are often buried in the mud substrate (*lower left*), clam worms are also found crawling over plants in search of algae and soft-bodied invertebrates. Up to 6 in (15.2 cm) long, the clam worm is reddish brown with a noticeable red blood line down its back; it has numerous and distinct leglike appendages, called *parapodia,* along its body length.

The **seaweed snail** (*Hydrobia* sp.; **2**) occupies the same niche as the river snail upstream (p. 64) and the variable bittium downstream among the eelgrass beds of the lower Bay (p. 167); it glides over submersed grasses, cleansing them of algae, fungi, and bacteria. This brown, brackish-water snail is almost translucent and less than $1/4$ in (0.6 cm) long. Other molluscs occupy the river bottom, most notably the **brackish-water clam**, *Rangia cuneata* (**3**), an introduced species with an expanding range (see p. 170). Here, near two old shells, siphons appear above the sediment, which shelters the live clams underneath from predatory crabs.

As elsewhere in brackish waters, the common grass shrimp (*Palaemonetes pugio;* p. 167) forages and is foraged upon in the grass beds and river shallows. And, in summer, molting **blue crabs** (*Callinectes sapidus;* **4**), and "soft shells," find shelter in the protective weed beds as they grow a new and larger hard shell.

ESTUARINE FISHES are the only year-round residents of the lower sections of major tributaries and the moderately brackish (i.e., mesohaline) reaches of the main Bay (see fig. 3; p. 12). From late spring to early fall, however, these regions are a melting pot: Young of anadromous herrings and shad (Clupeidae; pp. 65 and 185), and of marine species such as Atlantic menhaden (*Brevoortia tyrannus*, p. 185) and drums (Sciaenidae; p. 186) forage here in large schools. The area is a nursery for these species. A few freshwater forms, such as channel catfish (p. 66), invade the less salty rivers at this time. *Estuarine species*, which spend their entire lives within the estuary, are few; less than 30 are found in the Bay. These include various anchovies and silversides (p. 171), killifishes (p. 172), nonmarine blennies and gobies (p. 188), and the ubiquitous hogchoker (*Trinectes maculatus*; p. 189). Best known perhaps are the temperate basses below. Both are *semi-anadromous* (see p. 201), though part of the rockfish population is marine.

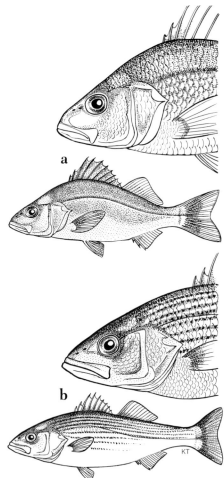

TEMPERATE BASSES (Percichthyidae) differ from other Bay "basses"—a name commonly and confusingly used for a number of unrelated genera—by the 2 spines that appear on the gill cover. Dorsal fins are deeply notched or separate. Sea basses (Serranidae; p. 187) have 3 spines on gill cover; dorsal fin continuous. Largemouth bass are sunfish (Centrarchidae; p. 67) and lack spines on gill cover; fins deeply notched.

White perch, *Morone americana* (**a**), is an estuarine species, restricted to the Bay and its tributaries year-round. Grayish (sometimes black) above, the sides are silvery and plain. Dorsal fins are deeply notched but joined. Tail is mildly forked. Anal fin has 3 spines. Body is deep and compressed. *Size:* to 19 in (48 cm). *Confusing species:* Yellow perch, *Perca flavescens*, a true perch (Percidae), is a freshwater species; dorsal fins widely separate (p. 65). Silver perch, *Bairdiella chrysoura*, is a drum (p. 186); tail rounded.

Striped bass, *Morone saxatilis* (**b**), or "rockfish," differs from white perch in having distinctly separate dorsal fins and stripes on sides. Second anal spine (of 3) is shorter than on *M. americana*. Greenish olive to blue above and white below, the silvery sides have black spots forming 7-9 stripes from head to slightly forked tail. Lower jaw projects; mouth extends to middle of eye. *Size:* to 6 ft (1.8 m).

REPTILES AND AMPHIBIANS of estuarine wetlands show a

marked difference in their tolerance of brackish water. *Amphibians*, which by definition are rarely far from water, have moist glandular skin that is prone to dessication. Consequently, few frogs and toads (or salamanders) inhabit salty water since it has a drying effect on the skin. In the Bay region at least one treefrog (Hylidae), true frog (Ranidae), and true toad (Family Bufonidae) are tolerant of brackish water, which marks the limit of their downstream ranges (see below). None are found in salt marshes or the marine environment. On the other hand, a number of *reptiles*, which have protective scales on their skin, readily inhabit brackish water and a few (e.g., the diamondback terrapin) are endemic to this environment. Besides the aquatic reptiles dicussed here, the eastern mud turtle (p. 45) and eastern ribbon snake (*Thamnophis s. sauritus*; p. 126) venture downstream into brackish habitats.

treefrogs

true frogs

toads

pads and webbing

only webbing

no pads, no webbing

a

b

c

e

KT

FROGS AND TOADS (Salientia) are aided in their ability to climb and swim by the presence of toe pads and webbing. Treefrogs (*Hyla* spp.) have large adhesive pads and are good climbers, though some relatives are not (see p. 69). True frogs (Ranidae) have webbing and are adept swimmers. True toads (Bufonidae) have neither pads nor webbing and are restricted to the ground or water when breeding.

Green treefrog, *Hyla cinerea* (**a**), a resident of fresh and slightly brackish wetlands, is well camouflaged on plants such as bultongue *at left*. Note large toe pads (for climbing). A white or yellowish stripe marks each side; green body turns grayish when dormant. Male call (in May) is a ringing "queenk," repeated once each second, or faster. *Size:* to 2½ in (6.3 cm).

Southern leopard frog, *Rana sphenocephala* (**b**), a typical frog with smooth skin and long legs (for leaping), is named for its round spots. Two *dorsolateral ridges* run from back of head to groin; light spot on eardrum (*tympanum*). Spring mating call is a croak followed by trills. *Size:* to 5 in (12.7 cm).

Fowler's toad, *Bufo woodhousii fowleri* (**c**), a typical toad with warty skin and short legs (for hopping), is covered with dark spots, each containing 3-4 warts. A light middorsal stripe runs between two large *parotoid glands* that just touch cranial crests, one behind each eye. Male voice is a nasal bleat. *Size:* to 3¾ in (9.5 cm).

g juvenile

KT

d

f

Not to scale.

AQUATIC TURTLES (Testudines) of various genera inhabit brackish water, though only terrapins (*Malaclemys* sp.) are endemic.

Common snapping turtle, *Chelydra serpentina serpentina* (d), is a common resident of brackish waters (up to 12 ppt). The large, strongly jawed head and long sawtooth tail are characteristic. *Carapace* (upper shell) is light brown to black; *plastron* (lower shell) is very small. Diet consists of fish, invertebrates, and plants. *Size:* to 18½ in (47 cm). *Note:* Snappers rarely bask on land; dangerous to handle.

Redbelly turtle, *Pseudemys rubriventris rubriventris* (e, *opposite page*), is the largest basking turtle of fresh and brackish rivers. The red markings on black shell (*carapace*) and red underbelly (*plastron*) are distinctive. Light line on top of head meets lateral line (through eye) to form an arrow at snout. *Size:* to 15¾ in (40 cm). *Confusing species:* Painted turtle, *Chrysemys picta*, has yellow spots on head; shell less domed; smaller; enters slightly brackish water but more typical of freshwater streams (p. 69).

Northern diamondback terrapin, *Malaclemys terrapin terrapin* (f), is an estuarine species. Inhabiting brackish waters, the terrapin is sometimes seen basking in tidewater marshes or rising to the surface to breathe. Recognized by the deep, concentric rings on each scute of the carapace and its spotted head and limbs. *Size:* Female to 9 in (23 cm); male half as large.

WATER SNAKES (*Nerodia* spp.; Serpentes). Only one species is widespread in brackish waters. For other species see p. 70.

Northern water snake, *Nerodia sipedon sipedon* (g), is ubiquitous in wetland habitats ranging from swamps to salt marshes and brackish waters (up to 12 ppt). Note discontinuous bands; unpronounced in adults. Underbelly has spots shaped like half-moons (sometimes absent). *Size:* to 53 in (134 cm). *Confusing species:* Brown water snake, *N. taxispilota*, and Eastern cottonmouth, *Agkistrodon p. piscivorus* (VENOMOUS), have diamond-shaped heads; see other differences pp. 70 and 43, respectively; both may enter brackish water; SE Virginia only.

WATER BIRDS AND WATERFOWL of open wetlands and bays

frequent the main stems and mouths of major tributaries and the tidal wetlands that hug their shores. Long-legged waders and marsh ducks remain in the shallows, close to land, while rafts of migrating bay ducks, sea ducks, swans, and geese can be spotted offshore, often at midstream. In addition to the bitterns and herons (Ardeidae), waterfowl (Anatidae), diurnal birds of prey (Falconiformes), and gulls and terns (Laridae; Charadriiformes) described below, various other birds reside in brackish wetlands, including rails (Rallidae)—specifically the king rail (*Rallus elegans*; p. 112) and Virginia rail (*R. limicola*; p. 128)—and nesting wrens, blackbirds, and *marsh* sparrows (p. 129). Fall and spring migrants include plovers and sandpipers (Charadriiformes; p. 145). Kingfishers and swallows (p. 74) nest on steep banks of estuarine rivers and feed over river and marsh. In general, however, brackish marshes do not support the same diversity of birdlife that resides upstream.

HERONS AND EGRETS (Ardeidae) are long-legged waders with spearlike bills. The family also includes bitterns (Tribe Botaurini) and night-herons (Tribe Nycticoracini), which are uncommon breeders. For white herons (egrets) see p. 142.

Great blue heron, *Ardea herodias* (**a**), is a permanent resident of tidewater wetlands, rivers, and bays. *Field marks:* This long-necked heron is unmistakable due to its large size and bluish gray color. Adult has a white head and black plumes. *Flight:* Look for slow, deep wingbeats. On takeoff, neck forms S-shaped loop; legs hang low. *Size:* Length to 52 in (130 cm); wingspan averages 72 in (183 cm). *Call:* 3-4 harsh squawks. *Food:* Fish and invertebrates. *Season:* All year; less common in winter. Local colonial nester in wooded swamps and isolated islands, in trees or tall bushes.

Green-backed heron, *Butorides striatus* (**b**), is a transient and common summer resident of wooded streams, rivers, tidal marshes, and bays. *Field marks:* Head and neck are chestnut. Back and wings are bluish gray. Legs are greenish yellow. Sexes alike. *Flight:* Crowlike with long neck pulled in; short flights between cover. *Size:* Length to 22 in (55 cm); wingspan averages 26 in (66 cm). *Call:* A loud "skew" or "skuck." *Food:* Mostly fish, grass shrimp, and insects. *Season:* Spring, summer, and fall; rare winter visitor. Nests in shrubs and trees.

SWANS, GEESE, AND DUCKS (Anatidae), or waterfowl as they are collectively known, are large water birds. Swans (Tribe Cygnini) are huge and have longer necks than geese (Tribe Anserini), which have larger bodies and longer necks than ducks (Anatinae). On takeoff, swans and geese patter across the water. They feed at surface (or in fields) on grains, grasses, and aquatic plants (SAV).

Tundra swan, *Cygnus columbianus* (**a**), is a transient and winter resident of rivers and bays. *Field marks:* Body is all white; black bill at end of long neck. Sexes similar. *Flight:* Deep, ponderous wing strokes. *Size:* Length to 53 in (133 cm); wingspan averages 80 in (203 cm). *Call:* High mellow whooping. *Season:* Mostly spring and fall; less common in winter; rare summer visitor. Nonbreeder.

Canada goose, *Branta canadensis* (**b**), is a common transient and winter resident (and uncommon summer denizen) of tidal rivers and bays. *Field marks:* Body is dark brown; belly whitish. Long neck and head are black with white "chin strap." Sexes identical. *Flight:* Look for long black neck; wing strokes deep and powerful. *Size:* Length (variable) to 45 in (114 cm); wingspan (variable) averages 68 in (173 cm). *Call:* Loud honking heard in flight. *Season:* Abundant spring and fall; common in winter; uncommon and local summer breeder. Nests on shore or marsh; mates for life.

Snow goose, *Chen caerulescens* (**c**), is a transient and winter resident of tidewater wetlands and bays. *Field marks:* White body contrasts with black *primary feathers.* Sexes alike. **Blue goose (d)** is a color morph of snow goose; body gray-brown; head white; intermixes with white morph and is common at certain Bay locales (e.g., Blackwater and Presquile NWRs). *Flight:* Look for black wingtips; for blue phase, white head contrasting with dark body. *Size:* Length to 38 in (95 cm); wingspan averages 59 in (150 cm). *Call:* A muffled, nasal "haw-haw" or "houck-houck." *Season:* Fall, winter, and spring. Nonbreeder.

Marsh ducks spring from water on takeoff

. . . and tip up to feed at surface.

Dabbling Ducks (Tribe Anatini), or marsh ducks, as they are commonly called, feed at the surface on seeds, grasses, sedges, and other wetland plants (including SAV). Marsh ducks spring from water on takeoff. Wings have a bright patch on secondary feathers—the *speculum.*

Mallard, *Anas platyrhynchos* (**a**), is a common transient and winter resident and occasional to fairly common summer inhabitant of freshwater wetlands, rivers, and bays. *Field marks:* Note male's dark green head, white "collar," and chestnut chest; yellow bill; white tail. Female is mottled brown; orangish bill; whitish tail. *Flight:* Look for blue speculum with white borders front and back. *Size:* Length to 28 in (70 cm); wingspan averages 36 in (91 cm). *Call:* Male (drake) has low "kwek-kwek"; female (hen) quacks. *Season:* All year; less frequent in summer; uncommon nester on high ground near water.

American wigeon, *Anas americana* (**b**), or baldpate, is a transient and winter resident of freshwater wetlands, rivers, and bays. *Field marks:* Male has a white crown and green head patch. Note white forewing. Female is brownish with gray head. *Flight:* White patch on forewing is distinctive; also look for white belly. Nervous, bunched groups have fast, erratic flight, resembling a flock of pigeons. *Size:* Length to 23 in (58 cm); wingspan averages 34 in (86 cm). *Call:* Drakes whistle; hens have loud "ka-ow" and a low "qua-awk." *Season:* Mostly spring and fall; less common in winter; rare summer visitor. Nonbreeder.

American black duck, *Anas rubripes* (**c**), is a common transient and winter resident and locally common summer resident of rivers, bays, and tidal wetlands. *Field marks:* Body is dark brown, almost black at distance, in contrast to paler brown head. Sexes similar. *Flight:* Look for purple speculum; white linings underneath wings are distinctive. *Size:* Length to 25 in (63 cm); wingspan averages 36 in (92 cm). *Call:* Drake's "kwek-kwek" and hen's quack are same as mallards'. *Season:* All year; less common May-August; nests on dry ground near water or woods. Note: Winter population was formerly over 200,000; today, less than 50,000 winter on the Bay.

Bay ducks run and patter when taking wing

. . . and dive underwater to feed.

Diving Ducks (Tribe Aythyini), or bay ducks as they are often called, dive for their food, mostly submersed aquatic vegetation, and run along surface on takeoff. Most nest in northern wetlands and migrate to the Chesapeake Bay in fall.

Canvasback, *Aythya valisineria* (**a**), formerly more abundant, is now a locally common transient and winter resident of tidal rivers and bays. *Field marks:* The unusual, sloping head profile is distinctive. Male head is chestnut-colored. Breast and tail are black "bookends" in the water at either end of the large, canvas-white body. Female is a dull gray-brown. Both have long blackish bill. *Flight:* Look for white back and black chest (p. 193). *Size:* Length to 24 in (60 cm); wingspan averages 34 in (86 cm). *Call:* Drakes croak and growl; hens have mallard type quack. *Season:* Mostly spring and fall; less common in winter; rare summer visitor. Nonbreeder.

Redhead, *Aythya americana* (**b**), also reduced in numbers, is a transient and uncommon winter resident on tidal rivers and bays. *Field marks:* Male similar to lesser scaup, but body is grayer; rounded head is rusty red. Female is brown with light patch on face near bill. Bluish bill has white band next to black tip. *Flight:* Gray wing stripe is distinctive (p. 193). *Size:* Length to 23 in (58 cm); wingspan averages 33 in (84 cm). *Call:* Drakes purr; hens have a loud, high squawk. *Season:* Mostly spring and fall; less common in winter; rare summer visitor. Nonbreeder.

Lesser scaup, *Aythya affinis* (**c**), is a common transient and winter resident of tidal rivers and bays. *Field marks:* Scaup are distinctive in water—white body with black breast and tail. Male has purple gloss on his domed head. Brown female has white patch at base of bill. *Flight:* White wing stripes shorter (half-length) than on greater scaup (p. 193). *Size:* Length to 18 in (45 cm); wingspan to 29 in (74 cm). *Call:* Drakes purr; hens "scaup" or are silent. *Season:* Mostly spring and fall; less common in winter; rare summer visitor. Nonbreeder.

Mergansers and Allies (Tribe Mergini) include the fish-eating mergansers and the familiar diving sea ducks below.

Hooded merganser, *Lophodytes cucullatus* (**a**), is a transient and local winter and summer resident of tidal rivers and bays. *Field marks:* Male has a distinctive white fanlike hood, bordered with black. Body is black above, rusty on sides. Saw-toothed bill is slender. Female has reddish crest. *Flight:* Look for white wing patch on rear edge. Springs from water on takeoff. *Size:* Length to 19 in (48 cm); wingspan averages 26 in (66 cm). *Call:* A low croak. *Season:* Mostly spring and fall; less common in winter and summer. Local nester (Maryland only) in wooded swamps.

Common goldeneye, *Bucephala clangula* (**b**), is a transient and winter resident. *Field marks:* Round white spot on face of male is distinctive. Body is white; head black, glossed with green. Female is gray with brown head; white "collar." *Flight:* Note large white wing patches (p. 195). *Size:* to 20 in (50 cm). *Call:* Drakes have piercing "spear-spear"; hens a low quack. *Season:* Mostly spring and fall; less common in winter; rare summer visitor. Nonbreeder.

Bufflehead, *Bucephala albeola* (**c**), is a small transient and winter resident. *Field marks:* Note white head patch on male (compared to crest of hooded merganser); back is black; white underneath. Gray female has white patch behind eye. *Flight:* Look for black-and-white body pattern and white wing patch (p. 195). *Size:* to 15 in (38 cm). *Call:* Drakes squeak; hens quack weakly. *Season:* Spring and fall; less common in winter. Nonbreeder.

Stiff-Tailed Ducks (Tribe Oxyurini)

Ruddy duck, *Oxyura jamaicensis* (**d**), is a common transient and winter resident. *Field marks:* Male has white cheek patch; body is dull brown in fall. Female has dark cheek stripe. *Flight:* Dark; note cheek patch (p. 195). *Size:* to 16 in (40 cm). *Season:* Mostly spring and fall, less common in winter; rare summer visitor. Nonbreeder.

OTHER BIRDS of estuarine rivers and shores include predatory and scavenging species, such as those illustrated here. For other birds of prey see p. 111; other gulls and terns see p. 159. Typical perching birds of brackish wetlands (in addition to fish crow) are shown on p. 129.

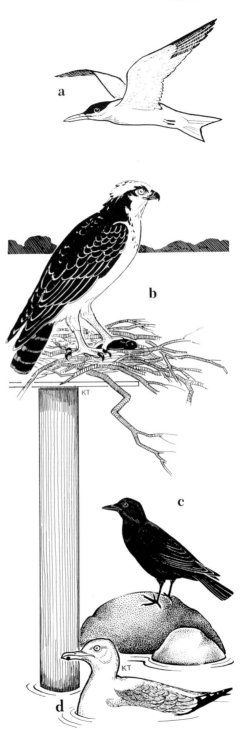

Caspian tern, *Sterna caspia* (**a**), is a fairly common migrant along lower reaches of tidal rivers. *Field marks:* Caspians have heavy red bills, slightly forked tails, and dark primaries below wings; black cap is mottled brown in fall. *Flight:* Terns hover and dive headfirst for fish. *Size:* Length to 20 in (51 cm); wingspan averages 50 in (127 cm). *Call:* A harsh "kraah," "karr," or "kaak." *Season:* Spring and fall; rare winter visitor; uncommon summer visitor. Nonbreeder (except on Virginia barrier islands).

Osprey, *Pandion haliaetus* (**b**), is a common summer resident and transient along tidal rivers. *Field marks:* Hawklike body is dark above, light below. Black cheek patch runs from eye to back of head. *Flight:* Hovers and plunges feetfirst for fish. Shows a dark patch at crook on underside of wings (p. 146). *Size:* Length to 25 in (64 cm); wingspan averages 65 in (165 cm). *Call:* A whistled cheep-cheep; or (near nest) a sharp "cheereeek." *Season:* Spring, summer, and fall; rare winter visitor (November-February). Nests on trees, platforms, and buoys.

Fish crow, *Corvus ossifragus* (**c**), is a permanent resident and transient along tidewater shores. *Field marks:* A small black crow distinguishable from American crow (*C. brachyrhynchos*) only by voice. *Size:* to 20 in (50 cm). *Call:* A short "ca" or "car" rather than the (larger) American crow's typical caw. *Season:* All year; most common in spring and fall; less common, winter. Common breeder.

Herring gull, *Larus argentatus* (**d**), is a common permanent resident of tidal rivers. *Field marks:* Note gray back and black wing tips. Yellow bill has red spot. *Flight:* Commonly soars (p. 196). *Size:* to 26 in (65 cm). *Call:* Often a "ga-ga-ga." *Season:* All year; less common in summer than fall-spring. Highly local breeder (p. 159). *Note:* This species is the common "sea gull" of harbors and spoil sites.

THE MAMMAL DIVERSITY of brackish wetlands, in contrast to that of nesting birds, is nearly as high in terms of numbers of species as one finds in freshwater marshes. Meadow voles (p. 75), muskrats, and marsh rice rats thrive here. These rodents forage on the stems, leaves, and rhizomes of narrow-leaved cattail, Olney three-square, and other salt-tolerant plants. Along tidal creeks, dense stands of big cordgrass also serve as shelter for *wetland mammals*. Here, muskrats and nutria (*Myocastor coypus*, p. 115) build houses and feeding platforms (see p. 131), while rice rats and meadow voles utilize leaves and detritus to build their smaller nests. *Upland mammals* such as white-footed mice (*Peromyscus leucopus*), house mice (*Mus musculus*), and meadow jumping mice (*Zapus hudsonius*) are usually restricted to the marsh edge. Attracted by these various rodents, the red fox (p. 53) and long-tailed weasel (*Mustela frenata*) enter brackish marshes to feed.

The familiar **raccoon** (*Procyon lotor;* **a**) can be seen at the river's edge (*at left*), looking for frogs, clams, insects, or seeds along the shore. Recognized by its black mask and alternating tail rings of yellowish white and black, the raccoon grows to 28 in (70 cm), not including its 12 in (30 cm) tail, and can weigh 35 lbs. Though visiting all types of wetlands from swamps to salt marshes, it typically nests in upland areas, choosing hollow trees, logs, or crevices to make a den.

The **marsh rice rat** (*Oryzomys palustris;* **b**) builds a nest above high tide like the one *at far left*, attached to the stems of big cordgrass. Sometimes rice rats take over marsh wren nests, which are also globular (though more oblong). Identified by their grayish brown fur and white feet, rice rats grow to 5 in (12.5 cm) with a sparsely furred, scaly tail often longer than the body. Rice rats typically feed on seeds and leaves of grasses, sedges, and aquatic plants and, like meadow voles, make surface runways throughout the marsh.

Often feeding on marsh plants in broad daylight, the **muskrat** (*Ondatra zibethicus;* **c**; *below left*) supplements its vegetarian diet with an occasional clam or fish. Muskrats are distinguished from nutria (pp. 115 and 131) by their smaller size (14 in; 36 cm) and naked, scaly tail (about 10 in; 25 cm long), which is flattened from side to side.

The Bay and Its Marshes and Shores

Fresh Bay Marshes

Brackish Bay Marshes

Salt Marshes

Beaches and Tidal Flats

Shallow Water Habitats

Deep, Open Water

Fresh Bay Marshes

AT the head of the Bay one finds a 12-mile (variable) stretch of "tidal fresh water" between the mouths of the Susquehanna and Sassafras rivers. Bordering these waters and south to the Gunpowder delta is a limited acreage of fresh bay marsh, similar in plant composition to the wetlands along freshwater streams. These isolated, exposed marshes differ from riverside wetlands in subtle ways. Tidal flooding or freshwater seepage inundates the marsh more often than streamflow. Quiet, sheltered ponds are more common and are a preferred habitat of marsh ducks.

Another extensive area of fresh bay marsh is located landward of the brackish bay marshes in Dorchester County, Maryland. Though separated by 70 miles, these two major expanses of freshwater wetlands are remarkably similar. In this chapter the two regions are considered a single habitat type. *Marshes*, by definition, are wetlands, above mean low water, dominated by herbaceous plants. In this regard, they differ from swamps (p. 27) and SAV (p. 163), which often border these emergent wetlands.

Fresh bay marshes are an oasis of aquatic and wetland life. Amphibians are found here; frogs in particular chorus in the spring in huge congregations. These moist-skinned creatures are rare in brackish environments farther along the Bay. Redwinged blackbirds and other marsh-nesting birds are common in stands of cattail. Muskrat houses dot the American three-square meadows, and violet-blue flowers of pickerelweed (*at left*) adorn the open shallows.

The term "fresh bay marsh" is, to some scientists, a misnomer—a not-surprising bias. Since the estuary, by definition, has a measurable salinity gradient along its length, one may logically expect "fresh water" to be absent, a pure form sequestered

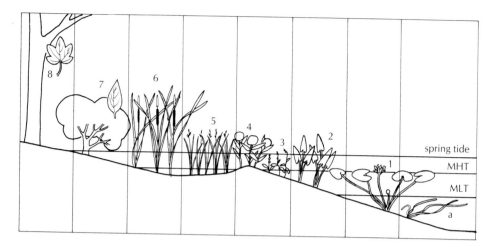

Figure 8. Plant zonation in a typical mixed freshwater marsh community (key *opposite*).

only in the headwaters of tidal tributaries. However, marsh types are defined by plant composition, not by rigid salinity zones. While a fresh bay marsh may be flooded by tidal fresh waters (0-0.5 ppt) in spring, those waters may be oligohaline (0.5-5 ppt) in late summer or fall (see fig. 3; p. 12). As long as the brackish inundation does not hold court for too long (e.g., over several years of drought), the wetland profile will remain a fairly typical freshwater marsh.

Major indicator plants of fresh bay marshes include narrow-leaved cattail, Walter's millet, American three-square (which may grow in extensive meadows), tearthumb and smartweed, fragrant waterlily, and spatterdock (which is often associated with arrow arum and pickerelweed).

These and other emergent freshwater plants typically segregate in zones according to soil type and water depth (see fig. 8; *above*). However, because of the high diversity of plants and occasional random distribution, these bands are often obscured. They are simplified for a discussion of zonation (*opposite page*).

Freshwater marshes, like other wetlands, offer a variety of important benefits. In addition to hydrological benefits, such as flood control and groundwater replenishment, wetlands enhance the water quality of the Bay by recycling nutrients, trapping silt, and breaking down pollutants. Marshes also supply food (e.g., *detritus*) to aquatic organisms and provide habitat for wildlife. Fishes invade the shallows at high tide (p. 171) and shorebirds forage along mud flats when the tide is out (p. 157).

A few interesting pockets of freshwater marsh are accessible by boat in the upper Bay. In the vicinity of Susquehanna Flats, visit Elk Neck State Park, Stemmers Run WMA, or the bayside section of Gunpowder Falls State Park. Fresh bay marshes can be observed in the western half of Blackwater NWR in Dorchester County. They are also in evidence north of Elliott Island at Savannah Lake.

THE PLANT PROFILE of tidal freshwater marshes shows the highest diversity of Chesapeake wetlands.

Plants often colonize certain zones within the marsh relative to elevation, soil type, and tidal inundation (see fig. 8; *opposite page*). Below mean low tide (MLT), one finds submersed aquatic plants (**a**) and, riding at the water's surface, the leaves of floating-leaved plants such as fragrant waterlily (**1**). Emergent plants, which dominate the marshland, are erect regardless of the water level and are not submersed at MLT. At the marsh edge, one finds arrow arum (**2**), spatterdock, and pickerelweed. Tearthumb and smartweed (**3**) grow on mud flats near mean high tide (MHT), while swamp milkweed (**4**) and other "associated species" grow on raised hummocks. In wet pockets within the marsh one finds a variety of grasses, rushes, and sedges (**5**). Cattails (**6**) thrive at the edges of ponds or in shallows at the marsh border. Buttonbush (**7**) and red maple (**8**), both woody species, often mark the upland (or swamp) margin.

EMERGENT PLANTS of freshwater wetlands include the cattails and arums with their distinctive flowering spikes (*at right*). Grasses, sedges, and rushes follow. Unless noted otherwise, species are *perennial*.

Narrow-leaved cattail, *Typha angustifolia* (**a**), grows in colonies at creek or upland borders in fresh and brackish wetlands. *Narrow leaves* are of 2 types: *basal leaves*, which arise from the stem base, up to 6 ft (1.8 m) long; and *stem leaves*, which are alternate, up to 2¹/₂ ft (76 cm) long; both up to ¹/₂ in (12.7 mm) wide. *Stems* are upright; produced from rhizomes. *Flowers* are densely crowded on 2 terminal spikes: male flowers (often covered with yellow pollen) on the upper spike are separated from female flowers on lower spike; *bloom* May-June. *Seedlike achene* has silky bristles attached to base. *Size:* up to 6 ft (1.8 m).

Sweet flag, *Acorus calamus* (**b**), grows in fresh marshes and shallow water. *Basal leaves* are swordlike; aromatic; midrib is off center; up to 5 ft (1.5 m) long; fanning out at plant base. *Stem* is lacking. *Flowers* are small and yellowish on spikelike *spadix*. *Size:* up to 5 ft (1.5 m).

Dodder, *Cuscuta gronovii* (**c**), is a parasitic plant that grows over cattail and other plants. *Stem* (vine) is yellow or orange; resembles tangled string. *Tiny flowers* are 5-lobed "bells" in *sessile* clusters.

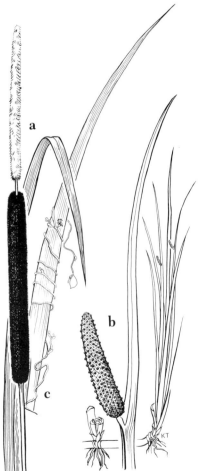

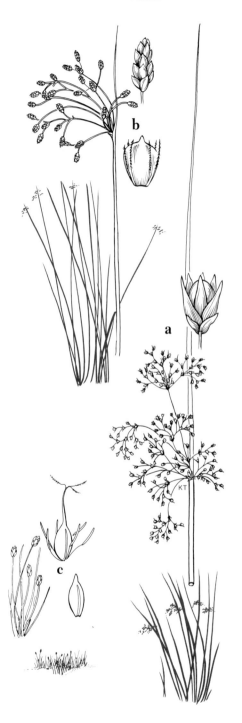

RUSHES (Juncaceae) generally have round, solid stems and fruit capsules that contain numerous tiny seeds.

Soft rush, *Juncus effusus* (**a**), grows in dense clumps (tussocks) in freshwater wetlands. *Leaves* lack blades; reduced to sheaths at stem base. *Stem* is soft, round, and grooved; grows from stout rhizome; tapers to a point, but not sharp (stiff) like black needlerush. *Flowers* are borne in loose branching clusters that arise on stem about one-third of the way down from tip; *bloom* July-August. *Seeds* are contained inside brownish capsule (shown) on spikelets. *Size:* up to 3$^{1}/_{2}$ ft (1 m).

SEDGES (Cyperaceae) include the bulrushes, three-squares, and spikerushes. Sedges have triangular or round, solid stems. Fruits are nutlets called *achenes*. Flowers are borne in the axils of overlapping scales, which may collectively resemble a bud.

Great bulrush, *Scirpus validus* (**b**), or soft-stemmed bulrush, is a tall species, resembling a rush, that colonizes fresh and brackish marshes. *Leaves* lack blades. *Stem,* either arching or upright, is round and soft; tapers to a point; grows from stout reddish rhizome. *Flowers* are borne in budlike oval spikelets, in drooping clusters near top of stem; *bloom* July-August. *Achene* (shown) is brownish gray with 4-6 bristles attached to base; grouped in drooping clusters near top of stem. *Size:* up to 8 ft (2.4 m).

Spikerushes (*Eleocharis* spp.) are leafless, grass-like plants with terminal flower heads. Freshwater species include square-stem spikerush, *E. quadrangulata*, and others (p. 58).

Dwarf spikerush, *Eleocharis parvula* (**c**), forms dense, low mats in the intertidal zone of brackish wetlands and (slightly brackish) "freshwater" marshes. *Leaves* are reduced to stem sheaths. *Stem* is wiry and erect but short; typically 2 in (5 cm) tall. *Flowers* inconspicuous on single, terminal budlike spikelet. *Achene* (shown) is a 3-angled nutlet. *Size:* up to 5 in (10 cm).

Umbrella sedge, *Cyperus esculentus* (**a**), or chufa, is a common sedge of freshwater wetlands. *Grasslike leaves* appear at base of stem and *leaflike bracts* are arranged just below flower clusters, the bracts of unequal lengths. *Stem* is stout and triangular in cross section. *Flower head* (umbel) is an umbrella-shaped complex of rays, each bearing numerous yellow-brown spikelets radiating in flat planes; *blooms* July-August. *Achenes* are small, elliptic nutlets. Seeds and nutlike tubers are eaten by waterfowl. *Size:* up to 3 ft (90 cm).

Tussock sedge, *Carex stricta* (**b**), grows in dense clumps, or tussocks, in freshwater wetlands. *Leaves* are long, narrow, and grasslike; up to 30 in (76 cm) long and $1/4$ in (6.4 mm) wide; channeled above and keeled below. *Stem* (when present) is 3-angled and slender, rising above the leaves. *Flowers* are grouped in spikes: male spikes (1-2) erect at top of stem; erect female spikes (2-6) are *sessile* or short-stalked in the axils of short upper leaves; *bloom* May-June. *Achene* is surrounded by an inflated paperlike sac (the *perigynium*). *Size:* up to $3^1/2$ ft (1 m). *Related species:* Sedge, *C. lurida* (p. 59), has thick barrel-like female spikes; perigynium has needlelike appendage.

American three-square, *Scirpus pungens* (**c**), is the only three-square in our area typical of freshwater wetlands. *Leaves* are not apparent at maturity; stem leaves (when present) are erect, up to 18 in (46 cm) long; ribbonlike basal leaves may surround base. *Stem* is sharply triangular; dark green; arising from a long dark rhizome and ending in a sharp point. *Flowers* are borne in 2-6 *sessile* (nonstalked) spikelets extending laterally from the stem up to 5 in (13 cm) below tip; *bloom* July-August. *Flowering scale* has a notched apex and needlelike bristle. *Fruits* arranged in similar conical clusters. *Size:* up to 6 ft (1.8 m). *Note:* Formerly named *S. americanus.* Seeds eaten by waterfowl; rhizomes consumed by muskrats. *Related species:* Olney three-square, *S. americanus* (p. 119), has concave 3-sided stem; seed clusters closer to stem tip; scale rounded; typical of brackish environs; formerly *S. olneyi.*

GRASSES (Gramineae) have jointed, round, hollow stems. Flowers are borne in spikelets. Fruits are grainlike seeds.

Wild rice, *Zizania aquatica* (**a**), grows in colonies in freshwater marshes. *Stem leaves* of mature plants have flat blades with rough, saw-toothed edges; up to 16 in (40 cm) long and 2 in (5 cm) wide. *Stem* is erect. *Flower head* (panicle) has 2 sections: upper branches bear the erect and close female flowers; lower branches spread horizontally, bearing the dangling short-lived male flowers; *blooms* June-August; panicle up to 2 ft (60 cm) long. *Rice grain* (shown) develops from the upper (pistillate) flowers; edible; important food for red-winged blackbirds and waterfowl. *Size:* up to 10 ft (3 m). Annual; propagates by seeds only.

Common reed, *Phragmites australis* (**b**), is an *introduced*, weedy species that grows in disturbed areas (e.g., dredge spoil sites and roadsides) as well as marshes, often outcompeting more important plants such as wild rice. *Leaves* are flat; up to 24 in (61 cm) long and 2 in (5 cm) wide. *Stem* is erect, arising from creeping rhizomes. *Flower cluster* (panicle) is a feathery multibranched plume, purplish at first, then light brown when mature; persists in fall; up to 12 in (30 cm) long; *blooms* July-August. *Fruits* are small grains; spreads also vegetatively by long rhizomes. *Size:* up to 12 ft (3.6 m).

Walter's millet, *Echinochloa walteri* (**c**), grows in tidal freshwater marshes and ditches. *Leaves* are long and tapering though not as rough-edged as wild rice or rice cutgrass; up to 20 in (50 cm) long and 1 in (25 mm) wide. *Stem* grows upright. *Flower head* (panicle) bears many reddish brown spikelets, each flower (floret) nearly concealed by an elongated bristle, or awn, up to 1 1/4 in (3 cm) long. *Blooms* in July. Panicle, which may be 4-12 in (10-30 cm) long, looks bristly and may become weighted down with seeds, nearly touching ground. Annual; propagates only by seeds. *Size:* up to 7 ft (2.1 m).

ASSOCIATED SHRUBS of freshwater marshes grow on elevated hummocks within the wetland or at the upland edge.

Buttonbush, *Cephalanthus occidentalis* (**a**), is a typical shrub of freshwater swamps and marshes. *Leaves* are shiny green above, veined, opposite (or in whorls of 3 or 4), and oblong. *Stems* are woody and branch frequently. *Tubular flowers* are small and white, radiating from a ball-like flower head; *bloom* July-September. *Spherical fruits* contain brown, clove-like nutlets. *Size:* up to 10 ft (3 m).

Other Common Shrubs and tree saplings that invade freshwater marshes:

Swamp rose, *Rosa palustris*, p. 32
Sweet pepperbush, *Clethra alnifolia*, p. 33
Silky dogwood, *Cornus amomum*, p. 33
Red maple, *Acer rubrum*, p. 34
Common alder, *Alnus serrulata*, p. 35
Black willow, *Salix nigra*, p. 35
Redbay, *Persea borbonia*, p. 36

ASSOCIATED HERBACEOUS PLANTS have nonwoody stems. Also see pp. 29-30, 32, and 61-63 for other herbs that colonize freshwater marshes.

Swamp milkweed, *Asclepias incarnata* (**b**), a member of the milkweed family (Asclepiadaceae), grows in freshwater marshes and swamps. *Leaves* are opposite and lance-shaped; up to 5 in (12.5 cm) long. *Stem* is leafy to the top. *Flowers* appear in small, pink umbrellalike clusters at top of stem; *bloom* July-August. *Seeds* are enclosed in spindle-shaped pods, each seed bearing a tuft of long silky hairs. *Size:* up to 4 ft (1.2 m).

Water dock, *Rumex verticillatus* (**c**), a member of the buckwheat family (Polygonaceae), inhabits freshwater marshes and swamps. *Leaves* are alternate and lance-shaped; up to 12 in (30 cm) long. *Stem* is grooved lengthwise and jointed. *Flowers* are small and green, borne singly on drooping stalks in whorls on main stalk; *bloom* June-July. *Fruits* are reddish brown heart-shaped nutlets. Size: up to 4 ft (1.2 m).

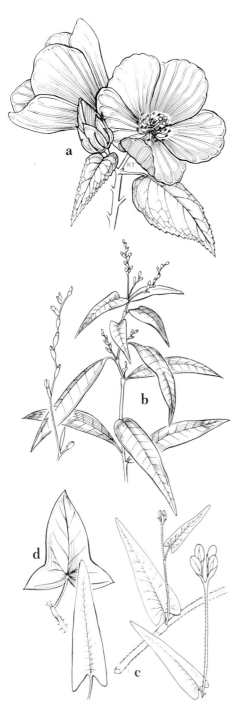

Marsh hibiscus, *Hibiscus moscheutos* (**a**), a member of the mallow family (Malvaceae), grows in fresh and brackish marshes, often at the upland edge. *Leaves* are alternately arranged, smooth above, and velvety below with toothed edges; often egg- or heart-shaped; up to 8 in (20 cm) long. *Stem* is round and smooth. *Large showy flowers* are pink or white with a distinctive red center; 5 petals; up to 6 in (15.2 cm) wide; *bloom* late July-August. *Seed pods* (p. 122) are rounded; distinctly 5-celled; remain on erect stem through winter. *Size:* up to 7 ft (2.1 m).

Smartweeds and Tearthumbs are members of the buckwheat family (Polygonaceae), all of which bear a membranous sheath (ocrea) on stem at each leaf node.

Dotted smartweed, *Polygonum punctatum* (**b**), is the most common smartweed in the Chesapeake area, growing in the intertidal zone in fresh marshes. *Leaves* are alternately arranged, punctuated with dots, and lance-shaped; up to 6 in (15 cm) long and 1 1/2 in (3.8 cm) wide. *Stem* typically grows upright. *Flowers* are small, white, and loosely clustered on spikes; *bloom* August-October. *Seed* is a 3-sided or biconvex (lens-shaped) nutlet; eaten by ducks. *Size:* up to 3 ft (90 cm).

Arrow-leaved tearthumb, *Polygonum sagittatum* (**c**), is a common associated herb of freshwater wetlands, often growing near smartweed in the intertidal zone. *Leaves* are alternate, narrow, and smooth; with arrow-shaped (sagittate) bases; up to 4 in (10 cm) long and 1 in (25 mm) wide. *Stem* is 4-angled, vinelike, weak, typically reclining on other plants, forming thickets (though erect when young); bears weak downward-pointing spines. *Flowers* are pink (or white or greenish white); in small loose clusters at end of long stalks arising from leaf axils; *bloom* July-August. *Fruit* is a 3-angled nutlet. *Size:* up to 4 ft (1.2 m). Annual; propagates only by seeds. *Related species:* **Halberd-leaved tearthumb,** *P. arifolium* (**d**), has broader leaves with pointed basal lobes (at right angles to axis); stronger prickles on stem.

Open Water Plants growing in tidal freshwater marshes typically are emergent species with a rooted base. The following 3 species from the water lily (Nymphaeaceae), arum (Araceae), and pickerelweed (Pontederiaceae) families, respectively, are common. Also see pp. 62-63.

Spatterdock, *Nuphar luteum* (**a**), or yellow pond lily, grows in large colonies with its characteristic leaves appearing to float at high tide, though they are clearly emergent (erect) at low tide. *Leaves* are heart-shaped or round; up to 10 in (25 cm) long; with a notch at each base where erect, rounded leafstalks (petioles) are attached. Petiole forms midrib below leaf. *Rootstalk* is a thick fleshy rhizome. *Flower* is a yellow, 6-petaled globe borne singly on a long stalk; up to 2 in (5 cm) wide; *blooms* June-September. *Fruit* is a many-seeded pod. *Size:* Petioles and flower stalks up to 4 ft (1.2 m) long. *Confusing species:* **Fragrant waterlily,** *Nymphaea odorata* (**b**), is a *floating-leaved plant*; leaf lacks midrib; flower (shown) is white and fragrant, with many petals; mostly nontidal waters.

Arrow arum, *Peltandra virginica* (**c**), grows on tidal flats or in shallow water. *Leaves* are thick, fleshy, and shaped like arrowheads; up to 18 in (46 cm) long; appearing on long stalks arising from base of flower stalk; basal lobes and main segment have a prominent midvein; another vein runs around leaf margin. *Rootstalk* is embedded in mud. *Flowers* cover a fleshy spike (*spadix*), concealed within a sheath (*spathe*); *bloom* May-July. *Fruits* are greenish berries borne on spike which droops at maturity. *Size:* up to 3 ft (90 cm).

Pickerelweed, *Pontederia cordata* (**d**), may be distinguished from arrow arum, with which it occurs, by the parallel veins on the leaf. *Leaves* are arrow- or heart-shaped, and of 2 types: either *basal leaves* (long-stalked) or *stem leaves* (short-stalked and alternate); up to 15 in (38 cm) long. *Stem* is stout, typically with one basal leaf. *Tubular flowers* are violet-blue, borne on terminal spires up to 4 in (10 cm) long. *Fruit* is a small sac bearing a single seed. *Size:* up to 3 ft (90 cm).

MARSHLAND INVERTEBRATES of the Bay proper (and its

tributaries) are most numerous and diverse within the freshwater regions of the watershed. Immediately apparent are the countless insects that inhabit the marsh. Dragonflies (Odonata) dart about on their predatory flights. Butterflies (Lepidoptera) and honeybees (Hymenoptera) visit swamp milkweed and other flowering plants. And, on cattail and wild rice, one finds numerous grasshoppers and crickets (Orthoptera), planthoppers (Homoptera), and true bugs (Hemiptera), all of which feed upon a variety of marsh plants. Mosquitoes, midges, and other obnoxious flies (Diptera) that are pests to man are abundant at certain times of the year (see p. 139). Fortunately, swallows, flycatchers, dragonflies, and a cohort of web-building and hunting spiders (Arachnida) keep them in check. The invertebrate world of the marsh is thus maintained in delicate balance. Below the water's surface roam a different array of creatures—mostly crustaceans, molluscs, and worms (see p. 64)—typical of freshwater aquatic vegetation.

river snail,
dextral (p. 64)

tadpole
snail,
sinistral

Not to scale.

KT

A **meadow grasshopper** (*Conocephalus* sp.; **1**, *at left*) rests on an arrow arum leaf at the edge of a cattail marsh, which may harbor several thousand per acre. This green orthopteran, up to 1 in (2.5 cm) long, feeds on marsh grasses and leaves; the male (shown) is a well-known songster, emitting a series of long buzzes separated by zips: "*bzzzzz-zip-zip-zip-bzzzzz.*" Crickets are also common grazers in the marsh, most notably the **ground cricket** (*Nemobious* sp.; **2**), which can even digest cordgrass. The female (shown) has a long *ovipositor*, used for laying eggs. A brownish cricket about 1/2 in (1.2 cm) long, the male has a high-pitched song full of trills and buzzes. Usually buried under litter or driftwood on the marsh floor, the **mole cricket** (*Gryllotalpa hexadactyla;* **3**) is among the strangest looking insects of the marsh. Brownish and hairy, the 1 in (2.5 cm) cricket has short antennae, and spadelike front legs it uses for burrowing; it eats decayed plant matter, thus helping to cycle nutrients within the marsh.

Ascending the stems of emergent and floating-leaved plants, one finds the **tadpole snail** (*Physa gyrina;* **4**)—an air-breathing (*pulmonate*) gastropod that deposits its gelatinous egg mass on the underside of arrow arum and spatterdock. This is the snail cultured for freshwater aquaria, easily identified by its black, *sinistral* (left-opening) shell (*above left*). The **river snail**, *Goniobasis virginica* (*above right*), has a *dextral* shell (the aperture positioned on the right).

AMPHIBIANS AND REPTILES populate freshwater marshes in

great numbers, though typically only the larger frogs, turtles, and water snakes are frequently seen. In addition to these familiar species (described below), a variety of smaller, secretive forms are present if one looks hard enough or at the right time. Under debris at the marsh edge, one can find various salamanders (Caudata), such as dusky salamanders (*Desmognathus* spp.), and toads (Salientia)—the American toad (*Bufo americanus*) and Fowler's toad (p. 86), for example. The marsh itself is an amphibian sanctuary. Treefrogs and their allies (Hylidae; pp. 69 and 86) are highly vocal in the spring. The high-pitched trill of the males can be deafening when hundreds join in the marsh chorus. After the short breeding season, few are heard and very few are seen. Terrestrial reptiles such as the five-lined skink (*Eumeces fasciatus*), northern black racer (p. 43), and other snakes (see p. 141) may wander into the marsh but are more typical of upland areas.

common
snapping
turtle
(p. 125)

KT

TRUE FROGS (Ranidae; Salientia) are larger than treefrogs and lack the toe pads necessary for climbing. Adept swimmers, *Rana* species have webbing between their hind toes. *Life cycle:* Females typically lay masses of eggs (**1**) underwater. Eggs hatch into newborn tadpoles (**2**) in 3 to 30 days. In growing tadpoles (**3**) water is drawn into the mouth, passes over gills, and exits through an opening (spiracle). Transforming tadpoles (**4**) develop limbs and absorb tail, which is absent in the air-breathing adult.

Green frog, *Rana clamitans melanota* (**a**), is a common resident of freshwater wetlands. Varying in color from light green to brown, the upper body has a distinct ridge at juncture of side and back extending two-thirds of length (but not reaching groin). Belly is white and often mottled. Voice is a deep "p'tung." Breeds May-July. *Size:* to 4 in (10 cm). *Related species:* Bullfrog, *R. catesbeiana* (p. 44), is twice the size; *dorsolateral ridge* ends at eardrum. Wood frog, *R. s. sylvatica*, has a dark face mask behind eye, bordered below by a pale line along jaw; typical of wet woods.

Southern leopard frog, *Rana sphenocephala* (**b**), resides in various wetland habitats from swamps to brackish marshes. Oval spots appear on back between conspicuous *dorsolateral ridges* that extend to groin. Belly is whitish. A white spot marks center of eardrum (*tympanum*), a white line the upper jaw. Voice is a short guttural chuckle. Breeds March-May. *Size:* to 5 in (12.7 cm).

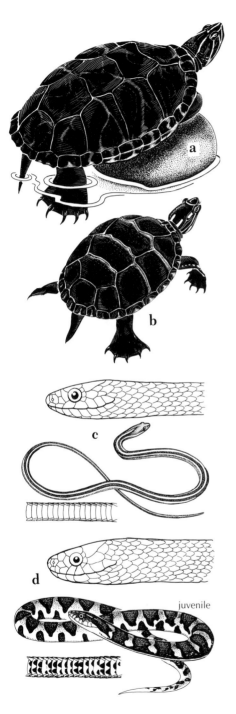

BASKING TURTLES (Emydidae; Testudines) control their body temperature by "sunning" on banks, stumps, and logs. Also see other freshwater turtles (p. 45).

Redbelly turtle, *Pseudemys rubriventris rubriventris* (**a**), is the largest basking turtle of Chesapeake marshes and rivers. The black upper shell (*carapace*) is highly domed; red bands (variable) run across middle of scutes; may only be visible when wet. Lower shell (*plastron*) is deep red or pink. Light lines on top and side of head meet at snout, forming an arrow; lines may be absent. *Size:* to 15¾ in (40 cm).

Eastern painted turtle, *Chrysemys picta picta* (**b**), is a resident of freshwater swamps, streams, and marshes. Distinguished from redbelly turtle at a distance by its smaller size, this colorful turtle has a flattened, black (or olive) carapace with a red border. The larger scutes are set in straight rows across carapace. Two yellow spots appear behind each eye. Plastron is yellow. *Size:* to 7 in (18 cm).

RIBBON SNAKES (Colubridae; Serpentes) typically swim at the water surface. Diet is mostly invertebrates, amphibians (including tadpoles), and fishes.

Eastern ribbon snake, *Thamnophis sauritus sauritus* (**c**), is semi-aquatic, rarely far from marsh or creek. Note ribbonlike body. Tail is nearly a third of body length. Three yellow stripes run along body, one on back, one on each side. Note dark *ventrolateral* stripe below yellow side stripes. Belly is plain. *Size:* to 38 in (96.5 cm).

WATER SNAKES (*Nerodia* spp.; Colubridae) swim both at surface and underwater. Diet is mostly frogs and fishes. Also see p. 70.

Northern water snake, *Nerodia sipedon sipedon* (**d**), the only water snake at the head of the Bay, is highly variable in color. Note alternating dorsal and lateral bands (most apparent on juveniles) with markings wider than spaces between. Belly variable: spots (crescents) present or not. *Size:* to 53 in (134 cm).

MARSH BIRDS of the Chesapeake

vary greatly—from the myriad inhabitants of freshwater wetlands near the Susquehanna Flats to the hardy denizens of salt marshes along the lower Bay. The diversity of birdlife in freshwater marshes is, nonetheless, highly seasonal and corresponds to the presence of food and cover. While cattail and common reed may remain erect throughout the winter, the leaves and stems of most other herbaceous plants decay rapidly, leaving most of the marsh devoid of cover from late fall until spring. At these times birds are scarce (except for migrating marsh ducks and swans and geese offshore), but the marsh comes alive in the spring, the avifauna peaking in late August when seed production is at a maximum. In addition to the families described below, you may find grebes (Podicipedidae; p. 175) swimming in the shallows and a variety of shorebirds (Charadriiformes), including plovers (Charadriidae; p. 157) and gulls and terns (Laridae; p. 159), during migration.

HERONS AND EGRETS (Ardeidae) are long-legged wading birds with long necks and spear-like bills. They hunt for fish, frogs, and aquatic invertebrates by slow ambush. However, hunting postures differ (see below). Sexes alike. Also see p. 127.

Great blue heron, *Ardea herodias* (**a**), is a local permanent resident of tidewater marshes. *Field marks:* A large blue-gray heron with a whitish head bearing black plumes (adults only). Immature has solid black crown; no plumes. When fishing, "GBH" walks slowly with neck in S-shaped loop or stands patiently with head on shoulders. *Flight:* Flies with head and neck folded back. *Size:* Length to 52 in (130 cm); wingspan averages 72 in (183 cm). *Call:* Deep hoarse croaks. *Season:* All year; very local breeder. Nests colonially in wooded swamps and on isolated islands in trees or shrubs.

Great egret, *Casmerodius albus* (**b**), is a transient and local summer resident of tidewater marshes. *Field marks:* A large all-white egret with contrasting yellow bill and black legs and feet. At breeding, plumes extend beyond tail (p. 71). When fishing, it leans forward with neck outstretched. *Flight:* Like "GBH," except neck held in open curve (see p. 142). *Size:* Length to 39 in (99 cm); wingspan averages 55 in (140 cm). *Call:* A low hoarse croak. *Season:* Spring-fall; very local breeder. Nests colonially in trees or shrubs near water.

American wigeon
(p. 90)

MARSH DUCKS (Tribe Anatini; Anatidae) feed at the surface on seeds and submersed plants. Colorful males (drakes) as well as drab females (hens) have bright *speculum* on rear of wing.

Mallard, *Anas platyrhynchos* (**a**), is a transient and winter resident of freshwater wetlands. *Field marks:* Drakes have bright green head and rusty chest. Hens are mottled brown. *Flight:* Look for blue speculum (with white borders) on wing. *Size:* Length to 28 in (70 cm); wingspan averages 36 in (91 cm). *Call:* Hen has loud quack; drake has low "kwek-kwek." *Season:* All year; uncommon summer breeder. Nests near water on dry ground. *Confusing species:* American black duck, *A. rubripes* (p. 128), is darker than female mallard. Sexes alike.

Green-winged teal, *Anas crecca* (**b**), is a transient and winter resident of tidal wetlands. *Field marks:* Drake has chestnut head with green patch. Note white vertical line on body ahead of wing. Hen is light brown. *Flight:* Look for green speculum. *Size:* Length to 14 1/2 in (37 cm); wingspan averages 24 in (60 cm). *Call:* Drakes whistle; hens quack. *Season:* Mostly spring and fall; less common in winter. Former breeder.

Blue-winged teal, *Anas discors* (**c**), is a transient and local summer resident of tidal marshes. *Field marks:* Drake has white crescent on face. Hen is brown and mottled. *Flight:* Look for blue shoulder patch on front of wing. *Size:* Length to 16 in (40 cm); wingspan averages 24 in (61 cm). *Call:* Drakes peep; hens have a low quack. *Season:* Mostly spring and fall; rare in winter; uncommon and local breeder.

Northern pintail, *Anas acuta* (**d**), is a transient and winter resident of tidal marshes. *Field marks:* Drake has a white neck stripe and pointed, needlelike tail. Hen is brown and mottled. *Flight:* Look for brown speculum with white border. *Size:* Length (male) to 30 in (75 cm); wingspan averages 35 in (89 cm). *Call:* Drakes whistle; hens quack. *Season:* Mostly spring and fall; less common in winter. Nonbreeder.

BIRDS OF PREY—other than owls—are diurnal (Falconiformes). The three diurnal (i.e., daytime) raptors most often seen over Chesapeake marshes are described below. Also see p. 146.

Bald eagle, *Haliaeetus leucocephalus* (**a**), is a transient and very local permanent resident of rivers and bays and associated wetlands. A designated endangered species. *Field marks:* Distinguished from other large birds of prey by its larger size, great wingspan, and white head and tail (adults only). Immatures are mostly brown with white mottling underneath. *Flight:* At distance look for long straight wings. *Size:* Length to 43 in (108 cm); wingspan averages 80 in (203 cm). *Call:* Often a "kak-kak-kak." *Food:* Mostly dead or dying fish. *Season:* All year; more common in spring and fall when migrants visit; local breeder. Nests atop tall trees (mostly loblolly pines) near water. *Confusing species:* **Turkey vulture**, *Cathartes aura* (**b**), flies with wings in a V.

Osprey, *Pandion haliaetus* (**c**), is a transient and common summer resident throughout the Bay. *Field marks:* Body is blackish above; white below. Black patch on cheek begins at eye and wraps around head. *Flight:* Look for crook in wings; dark patch at midcenter under wing (p. 146.) *Size:* Length to 25 in (64 cm); wingspan averages 65 in (165 cm). *Call:* A sharp cheep-cheep. *Food:* Live fish. *Season:* Spring-fall; rare in winter; common breeder. Nests on trees, buoys, or platforms (p. 128) near water.

Northern harrier, *Circus cyaneus* (**d**), is a transient and winter resident of tidewater wetlands. *Field marks:* Female (shown) is brown above, streaked with brown below. Male is gray above, mostly white below. *Flight:* Look for white rump; glides over marsh with wings held in shallow *dihedral* (p. 146). *Size:* Length to 23 in (58 cm); wingspan averages 42 in (107 cm). *Call:* A series of whistles: "pee-pee-pee." *Food:* Mostly rodents. *Season:* All year; common spring and fall; less common in winter; highly local and uncommon breeder.

Turkey vulture soars with wings in a dihedral.

Bald eagle soars with flat wings.

RAILS AND COOTS (Rallidae)

King rail, *Rallus elegans* (**a**), is a transient and local summer resident of fresh and brackish marshes. *Field marks:* A chickenlike rail with a long, slender *decurved* bill. Note black bars on flanks, rusty breast, and brown cheek. Sexes alike. *Size:* Length to 19 in (48 cm); wingspan averages 24 in (61 cm). *Call:* A low "kuk-kuk-kuk." *Season:* All year; uncommon in winter; local to uncommon breeder. *Confusing species:* Virginia rail, *R. limicola* (p. 128), is smaller; gray cheeks.

American coot, *Fulica americana* (**b**), is a transient and winter resident along rivers, marshes, and bays. *Field marks:* A slate gray, ducklike rail with a white bill. Note 2 white patches underneath tail. *Size:* Length to 16 in (40 cm); wingspan averages 25 in (64 cm). *Call:* Short croaks and cackles. *Season:* Mostly spring and fall; less common in winter; uncommon in summer; rare to local breeder (status uncertain).

SANDPIPERS AND ALLIES (Scolopacidae). See other migrant shorebirds, pp. 157-158.

Lesser yellowlegs, *Tringa flavipes* (**c**), is a common transient and uncommon winter resident of tidal wetlands and shores. *Field marks:* A slim gray sandpiper with yellow legs. Slender bill is very straight. *Flight:* Similar to greater yellowlegs (p. 158). *Size:* to 11 in (28 cm). *Call:* Only 1 or 2 soft notes: "yew-yew." *Season:* Spring and fall; uncommon and irregular in winter. Nonbreeder. *Related species:* Greater yellowlegs, *T. melanoleuca* (p. 158), is larger; longer, heavier, upturned bill.

Least sandpiper, *Calidris minutilla* (**d**), is a common transient of freshwater marshes and tidal flats. *Field marks:* Small. Brown above with a streaked breast; yellowish legs. *Size:* to 6 in (15 cm). *Call:* A high "kre-eep." *Season:* Spring and fall; uncommon and local in winter. Nonbreeder. *Related species:* Semipalmated sandpiper, *C. pusilla* (p. 158), has black legs; grayer; less streaking on breast.

PERCHING BIRDS (Passeriformes) of fresh-water wetlands include the nesting species below, and migrants such as the bobolink (*Doli-chonyx oryzivorus*) and swamp sparrow (*Melo-spiza georgiana*).

Marsh wren, *Cistothorus palustris* (**a**), is a transient and summer resident of tidewater marshes. *Field marks:* Note white eyebrow stripe and white streaks on back. The slim bill is slightly *decurved*. Sexes alike. *Size:* to 5 in (13 cm). *Call:* Often a reedy, rattling "cut-cut-trrrrrrrrr-ur." *Season:* Mostly spring-fall; uncommon in winter; local to common breeder. Oblong (globular) nest (with side entrance) is lashed to cattail or marsh grasses.

Common yellowthroat, *Geothlypis trichas* (**b**), a wetland warbler, is a common summer resident and transient of fresh, brackish, and salt marshes. *Field marks:* Male has a distinctive black mask. Female lacks mask but is otherwise similar: olive-brown above with yellow throat and breast; belly white. *Size:* to 5 in (13 cm). *Call:* A rapid "witchity-witchity-witchity-witch." *Season:* Spring-fall; uncommon in winter; common breeder. Nests near ground in brushy areas near water. Open, cupped nest built mostly with grasses; 3$^{1}/_{4}$ in (8 cm) wide.

Red-winged blackbird, *Agelaius phoeniceus* (**c**), is a common permanent resident of tidewater marshes. *Field marks:* Male is black with red shoulder patches. Female is dull brown. *Size:* to 9$^{1}/_{2}$ in (24 cm). *Call:* Male call is "konk-la-ree." *Season:* All year; common breeder. Deeply cupped nest is 4 in (10 cm) wide.

Sharp-tailed sparrow, *Ammodramus caudacutus* (**d**), is a local summer resident and common transient in tidal wetlands. *Field marks:* Note gray triangular ear patch, surrounded by yellowish orange. Breast is streaked with brown; belly white. Sexes alike. *Size:* to 5$^{1}/_{2}$ in (14 cm). *Call:* Two "chips," then a trill: "tut-tut-sheeeeeeeeee." *Season:* Spring-fall; uncommon in winter; local to uncommon breeder. Nests locally in brackish and salt marshes (see p. 129).

MAMMALS of freshwater marshes at the head of the Bay and at Blackwater

NWR include a mix of *terrestrial* and *aquatic* species. Some are difficult to classify. In fact, several nesting or foraging species could be termed "semi-aquatic" since they must contend with daily tidal inundations. Meadow voles and rice rats (*Oryzomys palustis;* p. 130) are excellent swimmers. The least shrew, *Cryptotis parva* (Insectivora), uses vole runways at low tide to hunt for invertebrates in the marsh. Star-nosed moles (*Condylura cristata*) use their broad front "digging" feet to swim effectively after aquatic insects. For terrestrial mammals that do not have such adaptations, wetlands are more inhospitable. Upland visitors, such as the Virginia opossum (p. 51), striped skunk (*Mephitis mephitis*), and long-tailed weasel (*Mustela frenata*) stalk frogs or voles at low tide or along the marsh border, but, once successful, quickly return to the woods. The wetland sanctuary, with few resident predators, permits small herbivores to flourish.

CARNIVORES (Carnivora) also include upland species such as the red fox (Canidae; p. 148) and raccoon (Procyonidae), which feed in the marsh, and true wetland species like the river otter (Mustelidae).

Raccoon, *Procyon lotor* (**a**), is a familiar visitor to the marsh, often foraging at creekside. *Field marks:* Note characteristic black mask and ringed tail. Upper body is typically reddish gray with a black tint. *Size:* Body length to 28 in (70 cm); tail to 12 in (30 cm). *Food:* Voles, bird and turtle eggs, fish, frogs, insects, clams, and fruits. May wash food. Typically nocturnal, the raccoon is a major predator of muskrats in the Bay.

HERBIVORES of the marsh are mostly rodents (Rodentia) and include terrestrial species like the meadow vole, which in wetland habitats is nearly semi-aquatic, and true aquatic species (see p. 115).

Meadow vole, *Microtus pennsylvanicus* (**b**), or meadow mouse, is the most abundant rodent in the marsh. *Field marks:* Upper body is rich chestnut brown to blackish brown; belly grayish or pale cinnamon. Tail is furry; typically longer than 1 in (25 mm). *Size:* Body length to 6 in (15 cm); tail up to 2½ in (6.6 cm). *Food:* Leaves, stems, roots, and, when available, seeds of wetland plants. *Note:* Surface runways (about 1-2 in wide) are lined with cut stems.

AQUATIC MAMMALS include the familiar muskrat (Cricetidae; Rodentia) and its larger South American relative, the nutria (Myocastoridae; Rodentia), as well as the playful river otter, a carnivore, and its relative, the mink (Mustelidae; Carnivora). Permanent ponds and channels within the marsh provide habitat for these animals.

Muskrat, *Ondatra zibethicus* (**a**), is the most common aquatic mammal in the marsh. *Field marks:* Upper body is dark brown to blackish; underparts silvery to cinnamon brown. Hind feet are partly webbed. Black tail, with few hairs, is flattened laterally. *Size:* Body length to 14 in (36 cm); tail to 11 in (28 cm). *Feeding behavior:* Though typically a vegetarian—consuming the rhizomes of marsh plants—the muskrat also eats mussels, insects, and fishes.

Nutria, *Myocastor coypus* (**b**), an introduced species, is mostly nocturnal and rarely seen. *Field marks:* Nearly the size of a beaver, the nutria has reddish brown fur. Tail is round and sparsely haired. *Size:* Body length to 25 in (63 cm); tail to 17 in (43 cm). *Feeding behavior:* A grazer rather than a root-consumer (except in winter); eats aquatic and wetland plants. *Note:* Less common than muskrat but may compete with it when populations are dense. *Similar species:* Beaver, *Castor canadensis* (p. 52), has a paddlelike tail.

River otter, *Lutra canadensis* (**c**), ranges between fresh and brackish marshes seasonally, often in search of food. *Field marks:* Otters have sharp teeth and long tails, but differ from other weasel-like animals in having webbed feet. Upper body is dark brown, underparts are grayish. Note white whiskers, small ears, and silver-white throat. *Size:* Body length to 30 in (76 cm); tail to 19 in (48 cm); males larger than females. *Food:* Fish, frogs, snakes, young muskrats (kits), crayfish, even blue crabs. *Similar species:* Long-tailed weasel, *Mustela frenata,* is smaller; black tip on tail and white underparts; feet not webbed. Mink, *M. vison,* is smaller; all brown except white on chin; feet unwebbed.

front, 1½ in
hind, 3 in

front, 2 in
hind, 4 in

r.f., 2¼ in
r.h., 2¾ in

KT

Brackish Bay Marshes

ALONG the middle Chesapeake immediately north and south of the Bay Bridge, brackish marshes rule the shoreline. From Rock Hall to Tilghman Island, from the Chester River to the Choptank, three-square marshes, cattail stands, and phragmites (*at left*) populate the river mouths and coves, and narrows such as Kent and Eastern Neck. In these slightly to moderately brackish waters we see a transition from the tall freshwater marshes of the upper Chesapeake to the low-lying salt meadows of the lower Bay.

While only small pockets of bayside wetlands remain on the western shore between the Patapsco and the Patuxent, large tracts of brackish wetlands are found even farther south on the Eastern Shore, mostly in Dorchester County, Maryland. Sandwiched between freshwater marshes landward and salt marshes toward the Bay, most of these brackish wetlands are three-square meadows (*Scirpus* spp.), with taller big cordgrass or narrow-leaved cattail along the margins of tidal creeks and ponds.

Like the brackish bay marshes near the Bridge, these *Scirpus* marshes differ from brackish river marshes (p. 77) in having a broad, ill-defined drainage system. Riverside wetlands tend to grow in narrower bands, with greater plant diversity and taller species. In mid-Bay rivers, such as the Choptank, brackish river marshes slowly grade into open brackish bay marshes near their mouths.

As in fresh bay marshes, dips in the marsh topography and muskrat "eat-outs" may foster shallow tidal pools, or marsh "ponds." These sheltered ponds, sometimes only visible from the air, are important habitat for migratory waterfowl. Submersed aquatics (SAV), particularly the pondweeds (*Potamogeton* spp.; p. 165), grow here.

Brackish bay marshes thrive in lowlands inundated by slightly brackish (oligohaline) to mod-

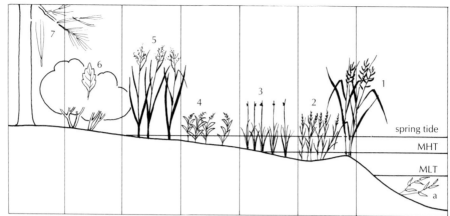

Figure 9. Plant zonation in a typical mixed brackish wetland community (key *opposite*).

erately brackish (lower mesohaline) waters. While the saltmarsh *Spartina* species may be present in various-sized patches, they are not dominant.

Perhaps the most important indicator plant of the brackish wetland is Olney three-square (*Scirpus americanus*), which grows in peaty soils with saltmarsh bulrush (*S. robustus*). Other major species include narrow-leaved cattail, big cordgrass, common reed, switchgrass, dwarf spikerush (*Eleocharis parvula;* p. 100) and black needlerush, the latter of which grows in large meadows, colonizing sandier soils. Associated species include low herbaceous plants such as seaside goldenrod and sea lavender (*Limonium carolinianum;* p. 137), as well as the saltbushes typical of elevated areas (i.e., hummocks) in the marsh. These wetland species grow in certain zones characterized by the soil composition and topography (relative to water depth) of the marsh floor. (See fig. 9 *above* and discussion of zonation *on opposite page*.)

The animal residents of the marsh in turn are concentrated in preferred zones that provide requisite food and cover. In the mud flats (p. 151) and shallows (p. 161) bordering the marsh are countless other invertebrates, as well as fishes, that endure (or count upon) the tidal rhythms of the marsh. Benthic invertebrates are dependent upon the enormous quantities of detritus that decay with the aid of anaerobic (oxygen-free) bacteria in the marsh soil. These lower animals serve as prey for aquatic reptiles and mammals, for wading birds, shorebirds, and waterfowl.

While many brackish bay marshes have been reclaimed for development, especially along the western shore and Kent Island, a few extensive tracts remain. Visit Eastern Neck NWR at the mouth of the Chester River; Horsehead Farm Wildlife Sanctuary on Eastern Bay; and, in Dorchester County, the east end of Blackwater NWR, Fishing Bay WMA (below Bestpitch), and the north side of Elliott Island to see three-square marshes and other important brackish-water communities. In Wicomico County, visit Ellis Bay WMA (north of Monie Bay), and, in Somerset County, Maryland, and Accomack County, Virginia, the headwaters of Pocomoke Sound above Saxis.

WETLAND PLANTS of brackish bay marshes represent a melting pot

of salt-tolerant varieties. Some species typical of freshwater marshes such as narrow-leaved cattail and common reed *(Phragmites australis*; p. 80) form extensive, sometimes pure, stands in slightly brackish water. In a *mixed brackish marsh community*, however, the marsh profile will include plants typical of salt marshes as well, in a distribution pattern dependent largely upon water depth (see fig. 9; *opposite page*). Below mean low tide (MLT), one finds submersed aquatics (SAV) tolerant of brackish conditions (**a**). At the water edge near mean high tide (MHT), grow big cordgrass (**1**) and, sometimes, saltmarsh cordgrass (**2**). Olney three-square (**3**) grows in extensive stands at MHT with associated species such as seaside goldenrod (**4**). Switchgrass (**5**) often claims sandy soils near the spring tide line, while groundsel tree (**6**) and other saltbushes grow on raised hummocks or at the marsh edge next to upland species like loblolly pine (**7**).

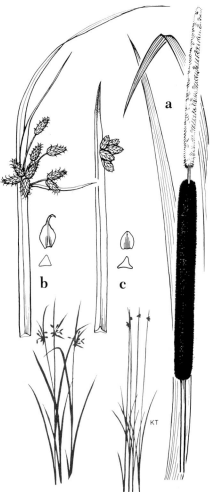

Narrow-leaved cattail, *Typha angustifolia* (**a**), is our only cattail (Typhaceae) tolerant of brackish conditions. *Leaves* are flat, narrow, and swordlike; up to ¹/₂ in (12.7 mm) wide. *Stems* are erect. *Flower spike* (when mature) has a gap between staminate (male) upper portion and pistillate (female) lower portion; the latter persists through winter. *Seeds* are tiny *achenes* with numerous silky bristles attached at base. *Size:* up to 6 ft (1.8 m).

THREE-SQUARES (*Scirpus* spp.) are sedges (Cyperaceae). Solid stems are triangular in cross section. *Fruits* are dark, single nutlets (*achenes*). Flowers are encased by overlapping scales, which collectively resemble a bud.

Saltmarsh bulrush, *Scirpus robustus* (**b**), is common in salt and brackish marshes. *Leaves* are long and narrow; up to ¹/₂ in (12.7 mm) wide. *Stem* is sharply triangular. *Flowers* are small, borne in (mostly) sessile spikelets, though a few are stalked; surrounded by erect leaflike *bracts; bloom* July-October. *Flowering scale* (shown) has recurved bristle. *Size:* up to 4 ft (1.2 m).

Olney three-square, *Scirpus americanus* (**c**), is restricted to brackish wetlands. *Leaves* are absent at maturity, restricted to base. *Stem* is deeply concave. *Flowers* are borne in sessile (nonstalked) spikelets, extending laterally from stem near tip; *bloom* June-August. Scale and achene are blunt. *Size:* up to 5 ft (1.5 m). *Note:* Formerly named *S. olneyi.*

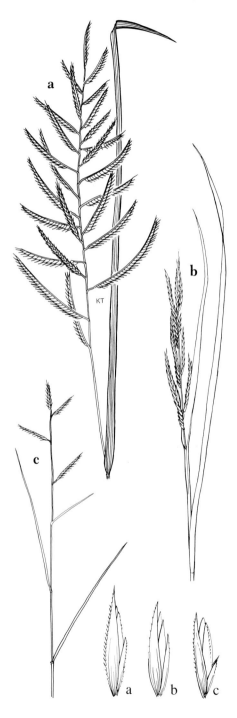

GRASSES (Gramineae) have jointed, round, hollow stems and grainlike seeds. The *Spartina* species below differ in height, panicle, and leaves; seeds (shown) have minor differences.

Big cordgrass, *Spartina cynosuroides* (**a**),

colonizes seepage areas at the upland edge and muddy banks along tidal creeks. *Leaves* are rough, swordlike blades, arranged along the stem in different planes; up to 28 in (71 cm) long. *Stem* is erect. *Flower head* (panicle) is an open green cluster consisting of 20-50 erect spikes up to $2^{1}/_{2}$ in (6.5 cm) long, each with dozens of densely packed spikelets. Entire panicle is up to 12 in (30 cm) long; turns tan when in seed. *Size:* up to 10 ft (3 m).

Saltmarsh cordgrass, *Spartina alterniflora* (**b**),

may grow in salt and brackish marshes right at creekside (tall form), behind big cordgrass (intermediate form), or in higher elevations near the salt meadows (short form). *Leaves* taper to a long point (and turn inward); up to 24 in (61 cm) long and $^{1}/_{2}$ in (12.7 mm) wide. *Stem* is typically stout and erect, though often soft at base. *Flower cluster* (panicle) is narrow; composed of 5-30 spikes; alternately arranged next to main axis; each spike consisting of 10-50 *sessile* spikelets. Panicle is whitish green. *Size:* Short form up to 2 ft (61 cm) in high marsh; intermediate form up to 4 ft (1.2 m); tall form up to 6 ft (1.8 m).

Saltmeadow cordgrass, *Spartina patens* (**c**),

typically grows in the higher elevations, above mean high tide, and forms dense meadows. *Leaves* are narrow and roll inward (appearing round); up to 18 in (46 cm) long; arranged in a single plane about stem. *Stem* is weak and wiry; bends in the wind, forming characteristic "cowlicks," or swirls, in the meadow. *Flower head* (panicle) is an open terminal cluster; up to 8 in (20 cm) long; typically composed of 3-6 spikes, alternately arranged and diverging from main axis; each spike consisting of 20-50 densely packed *sessile* spikelets. Panicle is a russet-brown. *Size:* Typically less than 2 ft (61 cm) tall; up to 5 ft (1.5 m).

Switchgrass, *Panicum virgatum* (**a**), grows in sandy soils at the upland edge of salt and brackish marshes. *Leaves* are tapered and smooth; up to 20 in (51 cm) long; some in basal clumps and typically one enclosing the terminal flower head. *Stems* are upright, arising from scaly rhizomes. *Flower head* (panicle) is an open delicate cluster of tiny florets, several appearing at each branch tip. The panicle is wiry in appearance and typically triangular (pyramidal) at top; *blooms* July-August. *Seeds* are tiny grains. *Size:* up to 6½ ft (2 m).

Saltgrass, *Distichlis spicata* (**b**), grows with saltmeadow cordgrass in the meadows that often characterize the higher elevations of salt and brackish marshes. *Leaves* are short, rolled inward (appearing round), and arranged in several planes about the stem; up to 5 in (10 cm) long. *Stem* is stiff and wiry, often forming dense mats. *Flower cluster* (panicle) bears either male or female spikelets, which occur on different plants; male spikelets are longer, with 8-12 flowers; female spikelets have 4-9 flowers. Entire panicle is whitish green; up to 3 in (7.5 cm) long. *Seeds* are tiny grains. *Size:* up to 2 ft (61 cm).

RUSHES (Juncaceae) have solid (rather than hollow), round stems. Fruits are multiseed capsules.

Black needlerush, *Juncus roemerianus* (**c**), colonizes sandier soils in the upper intertidal zone of salt and brackish marshes. *Leaves* are olive-brown, cylindrical, stiff, and resemble a stem, the uppermost leaf ending in a sharp point (often black); each leaf up to 8 in (20 cm) long. *Stem* is round and stiff. *Flowers* appear in a branched yellowish green cluster extending laterally about three-quarters of the way along stem; *bloom* June-August. *Seeds* are contained in capsules (shown) in cluster at upper leaf base. *Size:* up to 4 ft (1.2 m). *Related species:* Black rush, *J. gerardi*, up to 2 ft (60 cm), has elongated, more delicate leaves.

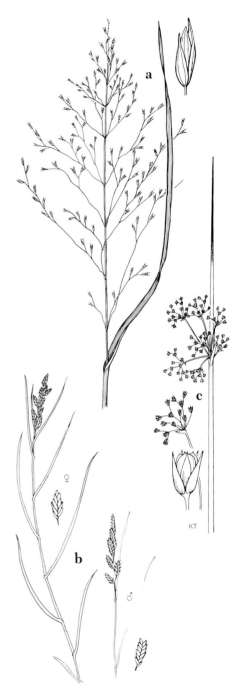

ASSOCIATED HERBACEOUS PLANTS (other than grasses, sedges, and rushes) typically have broader leaves and colorful flowers. Also see pp. 82 and 137-138. Many saltmarsh species invade brackish wetlands.

Marsh hibiscus, *Hibiscus moscheutos* (**a**), or rose mallow, a perennial, grows along the upland margins of brackish wetlands, near freshwater seepage. *Leaves* are alternate, toothed; smooth above and hairy below; typically wedge-shaped; up to 8 in (20 cm) long and 3 in (7.6 cm) wide. Lower leaves may have 3 lobes. *Stem* is round, smooth, and erect. *Flower* is pink or white with characteristic red center; 5 petals; up to 6 in (15.2 cm) wide; *blooms* late July-August. *Seedpod* (shown) has 5 cells; rounded at top; persists through winter. *Size:* up to 7 ft (2.1 m). *Related species:* **Seashore mallow,** *Kosteletzkya virginica* (**b**), may be distinguished by its smaller (2 in; 5 cm wide) pink flowers and triangular leaves (usually 3- or 5-lobed); *seedpods* (shown) are small, flattened globes. Salt and brackish marshes only.

Seaside goldenrod, *Solidago sempervirens* (**c**), a perennial, colonizes the edges and higher elevations of salt and brackish marshes. *Leaves* are alternately arranged along entire stem; thick and fleshy; lance-shaped or oblong; increasing in size toward bottom of stem; up to 16 in (40 cm) long. *Stem* is erect and smooth. *Flower clusters* are typical bright "golden rods" with many small flowers borne on terminal flower stalks; *bloom* August-September. *Seeds* are eaten by sparrows and voles. *Size:* to 6 ft (1.8 m), typically 3 ft (0.9 m).

Saltmarsh fleabane, *Pluchea purpurascens* (**d**), an annual, colonizes brackish marshes just above mean high tide, often near salt meadows. *Leaves* are velvety, lance-shaped, and alternate; edges are serrated; aromatic—like camphor—a medicinal odor; up to 4¾ in (12 cm) long. *Stem* is erect and hairy. *Flowers* are small and pink (or purple), clustered in flat or slightly domed flower heads; *bloom* late July-October. *Size:* up to 3 ft (90 cm).

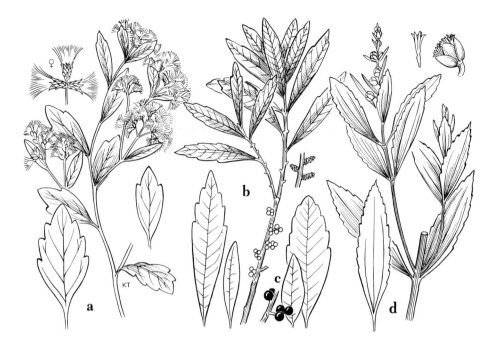

SHRUBS of brackish marshes consist of the saltbush community, made up of *Baccharis* and *Iva* species, and upland species, such as wax myrtle, which delineate the marsh edge.

Groundsel tree, *Baccharis halimifolia* (**a**), colonizes elevated hummocks in salt and brackish marshes. *Leaves* are of 2 types: *lower leaves* are wedge-shaped with large teeth, and are larger (up to 2½ in; 6.35 cm long); *upper leaves* have fewer (or no) teeth, and are smaller, more lance-shaped; alternate. *Stem* is woody and branches into distinctive green hairless twigs. *Flowers* on separate male and female plants *bloom* during August-October, forming yellow-white clusters. *Fruits* are tiny nutlets attached to white silky hairs; remain in *cottony clusters* on female plants through autumn. *Size:* up to 15 ft (4.5 m).

Wax myrtle, *Myrica cerifera* (**b**), an evergreen shrub, is often associated with the saltbush community at the upland edge. *Leaves* are alternate, wedge-shaped or lance-shaped,

leathery, and toothed (or not) toward tip; highly aromatic; up to 3 in (7.5 cm) long and less than ½ in (12.7 mm) wide. *Twigs* are hairy and brown, with resin dots. *Flowers* are borne in cone-shaped catkins; *bloom* April-June. *Fruits* are small wax-covered, blue-gray nuts (up to ⅛ in; 3 mm wide); highly scented and conspicuous on branches below leafy tips. *Size:* to 30 ft (9 m), though often a 6 ft (2 m) shrub. *Related species:* **Bayberry**, *M. pensylvanica* (**c**), has nonleathery, deciduous leaves more than ½ in (12.7 mm) wide; larger fruits (up to ¼ in; 6 mm wide).

Marsh elder, *Iva frutescens* (**d**), occurs with groundsel tree in salt and brackish marshes. *Leaves* are thick (fleshy), opposite, and lance-shaped, with regular toothed margins; up to 4 in (10 cm) long. *Twigs* branch from stem and show vertical lines. *Small flowers* (greenish white) in terminal clusters *bloom* August-October. *Fruits* are small. *Size:* Typically 3 ft (1 m) tall; up to 10 ft (3 m).

THE INVERTEBRATE COMPONENT of brackish marshes is

similar to that of the salt marsh in there being a predominance of estuarine species. Freshwater and terrestrial forms are few—restricted mainly to insects and spiders within the marsh canopy or bottom litter. Of the insects, ground and mole crickets (p. 106) are characteristic, though to the casual visitor mosquitoes and deerflies (p. 139) may seem more prevalent. Most visible, on or near the marsh floor, are crustacean and molluscan species tolerant of the brackish ebb and flow. A typical scenario is found at Solomons Island, Maryland, where fiddler crabs forage within the intertidal zone, saltmarsh snails (*Melampus bidentatus*) wander under marsh debris, and periwinkles climb up and down cordgrass stems along tidal creeks. At low tide, the marsh flats can be explored for a variety of organisms typical of tidal flats (pp. 153-156). And, in adjacent creeks, one may find brackish SAV beds with a host of aquatic species (see p. 84).

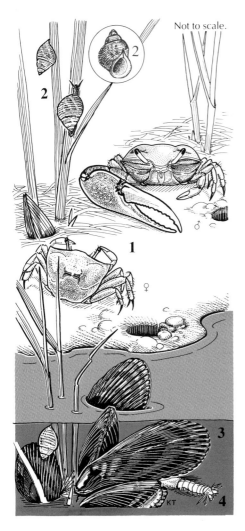

Not to scale.

At the base of *Spartina* at the edge of a three-square marsh sit two **red-jointed fiddler crabs** (*Uca minax;* **1**), the brackish-water variety of the genus *Uca* (p. 156). It is the largest fiddler crab, with a $1^1/_2$ in (3.8 cm) wide carapace. The large fiddle claw of the male reaches 2 in (5 cm) in length, and, here, he waves it to court a female who lacks the fiddle claw. These diurnal crabs prefer muddy areas where burrows are dug. They are omnivorous, feeding on algae, detritus, grass shrimp, even small fish. In turn, fiddlers are a favorite food of rails and raccoons.

A common snail clings to the stalks of saltmarsh cordgrass—the **marsh periwinkle** (*Littorina irrorata;* **2**), which has a *dextral* (i.e., right-handed) shell with reddish flecks on its spiral ridges. The periwinkle obtains oxygen from the water by means of a gill, and most likely climbs stems to avoid predators, such as the blue crab. The saltmarsh snail (*Melampus bidentatus;* p. 140) also inhabits the brackish marsh and is an important food for waterfowl, fishes, and blue crabs, as well as rice rats and seaside sparrows.

Attached by *byssal threads* to *Spartina* stems, the **Atlantic ribbed mussel** (*Geukensia demissa;* **3**) pumps more than a gallon of water each hour through its filter-feeding apparatus as it gleans bacteria, diatoms, and organic detritus from the water. Bent mussels (*Ischadium recurvum;* p. 169) are also found here and can be more common than ribbed mussels. Another typical invertebrate is the **common clam worm**, *Nereis succinea* (**4**), which, like the snails, is a menu item for killifishes and other predators.

REPTILES AND AMPHIBIANS of brackish bay wetlands are far

less numerous than the lineup found in freshwater marshes. This is due, in large part, to the paucity of amphibians in these wetlands. *Amphibians* have moist, smooth (or warty) skin that is susceptible to dessication. Consequently, few salamanders, frogs, or toads reside in brackish water since it has a drying effect on the skin. Moreover, their aquatic, gelatinous eggs cannot survive saltwater immersion. In the Bay region only the green treefrog (p. 86) and southern leopard frog (below), and one or two toads, namely Fowler's toad (p. 86) and (perhaps) the eastern narrowmouth toad (*Gastrophryne carolinensis*), are at all tolerant of brackish conditions. *Reptiles*, which have protective scales (or plates), do inhabit brackish water. Their leathery eggs are laid on land. The only reptile endemic to this environment, however, is the diamondback terrapin. At the marsh border, look for upland snakes mentioned on p. 141.

FROGS AND TOADS (Salientia) are anurans, meaning "without a tail." Anurans and other amphibians have moist, scaleless skin. Few can tolerate brackish conditions. Also see p. 86.

Southern leopard frog, *Rana sphenocephala* (**a**), a widespread species, is distinguished by its round leopardlike spots. Two *dorsolateral ridges* run from head to groin. Other marks include a light spot on eardrum and a light line on upper jaw. Mating call (in spring) is several croaks followed by trills— like a chuckle. *Size:* to 5 in (12.7 cm).

TURTLES (Testudines) are typical reptiles (like lizards) with scaly skin and clawed feet, but differ in bearing a shell. The shell has an upper part (*carapace*) and lower part (*plastron*), each covered with plates called *scutes*.

Eastern mud turtle, *Kinosternon subrubrum subrubrum* (**b**), inhabits fresh and brackish wetlands, up to 12 ppt salinity. Shell is yellowish brown. Plastron has 2 hinges. *Size:* to 4 in (10 cm). *Note:* Musk glands (shown) on the bridge between carapace and plastron are more potent in musk turtles (*Sternotherus* spp.), such as the freshwater stinkpot (p. 45).

Common snapping turtle, *Chelydra serpentina serpentina* (**c**), is common in brackish waters (up to 12 ppt). The massive carapace is light brown to black; the plastron is very small and cross-shaped. Tail is long and saw-toothed. *Size:* to 18½ in (47 cm). *Note:* Snappers rarely bask, but females lay eggs on land in spring.

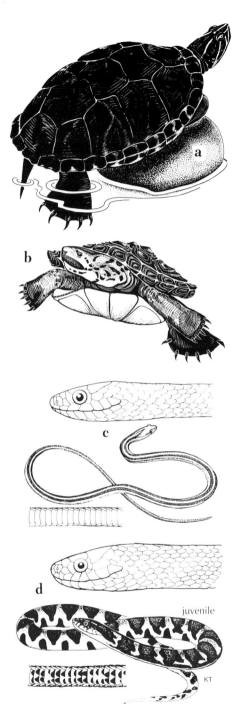

Redbelly turtle, *Pseudemys rubriventris rubriventris* (**a**), is the largest basking turtle of fresh and brackish marshes. The black carapace and red plastron are distinctive. Light line on top of black head may meet lateral line (through eye) to form an arrow at snout. *Size:* to 15³/₄ in (40 cm). *Confusing species:* Painted turtle, *Chrysemys picta* (p. 108), has yellow spots on head; shell less domed; enters only slightly brackish water.

Northern diamondback terrapin,

Malaclemys terrapin terrapin (**b**), is an estuarine species, restricted to brackish waters and coastal marshes. Carapace has rings and concentric ridges on each *scute*. Note dark flecks on head and limbs. *Size:* Female to 9 in (23 cm); male to 5¹/₂ in (14 cm). *Note:* Terrapins may bask in the marsh but feed mostly underwater.

RIBBON AND GARTER SNAKES (*Thamnophis* spp.; Colubridae; Serpentes) differ from water snakes (*Nerodia* spp.) in having single (non-divided) *anal plates* (see p. 43).

Eastern ribbon snake, *Thamnophis sauritus sauritus* (**c**), swims at the surface and is rarely far from marsh or creek. The body is very narrow; tail is almost a third of body length. Three yellow stripes extend along body; high lateral stripes run along rows 3 and 4 of the dorsal scales (as counted from ventral scales). Note dark (brown) *ventrolateral* stripe below lateral stripe. Belly is plain yellowish or green. *Size:* to 38 in (96.5 cm). *Confusing species:* Eastern garter snake, *T. sirtalis sirtalis*, an upland and wetland species, has lower stripes (rows 2 and 3); tail less than one-fourth of body length.

WATER SNAKES (*Nerodia* spp.; Serpentes). Only 1 species is widespread in brackish waters. For other species see pp. 70 and 87.

Northern water snake, *Nerodia sipedon sipedon* (**d**), inhabits a variety of wetland habitats from swamps to salt and brackish marshes (up to 12 ppt). Note alternating dorsal and lateral bands. Adults may appear plain black (especially when basking). Underbelly has spots shaped like half-moons (sometimes absent). *Size:* to 53 in (134 cm).

juvenile

WETLAND BIRDS are less numerous as one travels from freshwater areas toward the salt marshes of the lower Bay. In brackish bay wetlands the larger wading birds and waterfowl (pp. 89-92) are among the groups most often seen. The more secretive rails and small passerines are often concealed in the marsh. They nest in dense stands of narrow-leaved cattail, three-square, needlerush, or saltmarsh bulrush. Listen for their distinctive songs, which may be the only clue to positive identification. In addition to the familiar egrets and herons (Ardeidae), ducks (Anatidae), birds of prey (Falconiformes), rails (Rallidae), and perching birds (Passeriformes) described below, few other birds reside in brackish bay wetlands. However, in fall and spring, migratory waterfowl feed in the shallows, and a variety of shorebirds (Charadriiformes) typical of salt marshes (p. 145) and tidal flats (pp. 157-159) pass through, feasting on marsh invertebrates. Overhead, kingfishers and swallows compete with terns in aerial acrobatics.

HERONS AND EGRETS (Ardeidae) are long-legged waders with daggerlike bills. The family also includes bitterns (Tribe Botaurini) and night-herons (Tribe Nycticoracini), which are uncommon to local breeders in Chesapeake marshes and streamsides. Sexes alike. Also see p. 142.

Great blue heron, *Ardea herodias* (**a**), is a permanent resident of tidal wetlands and bays. *Field marks:* This long-necked heron is recognized by its large size and bluish gray color. Bill is yellowish. Adults have white head and black plumes. *Flight:* On takeoff neck forms S-shaped loop. *Size:* Length to 52 in (130 cm); wingspan averages 72 in (183 cm). *Call:* Harsh squawks when alarmed. *Season:* All year; less common in winter; highly local breeder. *Confusing species:* Little blue heron, *Egretta caerulea* (adult), is smaller; has maroon head and neck; gray bill with black tip.

Green-backed heron, *Butorides striatus* (**b**), is a transient and summer resident of tidal marshes. *Field marks:* A small, dark heron with a chestnut head and neck (adult). Immature is brown; streaked with brown below. When alarmed, it may stretch neck, raise crest, and jerk its tail. *Flight:* Look for short, dark wings (p. 143). *Size:* Length to 22 in (55 cm); wingspan averages 26 in (66 cm). *Call:* A sharp "skew." *Season:* Spring, summer, and fall; rare winter visitor. Common breeder.

osprey
hovering,
at far right

a

b

♂

♀

c

KT

BIRDS OF PREY (Falconiformes) frequent Bay wetlands in search of food.

Osprey, *Pandion haliaetus* (**a**), or fish hawk, is a common summer resident and transient of tidal wetlands. *Field marks:* Hawklike body is dark above, white below. Note black cheek patch. *Flight:* Hovers and plunges feetfirst for fish. *Size:* Length to 25 in (64 cm); wingspan averages 65 in (165 cm). *Call:* A whistled cheep-cheep, or (near nest) a sharp "cheereeek." *Season:* Spring-fall; rare winter visitor; common breeder. Nests on trees or platforms.

WATERFOWL (Anatidae) include swans, geese, and ducks, all of which frequent tidewater wetlands. Other marsh ducks, or surface-feeding ducks, are discussed on p. 110. For diving ducks, including bay ducks, mergansers, and sea ducks, see pp. 193-195.

American black duck, *Anas rubripes* (**b**), is a transient and winter resident of tidewater wetlands and bays. *Field marks:* Body is dark brown, almost black at distance, in contrast to paler brown head. *Size:* Length to 25 in (64 cm); wingspan averages 36 in (92 cm). *Call:* Drakes "kwek-kwek" and hens quack. *Food:* Grains, grasses, and SAV. *Season:* All year; less common in summer; local to common breeder.

RAILS (Rallidae) are hen-shaped marsh birds. The black rail, *Laterallus jamaicensis*, is a highly local breeder in brackish bay marshes (e.g., Elliott Island).

Virginia rail, *Rallus limicola* (**c**), is a transient and summer resident of fresh and brackish marshes. *Field marks:* A small rusty brown rail with a long, reddish, slightly *decurved* bill. Note gray cheek behind eye. *Size:* Length to 9½ in (24 cm); wingspan averages 14 in (36 cm). *Call:* "Ki-dick, ki-dick, ki-dick," or descending "qwak-qwak." *Season:* All year; uncommon and irregular in winter; uncommon to locally common breeder. Nests in tidal marshes (except salt marshes) in dry areas amidst vegetation. *Related species:* King rail, *R. elegans* (p. 112), is twice as large; brownish cheek.

PERCHING BIRDS (Passeriformes) are less varied in brackish wetlands. Also see common yellowthroat (p. 113).

Marsh wren, *Cistothorus palustris* (**a**), is a common transient and summer resident of most tidewater wetlands. *Field marks:* Note slightly *decurved,* slender bill. The white eyebrow stripe and white stripes on black upper back are diagnostic. Cocks tail. Sexes alike. *Size:* to 5 in (13 cm). *Call:* A rattling, sewing machinelike "cut-cut-trrrrrrrr." *Season:* Mostly spring-fall; uncommon in winter; local to common breeder. Female builds football-shaped brood nest in tall grasses. Male defends territory mostly by song.

Red-winged blackbird, *Agelaius phoeniceus* (**b**), is a common permanent resident of fresh and brackish wetlands. *Field marks:* The spectacular male is known by its red "epaulettes." Female is brown with dark streaks on breast. *Flight:* Look for flashing red on males. *Size:* to 9½ in (24 cm). *Call:* A spirited "oak-la-ree." *Season:* All year; common breeder. Female constructs cupped nest; male defends territory

with song, displays, and valiant chases, often against larger birds.

Sharp-tailed sparrow, *Ammodramus caudacutus* (**c**), is a transient and locally common summer resident of tidewater marshes. *Field marks:* A small brown sparrow. Note the yellowish orange border around the gray ear patch. Breast is streaked with brown; belly white. *Size:* to 5½ in (14 cm). *Call:* "tut-tut-sheeeeeeee." *Season:* Mostly spring-fall; uncommon in winter; local to uncommon breeder. Nests in brackish and salt marshes. Cupped nest is 4 in (10 cm) wide; not defended by male.

Seaside sparrow, *Ammodramus maritimus* (**d**), is a transient and locally common summer resident of salt and brackish marshes. *Field marks:* A dark olive-gray sparrow. Note yellow blotch ahead of eye and white line along jaw. Breast is streaked with gray; belly is buff. *Size:* to 6 in (15 cm). *Call:* Strongly accented "tut-tut-zhee-eeeeeeee." *Season:* Mostly spring-fall; uncommon in winter; local to uncommon breeder. Nests in salt marshes (see p. 147).

WETLAND MAMMALS of brackish marshes employ various be-

havioral adaptations to survive the rigors of the tidal environment. In this chapter we focus on rodents (Rodentia), the gnawing mammals that are the most abundant mammals in any marsh—fresh, brackish, or salt. To escape the fingers of the tide, rice rats build elevated spherical nests (or take over marsh wren nests), lashed to cattail, big cordgrass, or common reed. Muskrats build houses above the marsh floor, with an underwater entrance that protects them from both predators and the winter cold. Nutrias, lacking such protection, often freeze to death in winter. Meadow voles (and most other marsh mammals) frequently burrow in muskrat lodges to escape high water or dropping temperatures. A variety of predators (p. 148) prowl the marshes and tear up muskrat houses in search of prey. Minks prefer muskrat kits to any other food. The river otter (p. 115) is also found in brackish marshes in late summer. Least shrews (*Cryptotis parva*) are fairly common.

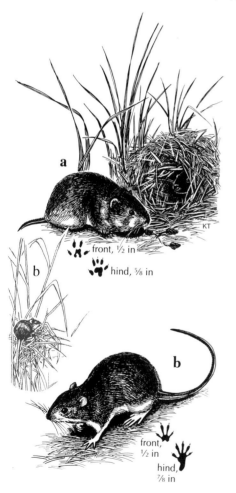

Meadow vole, *Microtus pennsylvanicus* (**a**), is common in brackish, as well as salt and freshwater, marshes. *Field marks:* Color is variable from light brown to blackish above, grayish below. Feet are dark brown. Teeth are ungrooved. *Size:* Body length to 5 in (12.5 cm); tail to 2½ in (6.6 cm). *Breeding:* Often nests in depression under marsh litter. Typically 3-5 young (up to 9), born naked and blind; several litters each year. *Feeding behavior:* Voles eat the stems and leaves of grasses, sedges, and rushes along runways. *Similar species:* Southern bog lemming, *Synaptomys cooperi,* has a very short tail (less than 1 in; 25 mm) and grooved upper incisors.

Marsh rice rat, *Oryzomys palustris* (**b**), is common throughout brackish marshes, and also invades freshwater wetlands. *Field marks:* Long and slender, the rice rat looks like a cross between a white-footed mouse and an Old World rat. The upper body has coarse, dark brown fur; underparts and feet are grayish white (never pure white). Tail is long and scaly; bicolored—darker above, paler below. *Size:* Body length to 5⅕ in (13.2 cm); tail to 7⅕ in (18.3 cm). *Breeding:* Nests under debris or in globular nest lashed to tall grasses. Typically 3-4 (up to 7) young, born naked and blind; several litters a year. *Feeding behavior:* Forages for plants, insects, crabs, and snails along runways. Feeding platforms (12 in wide) are often apparent.

a

front,
1½ in

hind,
3 in

b

front,
2 in

hind,
4 in

Muskrat, *Ondatra zibethicus* (**a**), is our most common aquatic mammal. *Field marks:* The only species with a laterally flattened black tail. Dark brown to blackish above and typically silvery below; sometimes white on throat. Hind feet only are partly webbed. Fur is thick (especially in winter) and oily (waterproofed). When swimming, head appears wedge-shaped; low in water. In contrast, beaver and nutria heads look squarish; river otter (p. 115) head appears round, may rise above water while swimming. *Size:* Body length to 14 in (36 cm); tail to 11 in (28 cm). *Breeding:* In marsh, muskrat constructs cone-shaped house, 5 ft in diameter at base, rising up to 3 ft above marsh. Construction is of grasses, sedges, and mud with underwater entrance. Typically 5-6 young (kits) born naked and blind; up to 3 litters per year. *Food:* A root consumer. Prefers cattail but rhizomes of bulrush and three-square are also consumed. *Feeding behavior:* Feeding shelters and lodges are connected by tunnels, called "leads." Overpopulation may produce characteristic "eatouts"—areas devoid of vegetation.

Nutria, *Myocastor coypus* (**b**), imported to Maryland in the 1940s for breeding on fur farms, escaped or was released into the wild. *Field marks:* Large size and round naked tail distinguish nutria from muskrat, which it closely resembles. Brown above and slightly lighter below. Snout and chin are grayish white. Inner 4 toes of hind feet are webbed. *Size:* Body length to 25 in (63 cm); tail to 17 in (43 cm). *Breeding:* Does not build a "house," but may take over abandoned muskrat lodge. Digs shallow burrow in mud bank with nesting chamber at rear, or sleeps in the open. Usually 5 *precocial* young, which can swim within a day of birth. Female has 4 pair of mammae (nipples) on sides, permitting the young to nurse in the water. *Feeding behavior:* A grazer (unlike the muskrat), nutria forages mostly upon stems and leaves. *Food:* Prefers American and Olney three-square over cattail; other menu items include most freshwater plants. *Note:* Feeding platforms (*above right*) are used for feeding, resting, and grooming. Nutria typically retreats into water with a loud splash; muskrat is quieter on retreat.

Salt Marshes

THE salt marshes of the lower Bay have a unique, primordial quality. For miles and miles, encompassing Taylors Island, the Honga River, Tangier Sound, and farther south, cordgrass meadows, dominated by only one or two species, stretch toward the mouth of the Chesapeake Bay. In some cases, entire islands, such as Bloodsworth and Great Fox, are overrun with cordgrass; dry land is absent. These vast wetlands are flat and monotonous. Only where small elevated islands appear does the eye find relief. There, in wax myrtle and loblolly pine, egrets and some relatives nest in colonial heronries. On the mud flats at low tide other birds appear, though most, like the dunlins (*at middle left*), are visitors. Only the willet, the clapper rail, and a few others reside in the marsh. Salt marshes are a hostile environment. Few species—both plant and animal—can survive.

A *salt marsh* may be defined quite simply as a *Spartina*-dominated wetland. Typically, only two species predominate: saltmarsh cordgrass, *S. alterniflora*, and saltmeadow cordgrass, *S. patens*. Saltmarsh cordgrass grows in tall colonies along tidal creeks below mean high tide (MHT) and in shorter stands at or above MHT. The tall form characterizes what is often referred to as the "regularly flooded salt marsh," or *low marsh*, while the short form of cordgrass (growing behind this zone) intergrades with the salt meadows of the "irregularly flooded salt marsh," or *high marsh*. Saltmeadow cordgrass grows in large meadows in the high marsh where the soil is well drained; in wetter (lower) areas of the high meadow, saltgrass (*Distichlis spicata*) may persist.

The waters that flood these wetlands typically have salinities in the upper mesohaline range (10 to 18 ppt) and above. In this range black needlerush and saltmarsh bulrush (*Scirpus robustus*; p. 119)

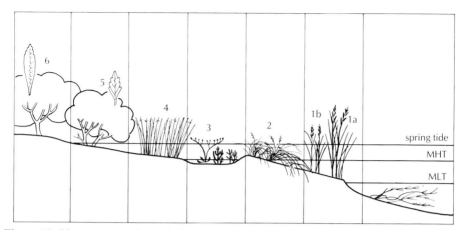

Figure 10. Plant zonation in a relatively diverse saltmarsh community (key *opposite*).

can still hold their ground, but in saltier waters (and lower elevations) they cannot compete with *Spartina*. In the lower (mostly southeastern) section of the Bay, where polyhaline waters (18-30 ppt) reign, only saltgrass (in dips at MHT) and the saltbushes (on hummocks) compete successfully within the cordgrass community. This transition to pure cordgrass meadows takes place at a point farther north on the Eastern than on the western shore, partly due to the Coriolis force (see p. 15). At sea level, in the *coastal embayment marshes* that fringe Assawoman and Chincoteague bays and the Virginia barrier islands, saltmarsh cordgrass grows in almost pure stands.

In the Chesapeake Bay, various "associated species" can compete by colonizing special zones and soils in the marsh. The elevation of the wetland floor relative to tidal inundation is the most important parameter of this zonation within a given (narrow) salinity band (see fig. 10; *above*). The spring tide line is often conspicuously marked with a wrack line of dead grass and debris. A summary of saltmarsh zonation follows (*opposite page*).

Salt marshes are among the most productive plant communities on earth. Cordgrass production can range from 4 to 10 tons of organic matter per acre per year, supplying great quantities of detritus and nutrients to the estuary and its inhabitants. Salt marshes are refuges for invertebrates, bull minnows, and other fishes that wander the network of tidal creeks which thread the marsh (see pp. 167-172).

To view a Chesapeake salt marsh in its purest form, one should sail or motor to one of the marsh islands such as South Marsh Island WMA, Smith Island (e.g., Martin NWR), Cedar Island WMA, or Tangier. By car or on foot, you can explore salt marshes at Point Lookout State Park (at the mouth of the Potomac), Hooper Island, lower Fishing Bay (below Toddville and Elliott), Dames Quarter Marsh (Deal Island WMA), and Janes Island State Park near Crisfield; or, in Virginia, look for smaller salt marshes along the entire Bay shoreline, for example, in Mobjack Bay (near Gloucester), Plum Tree Island NWR (near Poquoson), and the lower Eastern Shore from Saxis Marsh to Fishermans Island NWR.

SALTMARSH VEGETATION in the Bay area (and mid-Atlantic coast)

is dominated by saltmarsh cordgrass, which grows in vast colonies. Only a small number of associated species can tolerate the harsh conditions of the salt marsh. Colonization by these associated plants depends on soil type, elevation, and water depth, as well as salinity (see fig. 10; *opposite page*). Below mean low tide, widgeon grass or eelgrass (p. 166) will dominate the submersed aquatic vegetation. In the marsh, emergent plants reign. Saltmarsh cordgrass grows in 2 forms: a tall form (**1a**) along the water's edge, and a short form (**1b**) that grows near mean high tide. Behind these grow the salt meadows (**2**) from MHT to the limit of spring tides. In depressions, or "pannes," in the marsh floor, glasswort grows with sea lavender (**3**) and other associated species. Black needlerush (**4**) grows in sandy soil above mean high tide at moderate salinities. At the edge of the marsh, one finds the saltbush community (**5**), and wax myrtle (**6**) in upland areas.

THE DOMINANT *SPARTINA* species of salt marshes are members of the grass family (Gramineae).

Saltmarsh cordgrass, *Spartina alterniflora* (**a**), in salt marshes may grow at creekside (tall form) or at higher elevations (short form). *Leaves* taper to a long point and turn inward; up to 24 in (61 cm) long and $^1/_2$ in (12.7 mm) wide. *Stem* is stout, round, and hollow. *Flower cluster* (panicle) is narrow; composed of 5-30 spikes, each up to 4 in (10 cm) long; alternately arranged close to main axis; each spike consisting of 10-50 sessile spikelets. *Seeds* are small grains. *Size:* Short form up to 2 ft (61 cm); tall form up to 6 ft (1.8 m).

Saltmeadow cordgrass, *Spartina patens* (**b**), or saltmeadow hay, typically grows in the high marsh, and forms dense, matted meadows. *Leaves* are narrow, roll inward, and appear round; up to 18 in (46 cm) long and $^1/_5$ in (5 mm) wide; arranged in a single plane about stem. *Stem* is weak and wiry, forming characteristic swirls, or "cowlicks," in the meadow. *Flower head* (panicle) is an open terminal cluster; up to 8 in (20 cm) long; typically composed of 3-6 spikes, up to 2 in (5 cm) long, alternately arranged and diverging from main axis; each spike consisting of 20-50 densely packed sessile spikelets. *Seeds* are small grains. *Size:* Typically less than 2 ft (61 cm) tall; up to 5 ft (1.5 m).

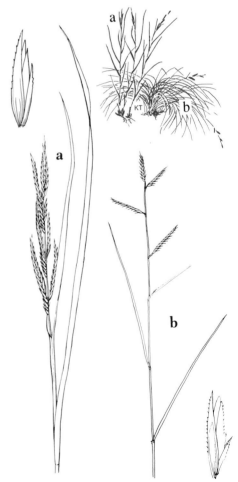

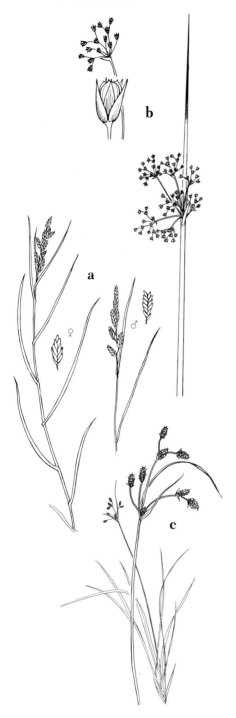

OTHER GRASSES, RUSHES, AND SEDGES
typically cannot compete with the *Spartina*
species in salt marshes, with the notable exception of the following species, one from each
family, that colonize special soils and zones.
Also see switchgrass (p. 121) and saltmarsh
bulrush (p. 119), which may also persist.

Saltgrass, *Distichlis spicata* (**a**), a true grass
(Gramineae), can withstand very high salinities,
growing in salt pannes within the high
meadows. *Leaves* are short, rolled inward (appearing round), and arranged in several planes
about the stem; up to 5 in (10 cm) long. *Stem* is
stiff and wiry, forming tangled mats. *Flower
cluster* (panicle) bears male or female spikelets
on separate (dioecious) plants: male spikelets
are longer, with 8-12 flowers; female spikelets
shorter, with 4-9 flowers. Entire panicle is
whitish green; up to 3 in (7.5 cm) long. *Seeds*
are tiny grains. *Size:* up to 2 ft (61 cm).

Black needlerush, *Juncus roemerianus*
(**b**), a rush (Juncaceae), typically grows in dense
stands near the high marsh, often in sandier
soils. *Leaves* are cylindrical, rigid, and resemble
a stem, the uppermost leaf ending in a sharp
point (often black, compared to dark green
lower leaf); each up to 8 in (20 cm) long. *Stem*
is rigid and round; gray late in season. *Flowers*
appear in a branched cluster extending laterally
approximately three-quarters of the way up
stem; *bloom* June-August. *Seeds* are contained
in capsules (shown). *Size:* up to 4 ft (1.2 m).

Saltmarsh fimbristylis, *Fimbristylis cas-
tanea* (**c**), a sedge (Cyperaceae), typically colonizes the higher elevations of salt and brackish
marshes. *Leaves*, arising from base of stem, are
linear, round (rolled inward), and shorter than
stem; up to 1$\frac{1}{2}$ ft (46 cm) long. *Stem* is slender
and rigid; triangular in cross section. *Flowers*
are small, one to each brown scale in budlike
spikelets on slender stalks; encompassed by 2-
3 leaflike bracts. *Fruits* (achenes) are grouped
in conelike clusters, nearly identical in appearance to the flowering heads. *Size:* up to 2$\frac{1}{2}$ ft
(76 cm).

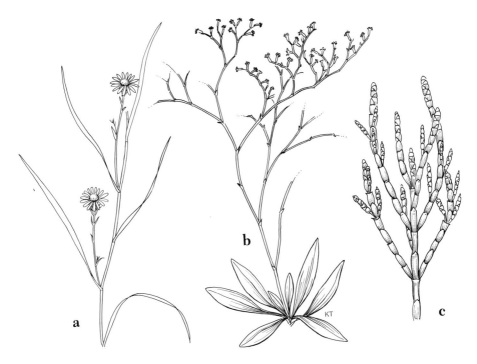

ASSOCIATED SPECIES of the salt marsh include the following herbs and shrubs.

Saltmarsh aster, *Aster tenuifolius* (**a**), a perennial herb, often grows within colonies of saltmarsh cordgrass. *Leaves* are linear or narrowly lance-shaped and fleshy; sparsely and alternately arranged on stem; up to 6 in (15 cm) long. *Stem* is smooth, arising from a slender, creeping rhizome. *Flowers* are pale purple or white and daisylike with 15-25 petal-like rays; heads grouped or solitary; up to 1 in (25 mm) wide; *bloom* August-September. *Size:* up to 3 1/2 ft (1 m). *Related species:* Annual saltmarsh aster, *Aster subulatus,* has more leaves and branches; smaller flowers; propagates by seeds.

Sea lavender, *Limonium carolinianum* (**b**), a perennial herb, is common in the higher elevations of salt and brackish marshes. *Leaves,* grouped in basal rosettes, are spoon-shaped, fleshy, leathery, and smooth; midvein prominent; arising from reddish leafstalks; up to 6 in

(15 cm) long. *Flower head* (panicle) is composed of tiny lavender tubular flowers, each with 5 lobes. Panicle branches broadly atop flower stalk that arises from basal leaves; *blooms* July-September. *Size:* up to 2 1/2 ft (76 cm). *Related species:* Sea lavender, *L. nashii,* has fine hairs at flower base.

Slender glasswort, *Salicornia europaea* (**c**), an annual herb, is an unusual plant of salt marshes, occurring in the saltier sandy pannes. *Leaves* are reduced to minute blunt scales, oppositely arranged at stem joints. *Stem* is fleshy (succulent), jointed, and multibranched; the lower branches creeping, upper branches erect. Stem is a jade green, turning ruby red in autumn. *Green flowers* are inconspicuous in upper joints of stem. *Size:* up to 2 ft (60 cm). *Note:* Succulent stems store water; edible. *Related species:* Dwarf glasswort, *S. bigelovii,* has sharp scales at joints and thicker branches; up to 1 ft (30 cm) tall. Perennial glasswort, *S. virginica,* has woody, unbranched stems; typically prostrate.

Sea oxeye, *Borrichia frutescens* (**a**), is a shrub that colonizes higher elevations in salt marshes from Virginia south. *Leaves* are thick and leathery; opposite; oblong and only scantily toothed near base. *Stem* is round with fine vertical lines. *Flowers* are yellow sunflowerlike blossoms with 15-25 short rays; *bloom* July-September. *Seed head* is a burlike brown globe, appearing in late autumn. *Size:* up to 2 ft (60 cm).

OTHER COMMON ASSOCIATED SPECIES of salt and brackish marshes:

Marsh orach, *Atriplex patula*
Sea blite, *Suaeda linearis*
Tidemarsh waterhemp, *Amaranthus cannabinus*, p. 82
Seashore mallow, *Kosteletzkya virginica*, p. 122
Saltmarsh loosestrife, *Lythrum lineare*, p. 82
Marsh pink, *Sabatia stellaris*
Seaside gerardia, *Agalinis maritima*
Saltmarsh fleabane, *Pluchea purpurascens*, p. 122
Seaside goldenrod, *Solidago sempervirens*, p. 122

The Saltbush Community is dominated by the following two shrub species, members of the composite family (Compositae).

Marsh elder, *Iva frutescens* (**b**), or hightide bush, occurs with groundsel tree on elevated hummocks. *Opposite leaves* are thick and fleshy; elliptic, with serrated margins; up to 4 in (10 cm) long. *Twigs* are branched with vertical lines. *Small flowers* (greenish white) appear on erect spikes; *bloom* August-October. *Size:* Typically 3 ft (90 cm); up to 10 ft (3 m) tall.

Groundsel tree, *Baccharis halimifolia* (**c**), grows in elevated areas in the marsh or at the upland border. *Alternate leaves* are of 2 types: on lower branches leaves are *wedge-shaped* and coarsely toothed, up to 2¹/₂ in (6.25 cm) long; *upper leaves* have fewer teeth (or none) and are smaller, more narrow or lanceolate. *Stem* is woody and branches into green, angled, hairless twigs. *Flowers* on male and female plants *bloom* during August-October, forming yellow-white clusters. *Size:* up to 15 ft (4.5 m).

SALTMARSH INVERTEBRATES are often highly specialized in their

ability to withstand both salinity and tidal inundation. The saltmarsh snail, for example, congregates in the high marsh above the normal reach of the tide. It is a pulmonate (i.e., air-breathing) snail and cannot survive lengthy submersion. During a spring tide hundreds of these snails can be seen climbing up plant stems to avoid drowning. Insects escape in the same manner or simply fly or swim to a dry refuge. Meanwhile, periwinkles can tolerate submersion as well as the high salinities and temperatures of tidal pools left standing within the marsh. They breathe via a gill and, to avoid desiccation, can seal their shells with a trap door (the *operculum*). While these invertebrates are readily seen in the marsh, the most abundant species remain well hidden. Underwater, crustaceans forage among submersed aquatic plants (p. 167), and, underground, marsh soils harbor the majority of invertebrate creatures (see pp. 153-155).

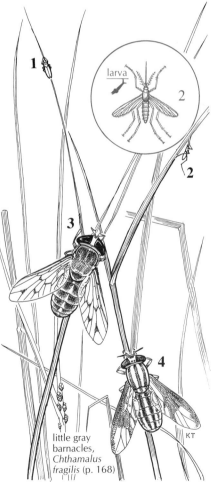

little gray
barnacles,
*Chthamalus
fragilis* (p. 168)

MARSH INSECTS are most visible in the herbaceous layer—on cordgrass, goldenrod, and saltbushes. Perhaps most abundant are the planthoppers and leafhoppers (Homoptera) such as the **planthopper,** *Prokelisia marginata* (**1**), *at right* (flightless form shown). Like the true bugs (Hemiptera), which are also common, planthoppers have piercing mouthparts (*stylets*) used to obtain sap from plants. Feeding directly on cordgrass and needlerush are a variety of grasshoppers and crickets (Orthoptera), which also occupy freshwater and brackish wetlands (see p. 106).

A host of flies (Diptera) are omnipresent within the marsh, though the annoying varieties are best known. First and foremost is the **saltmarsh mosquito** (*Aedes sollicitans;* **2**) which preys on warm-blooded vertebrates such as man. Secluded tidal pools provide breeding grounds for the mosquito and nurseries for their larvae (see silhouette). Marsh flies (*Dictya* spp. and *Haplodictya* spp.) prey on snails, particularly the marsh periwinkle, and robber flies (Asilidae) attack insects as large as grasshoppers. Aside from mosquitoes, the most bothersome flies to man are the **saltmarsh greenhead fly** (*Tabanus nigrovittatus;* **3**) popularly known as the horsefly, and the equally pugnacious **deerfly** (*Chrysops* sp.; **4**), known for their painful bites. These various insects may reach maturity at different intervals over the summer.

CRUSTACEANS AND MOLLUSCS of the salt marsh congregate in the intertidal zone (*above*) where algae, detritus, zooplankton, and worms are available as food. The voracious **marsh crab** (*Sesarma reticulatum;* **1**, *at left*) includes everything from grass shrimp to saltmarsh cordgrass in its varied diet. The 1⅛ in (2.8 cm) wide carapace is squarish with notches along the leading edges, just behind the eyes, which are situated at the front corners of the black to purplish shell. In contrast, the **marsh fiddler crab** (*Uca pugnax;* **2**), typical of saline marshes, is smaller, less than 1 in (2.5 cm) wide, and has a more tapered shell with central eyes situated on long stalks. Like other fiddler crabs (p. 156), the species can be distinguished by markings on the large "fiddle" claw of the male; in this case, a row of wartlike projections (*tubercles*) on the 1½ in (3.8 cm) long claw.

Marsh periwinkles (*Littorina irrorata;* **3**, *at left*) are conspicuous in sheltered marshes, where they feed on detritus and algae that they rasp from the surface of plants and the wetland floor. The grayish to yellowish tan right-handed (*dextral*) shell has spiral grooves with reddish flecks on the ridges. It reaches 1 in (25 mm) in length. Like men on a fire pole, periwinkles cover the stalks of cordgrass, climbing the stems to escape predation by blue crabs or terrapins. Meanwhile, **saltmarsh snails** (*Melampus bidentatus;* **4**) less than half that size, ascend marsh plants to avoid the rising tide, since they are strictly air-breathers. Half-buried in mud, the 4 in (10 cm) **Atlantic ribbed mussel** (*Geukensia demissa;* **5**) filters algae and zooplankton from the incoming tide. It attaches to plant stems, rhizomes, stones, or shells by means of a *byssus* (see illus., p. 124). In salt marshes, bent mussels (*Ischadium recurvum;* p. 169) may attach to *Geukensia* shells with their own byssal threads just as they cling to the shells of the American oyster (*Crassostrea virginica*) in subtidal areas. At *far right,* 2 **common mud nassas** (*Ilynassa obsoleta;* **6**, also p. 153) forage at the water's edge, searching with their outstretched siphons for dead crabs or fish.

FEW AQUATIC REPTILES can tolerate the saline conditions of the saltmarsh environment. Not surprisingly, this wetland type is devoid of *amphibians,* which lack the protective scales of *reptiles* and cannot keep their skins sufficiently moist in the drying salt water and air. Only the Fowler's toad (p. 86) may be common at the edge of the salt marsh. This warty-skinned toad is undoubtedly our most salt-tolerant amphibian. In addition to terrapins and water snakes in tidal creeks, one can usually find a few other reptiles at the *upland margin* of salt and brackish-water marshes. A variety of snakes forage in the shrubby saltbush communities that border these wetlands. Here black racers (p. 43), black rat snakes (*Elaphe o. obsoleta*), eastern hognose snakes (*Heterodon platyrhinos*), and eastern kingsnakes (*Lampropeltis g. getulus*) may hunt toads, marsh-dwelling birds, and voles. Garter and ribbon snakes (p. 126) are also found at the brackish or upland edge.

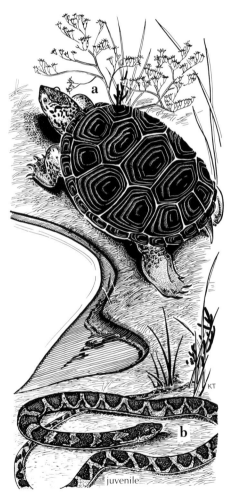

Northern diamondback terrapin,

Malaclemys terrapin terrapin (**a**), is the only turtle of saltwater (polyhaline) marshes. The terrapin is sometimes seen basking in salt and brackish marshes or caught rising to the surface of tidal guts for a breath of air. It derives its common name from the diamond-shaped rings on each scute of the *carapace* (upper shell), which is a dull gray, black, or brown. The lower shell, or *plastron*, is yellowish and often mottled with dark blotches. Note the dark spots or flecks covering the pale head and limbs. Diet consists of snails, crabs, worms, insects, and fishes. Females lay up to 21 eggs in a hole excavated from sandy soil above high tide. Longevity exceeds 40 years. *Size*: Female reaches 9 in (23 cm); male is half as large. *Note*: Formerly of great commercial importance, Bay populations were decimated by overharvesting in the 1920s. Still on the recovery, Chesapeake terrapins are now trapped in a limited fishery.

Northern water snake, *Nerodia sipedon sipedon* (**b**),

is the only snake widespread in moderately brackish (mesohaline) waters (up to 12 ppt). Note the alternating dorsal and lateral bands with markings wider than spaces between. Background color varies from gray to dark brown; markings vary from reddish brown to black. Underbelly is also variable: black or reddish crescent moons (p. 126) present or absent. Diet is mostly fish. *Size*: to 53 in (134 cm).

BIRDS of the salt marsh are few but typically are endemic to the environment. Clapper rails, laughing gulls, and seaside sparrows are strictly saltmarsh nesters. Willets and Forster's terns prefer this habitat as well. Other breeding birds, such as marsh wrens and red-winged blackbirds (p. 129), invade salt marshes but are more numerous in the taller (and more protected) fresh and brackish marshes northward or upstream. A few nesting black ducks (p. 128) or blue-winged teals (p. 110) may be found in saltmarsh cordgrass, but these and other waterfowl (e.g., gadwalls) are more numerous in winter. The migration season brings many shorebirds (Charadriiformes) into the marsh and onto its exposed mud flats. Migrating tree swallows (*Tachycineta bicolor*) and Savannah sparrows (*Passerculus sandwichensis*) also pass through. However, Chesapeake salt marshes differ significantly from Atlantic coastal salt marshes, such as Assateague. A number of terns and other shorebirds rarely wander inland and are best seen at Chincoteague NWR.

HERONS AND EGRETS (Ardeidae) are long-legged waders with spearlike bills. They stand with neck outstretched or with head hunched on shoulders. Sexes alike. *Food:* Fish, frogs, and invertebrates. *Note:* The family also includes bitterns (Tribe Botaurini) and night-herons (Tribe Nycticoracini), which are local and uncommon breeders in Chesapeake wetlands.

Great egret, *Casmerodius albus* (**a**), is a transient and summer resident of tidewater wetlands and shallow bays. *Field marks:* A large white heron with a yellow bill and black legs and feet. For breeding plumage see p. 71. *Flight:* Neck held in open curve. *Size:* Length to 39 in (99 cm), averages 38 in (96 cm); wingspan averages 55 in (140 cm). *Call:* A hoarse croak or "kuk-kuk-kuk." *Feeding behavior:* Leans forward, extending neck; remains still. *Season:* Spring-fall; highly local breeder. Nests in colonies.

Snowy egret, *Egretta thula* (**b**), is a transient and summer resident of tidewater wetlands. *Field marks:* A medium-sized white heron with a black bill and legs but yellow feet. For breeding plumage see p. 174. *Flight:* Head held back; neck in tight curve. *Size:* Length to 27 in (68 cm), averages 24 in (61 cm); wingspan averages 41 in (104 cm). *Call:* A low croak. *Feeding behavior:* Scurries about, stirring up prey with feet. *Season:* Spring-fall; very local breeder. Nests in low shrubs or trees near water.

Great blue heron, *Ardea herodius* (**a**), is a common permanent resident of tidewater marshes and nearby shallows. *Field marks:* The largest heron in North America, the "GBH" is known by its great size and slate blue color. Adult has black stripe above eye; black plumes (when breeding); yellow bill. Immature has black crown; no plumes. *Flight:* Head and neck held in tight curve. *Size:* Length to 52 in (130 cm), averages 47 in (117 cm); wingspan averages 72 in (183 cm). *Call:* Harsh squawks when alarmed. *Feeding behavior:* Walks slowly or waits patiently with head back on shoulders. *Season:* All year; less common in winter (except at Chincoteague NWR); very local breeder. Nests colonially. *Confusing species:* Little blue heron, *Egretta caerulea* (adult), has maroon head and neck. Tricolored heron, *E. tricolor*, has white belly and rump. Both are dark blue above; medium-sized like a snowy.

Green-backed heron, *Butorides striatus* (**b**), is a transient and common summer resident of tidal wetlands. *Field marks:* A small dark heron with short yellow legs (orange when breeding). *Flight:* Very rapid; neck in tight curve. *Size:* Length to 22 in (55 cm), averages 18 in (46 cm); wingspan averages 26 in (66 cm). *Call:* A piercing "skew" when alarmed. *Feeding behavior:* Typically keeps short neck folded back on shoulders, giving it a bitternlike appearance. *Season:* Spring-fall; common breeder. *Confusing species:* American bittern, *Botaurus lentiginosus*, and night-herons, *Nycticorax* spp., are larger, stockier birds.

IBISES (Threskiornithidae)

Glossy ibis, *Plegadis falcinellus* (**c**), is a transient and summer resident in tidewater wetlands. *Field marks:* A medium-sized wader with a long *decurved* bill. Color is a dark glossy purple; bill and legs dark gray. *Flight:* Unlike a heron, ibis flies with neck outstretched. *Size:* Length to 25 in (63 cm), averages 23 in (58 cm); wingspan averages 36 in (91 cm). *Call:* A low "kruk" or "ka-honk." *Food:* Small fish and aquatic invertebrates. *Season:* Spring-fall; local breeder on Atlantic barrier islands.

GULLS AND TERNS (Laridae) are closely related. The stockier gulls have slightly hooked bills and squared-off tails. The slimmer terns have pointed bills and forked tails. Terns hover and dive for fish. Gulls glide and seldom dive; but swim (terns do not). Also see p. 159.

Forster's tern, *Sterna forsteri* (**a**), is a common transient and summer resident along the salt marshes and shores of the Bay. *Field marks:* A medium-sized tern with light wing tips. Black cap extends from top of bill through eye to nape. Bill is orange, tipped with black. Tail is deeply forked; inner edge dark. *Size:* Length to 15 in (38 cm); wingspan averages 30 in (76 cm). *Call:* A nasal "karr." *Season:* Spring-fall; uncommon in winter (mostly SE Virginia); breeds in salt marshes of Atlantic Coast; in autumn, postbreeding flocks migrate up tidal rivers to *fall line. Related species:* Common tern, *S. hirundo* (p. 159), has redder bill; black wing tips; tail dark on outer edge.

Laughing gull, *Larus atricilla* (**b**), is a common transient and summer resident in salt marshes and shallow bays. *Field marks:* A small black-hooded gull. Feet are dark orange. In flight, dark mantle ends in black wing tips (see p. 196). *Size:* Length to 17 in (43 cm); wingspan averages 40 in (102 cm). *Call:* A laughing ha-ha-ha. *Season:* Spring-fall; rare in winter; in Maryland and Virginia breeds in Atlantic Coast salt marshes; postbreeding flocks move up tidal rivers in autumn.

RAILS (Rallidae) are hen-shaped birds.

Clapper rail, *Rallus longirostris* (**c**), is a transient and summer resident of salt marshes. *Field marks:* A large gray-brown rail. Note long, slightly *decurved* bill. Cheek and breast are grayish. Flanks are lightly barred. Note white patch under tail. *Size:* Length to 16 in (40 cm); wingspan averages 20 in (51 cm). *Call:* "Kek-kek-kek." *Food:* Marsh fiddler crabs and snails. *Season:* Mostly spring-fall; uncommon and irregular in winter; uncommon to local breeder. Nests in cordgrass or needlerush. *Related species:* King rail, *R. elegans* (p. 112), has rusty breast and darker (blackish) stripes on back and flanks.

SANDPIPERS AND ALLIES (Scolopacidae) are long-billed shorebirds. Also see p. 158. *Food:* Small invertebrates.

Willet, *Catoptrophorus semipalmatus* (**a**), is a summer resident (and transient) of Bay salt marshes and tidal flats. *Field marks:* A large gray sandpiper with a long straight stout bill. White band on wings is not always apparent at rest. Legs are bluish gray. *Flight:* Look for black-and-white wings. *Size:* to 17 in (43 cm). *Call:* At breeding, a melodious "will-will-willet." *Season:* Spring-fall; winters on coast and at mouth of Bay; uncommon breeder in Maryland, locally common in Virginia. Nests in salt marshes amidst short-growth cordgrass. *Confusing species:* **Greater yellowlegs,** *Tringa melanoleuca* (p. 158), has yellow legs; flight pattern (**b**) lacks black-and-white pattern.

Dunlin, *Calidris alpina* (**c**), is a transient and winter resident of tidewater wetlands and tidal flats. *Field marks:* A medium-sized gray-brown sandpiper. Note downward droop at end of long bill. *Size:* to 8¹/₂ in (22 cm). *Call:* A nasal

"treep." *Season:* Fall-spring. Nonbreeder.

Semipalmated sandpiper, *Calidris pusilla* (**d**), is a common transient along the tidal flats adjoining tidewater wetlands. *Field marks:* A small gray "peep" sandpiper. Note blackish legs. *Size:* to 6¹/₂ in (16 cm). *Call:* A short low-pitched "krip." *Season:* Mostly spring and fall; uncommon in summer. Nonbreeder. *Related species:* Least sandpiper, *C. minutilla* (p. 158), has yellowish legs; brown streaking on breast.

PLOVERS (Charadriidae) have shorter bills than sandpipers.

Semipalmated plover, *Charadrius semipalmatus* (**e**), is a common transient along the tidal flats of salt marshes and estuarine rivers. *Field marks:* A small brown-backed plover. In winter, characteristic breast band is dull brown. Legs are yellowish. *Size:* to 7¹/₂ in (19 cm). *Call:* A rising "too-wee." *Season:* Mostly spring and fall; uncommon in summer. Nonbreeder.

Osprey flies with crook in wings.

Turkey vulture soars with wings in a dihedral.

Bald eagle soars with flat wings.

Northern harrier flies low with vulturelike dihedral.

a
♀

b
♀

KT

BIRDS OF PREY of salt marshes may include hunting ospreys, eagles, and harriers. Less common species include the short-eared owl, *Asio flammeus*, and rough-legged hawk, *Buteo lagopus*; both appear in winter only.

Osprey, *Pandion haliaetus* (**a**), or fish hawk, is a common summer resident and transient of tidal marshes and bays. *Field marks:* Plumage brownish black above; white below. Black cheek patch runs from eye to back of head. Female has dark stippling on white breast. *Flight:* Hovers and plunges feetfirst for fish. Shows a dark "wrist" patch at crook on underside of wings. *Size:* Length to 25 in (64 cm), averages 23 in (58 cm); wingspan averages 65 in (165 cm). *Call:* A whistled cheep-cheep or "yew-yew-yewk." *Season:* Spring-fall; rare in winter; common breeder. Nests on trees, platforms, and buoys (p. 128). The nest is constructed of small to large sticks; up to 6 ft (2 m) in diameter. *Confusing species:* Bald eagle, *Haliaeetus leucocephalus* (p. 111), has pure white head; lacks black cheek patch.

Northern harrier, *Circus cyaneus* (**b**), or marsh hawk, is a transient and winter resident (and uncommon and local summer resident) of tidal marshes. *Field marks:* A slender hawk with a distinctive white rump. Female (shown) is brown above with brown stippling on whitish breast. Male is gray above; mostly white underneath. Note owl-like face patch. *Flight:* Note white rump; glides low over marshes and fields with wings in slight *dihedral*, tilting from side to side. Gray males have black wing tips. *Size:* Length to 23 in (58 cm), averages 20 in (51 cm); wingspan averages 42 in (107 cm). *Call:* Nasal whistles: "pee-pee-peee." *Food:* Mostly small rodents. *Season:* All year; mostly spring and fall; less common in winter; rare to local breeder. Nests in marshes on or near ground with structure made of sticks and grasses, up to 30 in (76 cm) in diameter. *Confusing species:* Rough-legged hawk, *Buteo lagopus*, has broad wings; shorter tail is white with black band at tip.

PASSERINE BIRDS (Passeriformes) are less common in salt than in freshwater marshes.

Marsh wren, *Cistothorus palustris* (**a**), is a common transient and summer resident of salt, fresh, and brackish marshes. *Field marks:* The slim, slightly curved bill and white stripes on back are distinctive. Also note the white eyebrow stripe and brown cap. *Size:* to 5 in (13 cm). *Call:* A buzzing rattle: "cut-cut-trrrrrrrrrr-ur." *Food:* Mostly insects. *Season:* All year; uncommon in winter; locally uncommon to common breeder. Nest is in rushes, sedges, or saltbushes typically 1-3 ft (1 m) above water; oblong (football-shaped) structure, woven from grasses; has side entrance.

Seaside sparrow, *Ammodramus maritimus* (**b**), is a common transient and summer resident of Chesapeake salt marshes. *Field marks:* Note relatively long bill and yellow dash ahead of eye. Upper body is olive-gray; belly buff-white. *Size:* to 6 in (15 cm). *Call:* A sharp "tut-tut-*zhee-eeeeeee.*" *Season:* Mostly spring-fall; uncommon in winter; local to uncommon breeder. Open cupped nest is made of grasses; 3-4 in (10 cm) wide; males territorial. *Related species:* Sharp-tailed sparrow, *A. caudacutus,* p. 129, has orangish triangle on face; browner; shorter bill; nest bulkier.

Boat-tailed grackle, *Quiscalus major* (**c**), is a local permanent resident of salt marshes, beaches, and tidal flats. *Field marks:* Male is a large blackbird with a distinctive large wedge-shaped tail. Female is brown; smaller; pale brown breast. *Size:* Length to 9^1/$_2$ in (24 cm), averages 8^1/$_2$ in (22 cm). *Call:* "chek-chek-chek." *Season:* All year; local to common breeder.

Fish crow, *Corvus ossifragus* (**d**), is a permanent resident and transient of the estuary. *Field marks:* A small black crow distinguishable by voice from common crow. Sexes identical. *Size:* to 20 in (50 cm). *Call:* A short "ca" or "car" rather than the (larger) American crow's typical caw. *Season:* All year; most common in spring and fall; less common in winter. Common breeder.

MAMMALS of coastal wetlands can be grouped into 2 categories: *upland species,* which nest in dry terrestrial habitats, and *wetland species,* which nest in the swamp or marsh. In salt marshes only a few mammals reside in the tidal zone, the most prevalent being the ubiquitous meadow vole. Cordgrass meadows offer little protection, however, for larger mammals. The nutria is absent from this habitat. The Blackwater population of river otters only visits in winter—to fish—when the freshwater marshes are frozen over. Even the durable muskrat considers the salt marsh a secondary habitat, only colonized once population pressures in cattail or three-square marshes become extreme. Muskrat populations are lower here, and animals consuming cordgrass are (on average) 10 percent lighter in weight. Upland visitors are more commonly seen. In addition to the 2 carnivores below, one may encounter a foraging striped skunk (*Mephitis mephitis*) or the insectivorous least shrew (*Cryptotis parva*), or, grazing at the marsh edge, a white-tailed deer (p. 53).

r.f., 3 in

r.h., 4 in.

a

r.f., 2½ in

l.h., 2 in

KT

b

CARNIVORES of the salt marsh are, for the most part, upland species that invade the marsh at dawn or dusk to feed upon voles, muskrat kits, or bird eggs, and invertebrates such as insects, crabs, or clams.

Raccoon, *Procyon lotor* (**a**), is an important predator in salt and brackish marshes. *Field marks:* Upper body is grizzled gray, often with a reddish or blackish tint. Underparts are gray. The distinctive tail has alternating yellowish white and black bands. Black mask is outlined in white. *Size:* Body length to 28 in (71 cm); tail to 12 in (30 cm). *Food:* Insects, crabs, rodents, fruits, and, in fresh and brackish marshes, frogs and freshwater clams.

Red fox, *Vulpes vulpes* (**b**), like the raccoon, steals into the marsh to forage upon resident animals. *Field marks:* Upper body is reddish gray to rust red. Feet and ears are black. Underparts and tip of bushy tail are grayish white. *Size:* Body length to 25 in (63 cm); tail to 16 in (41 cm). *Food:* Rabbits, rodents (especially voles and muskrats), small marsh birds and eggs, invertebrates, and berries. In fall, fruits and seeds may compose up to one-fourth of diet. In winter, hunting is restricted to upland areas. *Tracks:* Red fox oval prints (except in soft mud) can be distinguished from tracks of domestic dog in that heel pad appears far behind the toes.

HERBIVORES of the salt marsh are restricted to the small rodents that are hardy enough to survive the saline environment and the ebb and flow of the tides.

Meadow vole, *Microtus pennsylvanicus* (**a**), is the most common rodent in the salt marsh. *Field marks:* Voles are distinguished by a relatively short tail (less than length of body). Upper body is brown to almost black; belly usually grayish. Feet are brown. *Size:* Body length to 6 in (15 cm); tail to 2½ in (6.6 cm). *Breeding:* Typically builds a nest of grass on ground; 1-9 young per litter; several litters a year. *Food:* In salt marshes, stems, leaves, and rootstalks of grasses, bulrushes, and seaside goldenrod. Also insects. *Note:* Narrow runways are constructed in marsh. An excellent swimmer. Active day and night.

Marsh rice rat, *Oryzomys palustris* (**b**), common in a variety of wetlands, often constructs nest (p. 130) atop needlerush in salt marshes. *Field marks:* Rice rats are distinguished by a scaly, bicolored tail typically longer than body. This separates them from Old World rats (*Rattus* spp.). Note dark upper body and grayish white belly and feet. *Size:* Body length to 5⅕ in (13.2 cm); tail to 7⅕ in (18.3 cm). *Breeding:* Usually 3-4 young. *Food:* In salt marshes, a great deal of insects and crabs, in addition to seeds. *Note:* Excellent swimmers, rice rats may dive if threatened. They construct runways. Mostly nocturnal. *Similar species:* White-footed mouse, *Peromyscus leucopus,* an upland (edge) species, has pure white feet and a shorter tail. Norway rat, *Rattus norvegicus,* has a naked, scaly tail that is shorter than body; not bicolored.

Muskrat, *Ondatra zibethicus* (**c**), the well-known furbearer, is less common in salt marshes than in fresh and brackish wetlands. *Field marks:* Note laterally flattened tail, unique to this species. Upper body is brown to blackish; light brown below. *Size:* Body length to 14 in (36 cm); tail to 11 in (28 cm). *Breeding:* Dome-shaped houses dot the marsh. Up to 3 litters of 5-6 young each season. *Food:* Mostly rhizomes of plants, but also molluscs, insects, and an occasional fish. *Note:* Mostly nocturnal.

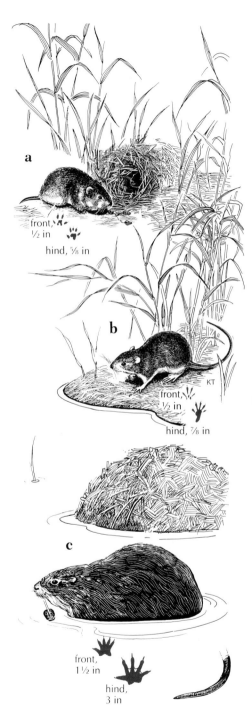

a

front, ½ in
hind, ⅝ in

b

KT

front, ½ in
hind, ⅞ in

c

front, 1½ in
hind, 3 in

Beaches and Tidal Flats

THE shoreline of the Chesapeake Bay stretches for more than 4,000 miles around the basin, inclusive of marshes, wooded bluffs, bulkheads, beaches, and tidal flats. The banks of tributary rivers and streams double this figure to over 8,000 miles, roughly the distance from Washington to Cape Town. While the preceding chapters have highlighted the vegetated wetlands of the Bay's prodigious coastline, here we explore a different habitat—the band of unvegetated wetlands surrounding the Chesapeake shallows.

Best explored at low tide, unvegetated wetlands border most marshes and beaches from the mouth of the Susquehanna to Capes Henry and Charles. Here, underneath or beside the empty shells of oysters, mussels, and clams left by the tide, the beachcomber can find a multitude of fascinating living creatures. In late May, the horseshoe crab (*at left*) comes ashore to lay its green gelatinous eggs. Gulls, terns, and sandpipers greet this annual spawning event with great chatter and appetite.

Unvegetated wetlands may be defined as wet substrates, devoid of rooted plants, that are subjected to tidal inundation. In its strictest sense, this definition includes streambeds, unvegetated shallows, and open water below mean low tide (MLT), which in this guide are treated as separate habitats. In this chapter, we consider the unvegetated wetlands *above* MLT, including sandbars and mud flats exposed at low tide as well as sandy beaches. Upper beaches represent the shoreline continuum above mean high tide (MHT), only reached by storm and spring tides and salt spray.

The shoreline is divided into four distinct zones based on elevation relative to tidal fluctuations (see fig. 11; p. 152). Below MLT is the *subtidal zone*, which includes submersed aquatic

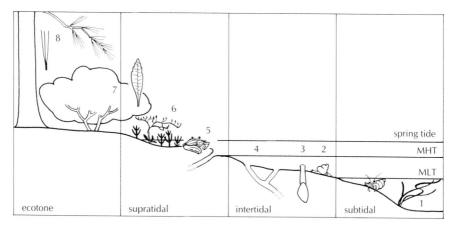

Figure 11. Tidal zonation of typical Chesapeake shoreline (key in text).

vegetation (**1**) and benthic algae, as well as unvegetated shallows (see p. 161). Between MLT and MHT is the *intertidal zone*, which may be muddy (composed of silt, clay, and organic material), sandy (composed mostly of sand, pebbles, or shells), or a mixture of these. In this zone, a variety of snails (**2**), clams (**3**), and burrowing worms (**4**) populate the substrate. Above MHT up to (and somewhat beyond) the limit of spring tides is the *supratidal zone*, which may support scattered plants. This is the area of dry sandy beaches, where sand fiddlers (**5**) dig their burrows, and where dips, or *pannes,* in the sand foster salt barrens where salt-tolerant plants (*halophytes*), such as glasswort (**6**), may gain a foothold. Above the supratidal zone is a transition zone or *ecotone,* colonized by species such as wax myrtle (**7**) and loblolly pine (**8**) at the upland edge.

The community profiles of beaches, sandbars, and mud flats vary—like all habitats within the estuary—with salinity. Freshwater, estuarine, and marine invertebrates are distributed according to their salinity tolerances. Bay beaches, for example, lack marine burrowing species such as mole crabs (*Emerita talpoida*) and *Donax* clams. Species also segregate according to elevation and soil type. In sandy areas of the supratidal zone, one finds various beach fleas (amphipods) such as *Orchestia platensis* and *Talorchestia longicornis*, but in intertidal flats another species, *O. grillus*, is more common. Densities of major invertebrate groups range from 330-3,000 individuals per square meter on sandbars to 5,300-8,300 individuals per square meter on richly organic sand-mud flats.

While Chesapeake shores lack the celebrated tidal pools of the northern rocky coast, the modest tides of the estuary still allow for some remarkable adaptations among intertidal residents. To avoid dessication at low tide, mud snails and periwinkles can seal off their apertures with a tiny trap door, the *operculum.* Clams and worms burrow into the mud or sand to avoid predation by shorebirds (and dessication) at low tide, and predation by blue crabs, fishes, terrapins, and waterfowl at high water. In turn, shorebirds have developed some remarkable tools and techniques for harvesting the secretive fauna of the flats (see p. 157).

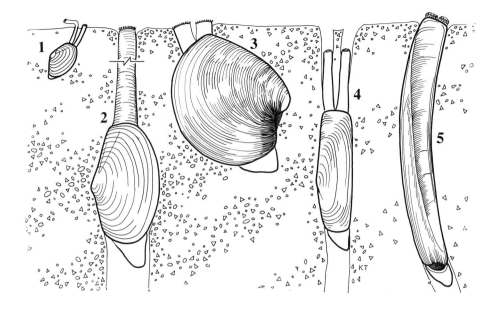

BURROWING CLAMS (Pelecypoda; Mollusca) have a characteristic hatchet-shaped foot for digging and extendable siphons. Prefer sand or sandy muds. Also see the brackish-water clam, *Rangia cuneata*, p. 170.

Baltic macoma clam, *Macoma balthica*
(**1**), a member of the tellin family (Tellinidae), extends its long movable siphon to suck up food (algae and protozoans) from the bottom. *Macoma* shells are dull, chalky white. *Size:* to 1 in (25 mm). *Range:* Intertidal to subtidal; 5 ppt to marine.

Soft-shelled clam, *Mya arenaria* (**2**), is a
member of the Myacidae family, which typically have long retractable siphons encased in a single, leathery tube. The elliptical white shell has a spoon-shaped depression (*chondrophore*) inside the left valve at the hinge (see p. 170). At maturity, *Mya* may be buried a foot or more (30-45 cm) in the substrate. *Size:* to 3 in (7.5 cm). *Range:* Intertidal to subtidal; 5 to 30 ppt.

Hard clam, *Mercenaria mercenaria* (**3**), is
the commonest venus clam (Veneridae) in the

Bay. Note the classic thick heart-shaped shell; bears concentric growth lines. Interior is white, a purple stain surrounds muscle scar and *pallial sinus* (see p. 170). *Size:* to 4 in (10 cm). *Range:* Intertidal to subtidal; 15 ppt to marine.

Stout razor clam, *Tagelus plebeius* (**4**), a
member of the Gariidae, has a rectangular shell; somewhat cylindrical (on end) with a gaping, open posterior end where the long siphons extend. Exterior is white with a brownish covering (*periostracum*) and fine concentric grooves; interior white. Hinge has 2 small teeth. *Size:* to $2^{1}/_{2}$ in (6.5 cm). *Range:* Intertidal to subtidal; 10 to 30 ppt.

Common jackknife clam, *Ensis directus* (**5**), a true razor clam (Solenidae), has short
siphons and a hatchet-shaped foot. The long, thin, fragile shell is gently curved with sharp edges. On end, the shell is cylindrical, gaping where siphons extend, and covered with a glossy, olive-brown covering (periostracum). Left valve has 2 *cardinal teeth*. *Size:* to 6 in (15 cm). *Range:* Intertidal to subtidal; 15 to 30 ppt.

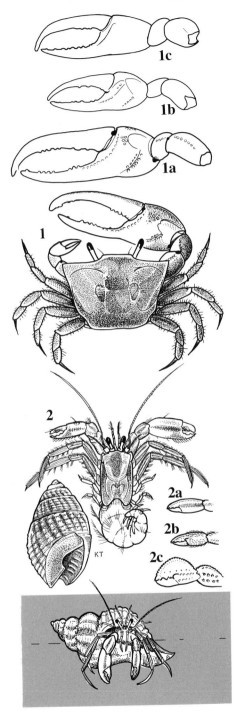

CRABS (Decapoda; Crustacea) have 5 pairs of legs, the first pair typically clawed. In the intertidal brackish zones of the estuary, mud crabs (Xanthidae; p. 183) are the most common.

Fiddler crabs, *Uca* spp. (**1**), have 4 pairs of well-developed walking legs. The fifth pair are modified pincers. Shell (*carapace*) is squarish and tapered to rear. Only the male sports an enlarged (right or left) "fiddle" claw. **Red-jointed fiddler crab**, *U. minax* (**1a**), has a distinctive groove on carapace (shown) behind each eye. Joints of major claw are red. *Tubercles* appear in 2 rows on inside of claw. *Size:* Carapace width to $1^1/_2$ in (3.8 cm); major claw to 2 in (5 cm). *Range:* Intertidal muds; brackish and salt marshes (0.5 to 18 ppt). **Marsh fiddler crab**, *U. pugnax* (**1b**), lacks groove behind eye. Major claw has 1-2 rows of tubercles on inside (palm). *Size:* Carapace width to $^7/_8$ in (22 mm); major claw to $1^1/_2$ in (3.8 cm). Range: Intertidal muds; salt marshes (5 to 30 ppt). **Sand fiddler crab**, *U. pugilator* (**1c**), lacks groove behind eye; carapace light tan. Major claw's inner palm is smooth; tubercles absent. *Size:* Carapace width to 1 in (25 mm); major claw to $1^5/_8$ in (4.1 cm). *Range:* Supratidal to intertidal sand; beaches or sandy flats (10-30 ppt).

Hermit crabs, *Pagurus* spp. (**2**), differ from true crabs (brachyurans) in that only the first 2 walking legs are well developed; the last pair are small and modified. Typically one claw is larger than the other on both sexes. Hermit crabs adopt bay shells as temporary homes but can change address at any time. **Long-clawed hermit crab**, *P. longicarpus* (**2a**), has a narrow major claw with a dark median stripe. *Size:* Carapace length to $^3/_8$ in (9 mm). *Range:* Intertidal to (mostly) subtidal; 10 ppt to marine. **Banded hermit crab**, *P. annulipes* (**2b**), has a hairy major claw. The walking legs (not shown) are banded with brownish rings. *Size:* Carapace length to $^1/_4$ in (6 mm). *Range:* Subtidal; 18 ppt to marine. **Broad-clawed hermit crab**, *P. pollicaris* (**2c**), has a broad, flat major claw covered with wartlike tubercles. *Size:* Carapace length to $1^1/_4$ in (3.1 cm). *Range:* Subtidal; 18 ppt to marine.

SHOREBIRDS of Chesapeake beaches

and tidal flats are dominated by migrant species that breed in Canadian marshes and tundra. There are, however, a few local breeders, most notably the American oystercatcher and some gulls and terns. In summer, one also finds a number of marsh breeders, for example the willet (p. 145), feeding on flats at the wetland edge. Like the transient species, these birds are attracted to the abundant invertebrates of the intertidal zone. Bill types suggest various adaptive feeding strategies. The oystercatcher pries open molluscs with its long flattened bill and can reach worms and clams buried in wet sand. Plovers have short bills and forage upon small invertebrates near or upon the surface. Sandpipers have longer bills for probing into mud flats, from which they glean crustaceans, molluscs, and worms. Gulls are scavengers and feed at the surface. Terns hover and dive for fish just offshore. Many shorebirds, such as the sanderling, *Calidris alba*, are more common on Atlantic beaches than inland along the Chesapeake Bay.

American oystercatcher, *Haematopus palliatus* (**a**), is a summer resident and transient on beaches and sand flats of the lower Bay. *Field marks:* A large shorebird with a long, vertically flattened, red bill. Note black head, dark brown back, and white belly. *Flight:* Look for white wing patches and rump. *Size:* to 21 in (53 cm). *Call:* A shrill "kleep." *Season:* Mostly spring-fall; uncommon winter visitor; highly local breeder (Tangier Sound); local to common breeder on Atlantic Coast sandy beaches.

PLOVERS (Charadriidae)

Semipalmated plover, *Charadrius semi-palmatus* (**b**), is a common transient along the tidal flats of salt marshes and sandy beaches. *Field marks:* A small brown-backed plover. In winter plumage, breast band is dull brown. Legs are yellowish. *Size:* to 7½ in (19 cm). *Call:* A clear, rising "too-wee." *Season:* Mostly spring and fall; uncommon in summer and winter. Nonbreeder.

Black-bellied plover, *Pluvialis squatarola* (**c**), is a common transient and winter resident of tidal flats in the lower Bay. *Field marks:* A large, stocky plover. Note short pigeonlike bill. In winter plumage, black belly is lacking; upper body gray, belly slightly streaked. *Flight:* Look for black "wing pits" (axillars). *Size:* to 13½ in (34 cm). *Call:* A slurred whistle: "wee-er-eee." *Season:* Mostly fall and spring; less common in winter; uncommon in summer. Nonbreeder.

SANDPIPERS AND ALLIES (Scolopacidae)

Greater yellowlegs, *Tringa melanoleuca* (**a**), is a common transient of tidal wetlands and associated mud flats. *Field marks:* A large, slender gray sandpiper with yellow legs and a long, slightly upturned bill. Upper body is checkered with black and gray. *Flight:* Note white rump and dark wings, which lack stripe of **willet** (**b**). *Size:* to 14 in (36 cm). *Call:* Often 3 sharp notes: "whew-whew-whew." *Season:* Mostly spring and fall; uncommon in summer and winter. Nonbreeder. *Related species:* Lesser yellowlegs, *T. flavipes* (p. 112), is smaller; shorter, thinner, straight bill. Willet, *Catoptrophorus semipalmatus* (p. 145), is stockier; thick, straight bill; dark legs.

Dunlin, *Calidris alpina* (**c**), is a transient and winter resident of wetlands, mud flats, and beaches. *Field marks:* A gray-brown sandpiper. In winter, a gray wash covers the breast. Note slight droop at end of long, stout bill. *Size:* to 8½ in (22 cm). *Call:* A nasal "treep." *Season:* Fall-spring; rare in summer. Nonbreeder.

Least sandpiper, *Calidris minutilla* (**d**), is a common transient of tidal wetlands and associated mud flats. *Field marks:* The smallest of the smaller sandpipers, commonly called "peeps." Brown above with a streaked breast; yellowish legs; thin bill. *Size:* to 6 in (15 cm). *Call:* A high "kre-eep." *Season:* Spring and fall; uncommon and local in winter. Nonbreeder. *Related species:* **Semipalmated sandpiper,** *C. pusilla* (**e**), is grayer above with less streaking on breast; stouter bill; blackish legs.

OTHER MIGRANT SANDPIPERS of Chesapeake beaches and tidal flats:

Lesser yellowlegs, *Tringa flavipes*, p. 112
Solitary sandpiper, *T. solitaria*
Spotted sandpiper, *Actitis macularia*, p. 73
Ruddy turnstone, *Arenaria interpres*
Sanderling, *Calidris alba*
Western sandpiper, *C. mauri*
White-rumped sandpiper, *C. fuscicollis*
Pectoral sandpiper, *C. melanotos*
Purple sandpiper, *C. maritima*
Short-billed dowitcher, *Limnodromus griseus*

GULLS AND TERNS (Laridae)

Common tern, *Sterna hirundo* (**a**), is a common transient and summer resident of beaches and bays. *Field marks:* A midsized tern with dark wing tips and a black cap. Bill is reddish with black tip. *Flight:* Look for dark primaries and forked tail with dark outer edge. *Size:* Length to 16 in (40 cm); wingspan averages 31 in (79 cm). *Call:* A harsh "key-urrr" or "kick-kick-kick." *Season:* Spring-fall; rare in winter; very local breeder on Bay islands; locally common breeder on Atlantic Coast.

Laughing gull, *Larus atricilla* (**b**), is a common transient and summer resident of wetlands, beaches, and bays. *Field marks:* In summer, adult has black hood (absent in winter). *Flight:* Look for dark wings ending in black tips (see p. 196). *Size:* Length to 17 in (43 cm); wingspan averages 40 in (102 cm). *Call:* A laughing hah-hah-hah. *Season:* Spring-fall; rare in winter; local to common breeder in salt marshes of Atlantic Coast (Maryland and Virginia); post-breeding flocks move up tidal rivers.

Herring gull, *Larus argentatus* (**c**), is a common transient and winter resident, as well as a locally common summer resident, along tidal rivers and shores. *Field marks:* The familiar sea gull. Note gray mantle of adult. Yellow bill has red spot. *Flight:* Look for gray wings ending in black tips with white spots (see p. 196). *Size:* Length to 26 in (65 cm); wingspan averages 58 in (147 cm). *Call:* A loud "yuk-yuk-yuk" or "ga-ga-ga." *Season:* All year; less common in summer; local colonial breeder on Atlantic Coast and Bay islands near Tangier Sound.

Great black-backed gull, *Larus marinus* (**d**), is another common permanent resident of beaches, tidal rivers, and bays. *Field marks:* Our largest gull. Note the solid black back and wings (obvious at distance). Massive bill is yellow with red spot. *Flight:* Look for solid black wings (see p. 196). *Size:* Length to 31 in (78 cm); wingspan averages 65 in (165 cm). *Call:* A deep, harsh "cow-cow-cow." *Season:* All year; less common in summer; locally common breeder (Tangier Sound); local to uncommon nester on Atlantic Coast (Maryland and Virginia).

Shallow Water Habitats

SHALLOW waters are the site for much of the Chesapeake's remarkable productivity. On average, the Bay is 21 ft (6.4 m) deep. Moreover, much of the basin is covered by less than 10 ft (3 m) of water. These shoal areas border the shoreline of the Bay and extend hundreds of feet (in some cases, miles) to the edges of deepwater channels. Sunlight reaches the Bay floor at these shallow depths, permitting photosynthesis in both the water and benthos.

Shallow waters host 3 important plant communities—phytoplankton, benthic algae, and submersed aquatic vegetation (SAV). Nutrient-enriched shallows also receive detritus (decayed organic matter) from nearby marshes and tributaries. These 2 sources of organic material—living aquatic plants and detritus—provide the basis for estuarine food chains.

The high primary productivity allows several shallow-water communities to flourish. These communities form a continuum with intertidal and deep-water communities. The water column hosts swimming organisms (*nekton*), like the killifish and juvenile spot *at left*, and floating organisms (*plankton*). SAV communities support benthic organisms, both attached plants (*epiphytes*), such as diatoms, and crawling and attached animals (*epifauna*), such as snails and barnacles. Man-made structures such as pier pilings, bulkheads, and rock jetties also support epifaunal communities. Finally, the unvegetated benthic community is rich with worms, molluscs, and crustaceans living in (*infauna*) or on (*epifauna*) the sand or mud. The benthos also includes some specialized communities such as oyster beds, which range into deeper waters (see pp. 182-183).

Shallow waters may be defined as the subtidal zone (see fig. 11; p. 152) lying between mean low tide (MLT) and a depth of 9 or 10 ft (3 m), which, in the murky Chesapeake, is the limit of light penetration permitting the growth of rooted aquatic plants. The intertidal community, which is covered by a foot or more (0.3 m) of water at high tide, is sometimes defined as a special class (or extension) of the shallow-water benthos that is tolerant of temporary exposure to air (see pp. 151-156).

When exploring the shallow-water habitat, it is important to remember that the species composition of a given community will depend upon the salinity of the local waters. A wild celery bed at the Susquehanna Flats is dramatically different from an eelgrass community in Tangier Sound. Seagrass meadows in the lower Bay tend to harbor a greater diversity of fishes and invertebrates because of the influx of marine species. A review of the estuarine salinity zones will be helpful in identifying aquatic invertebrates and fishes (see fig. 3; p. 12).

While not as harsh a habitat as intertidal flats or marshes, shallow waters compose a volatile zone where inhabitants are exposed to environmental extremes. In summer, the sun can superheat the entire water column. Rain storms can flood shallows with fresh water, depressing the salinity and temperature, and clouding the water with brown silt. To survive, sessile invertebrates must be tolerant of a wide range of local salinities. Excessive siltation may be lethal.

The surface of the Bay sometimes offers clues to what is growing, stationed, or swimming underneath. The flower heads of submersed plants may stand above the water, showing the extent of underwater grass meadows. Barnacles on an old pier suggest that other fouling organisms (epifauna) lurk lower on the pilings. In spring, mullet jump above the surface, and silversides, anchovies, young menhaden, and minnows flash in the sunlight as they school close to the shore. In elevated shoal areas along the Bay (e.g., Seven Foot Knoll, Holland Bar, and Shark Fin Shoal), menhaden may ripple the surface like rainwater, enticing marauding bluefish into a feeding frenzy.

Also, at the surface, one finds a variety of wading and swimming birds that feed in the shallows. Egrets and herons feed on small fishes and invertebrates that reside in the underwater grasses. Marsh ducks, such as the black duck, tip up to feed. In fall and winter, diving ducks such as canvasbacks and redheads feed upon aquatic plants in morning and evening while spending midday in large rafts offshore in deeper water (see p. 193). Ducks and geese segregate in salinity zones depending upon food preferences. Redheads prefer wild celery and pondweeds in fresher waters; brant (p. 192) favor eelgrass in saltier bays.

In addition to serving as a haven for molting blue crabs and other vulnerable juveniles, submersed aquatic vegetation provides additional benefits to the estuary. The root and rhizomal systems of plants trap and stabilize bottom sediments while the stems and leaves retard wave action. SAV recycles nutrients and oxygenates the water. More importantly, SAV, like emergent vegetation, yields a vast quantity of detrital material that fuels the indirect energy pathway in the estuary. More directly, a great number of waterfowl and aquatic mammals (e.g., muskrats and nutria) feed upon SAV, one of the reasons for the Bay's winter population of ducks and geese.

SUBMERSED AQUATIC VEGETATION, or SAV, is one of the most

important plant communities in the Chesapeake watershed. Historically, the Chesapeake estuary, because of its shallow depth, has supported healthy populations of underwater plants. However, in the last few decades the Bay has experienced a drastic decline in acreage and local diversity of submersed aquatic species due to pollution, siltation, and excessive nutrients, the latter two resulting in *turbidity* (cloudiness) that cuts off essential sunlight from rooted beds. Submersed aquatic plants are defined as those flowering plants that grow primarily below the water surface. All of those discussed here (with the exception of coontail) are rooted. Three nonflowering algal species that attach with *holdfasts* rather than roots are also illustrated. Surprisingly, there are only about a dozen common submersed aquatics in the Bay. These are distributed in rivers and open Bay shallows according to their tolerances of salinity, depth, turbidity, sediments, wave action, and interspecific competition.

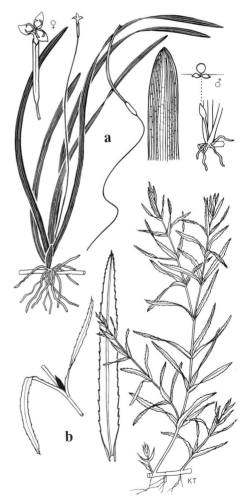

Wild celery, *Vallisneria americana* (**a**), a freshwater species, grows in rivers and the upper Bay into slightly brackish regions. *Basal leaves* are narrow and ribbonlike with fine veins and a light center stripe; up to 6 ft (1.8 m) long (though typically shorter); arising in small clusters from buried stems. *Stem* (white) is embedded horizontally in mud; rooted at intervals; *rhizomes* and tuberlike winter buds present. *Flowers* appear on separate plants: female flower solitary and floating at surface at end of long stalk (*peduncle*); male flower solitary, borne in sheathlike structure (*spathe*) on short submerged stalk, breaks off and rises to the surface at flowering; *bloom* July-September. *Fruit* is a cylindrical pod; up to 2 in (5 cm) long; attached to peduncle which coils in, drawing the fruit underwater when mature.

Southern naiad, *Najas guadalupensis* (**b**), grows in shallow, fresh to slightly brackish waters. *Leaves* are linear and finely toothed; oppositely arranged and clasping (at base) to stem; tapering to a fine point; up to 1 in (25 mm) long. *Stem* is multibranched, arising from a fibrous rooted base. *Flowers* are inconspicuous, arising in the axils of leaves and branches; males in upper axils, females in lower; *bloom* July-September. *Fruit* is cylindrical and purplish brown, containing a single pitted seed; one to each leaf or branch axil; up to ⅛ in (3 mm) long. *Related species:* Naiad, *N. minor*, has toothed leaves curving outward from stem; seeds ribbed lengthwise.

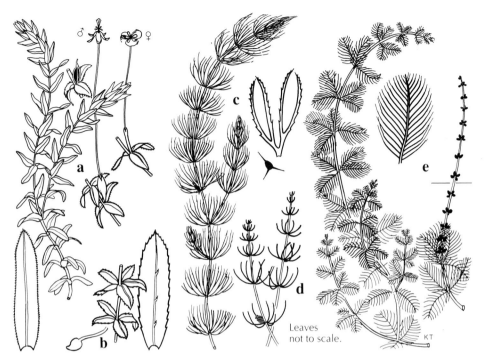

Leaves
not to scale.

Common waterweed, *Elodea canadensis* (**a**), grows in fresh to moderately brackish waters. *Leaves* are short, narrow, and finely serrated, ending in round or pointed tips; arranged in whorls of 2 or 3 and clasping (at base) to stem; typically drooping downward; up to ³/5 in (15 mm) long and ¹/5 in (5 mm) wide. *Stem* is multi-branched; arising from a horizontal, rooted base (stolon). *Flowers* appear on separate plants: male flowers are rare; female flowers more common, appearing (like males) on long stalks (pedicels) that arise from a tubular structure (*spathe*) in leaf axils; *bloom* July-September. *Fruit* is a several-seeded capsule typically in upper leaf axils. *Confusing species:* **Hydrilla,** *Hydrilla verticillata* (**b**), has 4-5 toothed leaves at each node, spines on leaf midrib, and fleshy tubers (shown). South American elodea, *Egeria densa*, has longer leaves arranged in whorls of 4-6. Both introduced; nuisance species.

Coontail, *Ceratophyllum demersum* (**c**), grows in fresh and slightly brackish waters. *Leaves* are compound (forked), dividing 2 or 3 times, the extremely narrow segments flat and finely toothed; arranged in whorls of 5-12 along stem, the whorls more crowded toward tip; up to 1¹/5 in (3 cm) long. *Stem* is multi-branched; flexible or stiff; free-floating (i.e., lacks roots). *Flowers* are inconspicuous; both males and females solitary and randomly placed in leaf axils; bloom July-August. *Fruit* (achene) is a dark brown nutlet with 3 spines; up to ¹/4 in (6 mm) long. *Confusing species:* **Muskgrass,** *Chara* sp. (**d**), an alga, has whorls of undivided leaves; reproductive (sporing) stage shown.

Eurasian water milfoil, *Myriophyllum spicatum* (**e**), grows in fresh to moderately brackish waters. *Leaves* are fan-shaped with featherlike segments; opposite or 4-whorled about stem; up to 1¹/2 in (4 cm) long. *Stem* is flexible and branched; the tip protrudes above surface at flowering; arises from rooted base; lower stems short. *Flowers* appear in whorls on spike above water surface; *bloom* July-August. *Fruit* is a 4-celled nutlike seed.

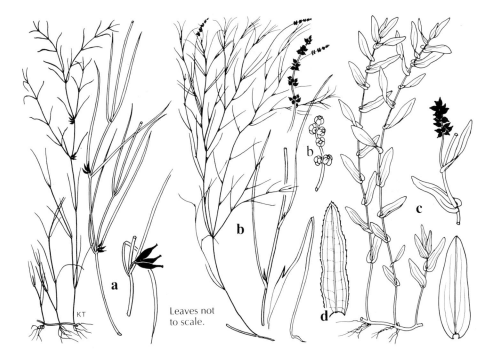

Leaves not to scale.

Horned pondweed, *Zannichellia palustris* (**a**), occurs in tidal fresh and brackish waters.

Leaves are linear and threadlike; paired (oppositely arranged) on stem; relatively short and sparse; up to 3 in (7.5 cm) long. *Stem* is very slender and branched, arising from a rooted base; often prostrate. *Flowers* are minute and enclosed in a sheath arising from leaf axils; *bloom* early (June-July). *Fruit* (achene) is a dark, oblong (crescent-shaped) nutlet. *Confusing species:* Southern naiad, *Najas guadalupensis* (p. 163), has shorter, wider (not threadlike), finely toothed, opposite leaves. Widgeon grass, *Ruppia maritima* (p. 166), has threadlike, alternate leaves.

Sago pondweed, *Potamogeton pectinatus* (**b**), grows in tidal fresh and brackish waters.

Leaves are linear (threadlike) with one central vein; tapering to a long point; alternate; up to 4 in (10 cm) long; bushy (i.e., densely clustered). Sheath at leaf base has delicate pointed tip. *Stem* is multibranched; arises from a rooted base. Long rhizomes often have tubers. *Flowers* are borne like beads in whorls of 2-5 on short spikes at end of stalks (*peduncles*) that are up to 4 in (10 cm)

long; *bloom* June-August. *Fruits* (achenes) are small, dark, blunt (unridged) nutlets with a pointed tip. *Related species:* Slender pondweed, *P. pusillus*, has linear leaves with small glands at unsheathed bases and 3-5 veins; seeds blunt (not ridged). Leafy pondweed, *P. foliosus*, has linear leaves with 3-5 veins; lacks glands at base; seeds ridged.

Redhead pondweed, *Potamogeton perfoliatus* (**c**), occurs in tidal fresh to moderately brackish waters.

Leaves are oval to oblong with rounded tips; alternately arranged and clasping (at base) on stem; up to 5 prominent veins; typically up to 1½ in (4 cm) long and ½ in (12.7 mm) wide. *Stem* (reddish or white) is slender and multibranched, arising from a rooted base; rhizomes extensive. *Flowers* are borne on densely crowded spike at end of long stalk (*peduncle*) that is up to 4¾ in (12 cm) long, rising above water surface; *bloom* June-August. *Fruit* (achene) is a dark, blunt nutlet with a pointed tip. *Related species:* **Curly pondweed**, *P. crispus* (**d**), has opposite, toothed leaves with wavy margins; introduced; native to Europe.

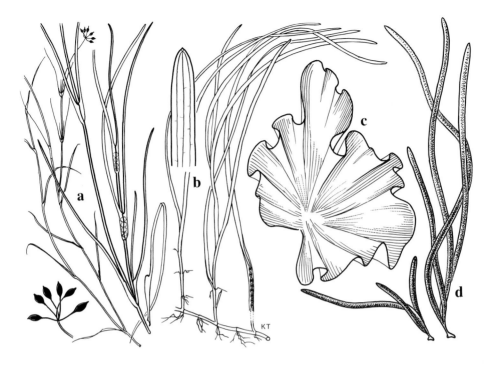

Widgeon grass, *Ruppia maritima* (**a**), grows in slightly to highly brackish waters. *Leaves* are linear (threadlike); alternately arranged with basal sheaths at stem with distinctive firm rounded tip; up to 4 in (10 cm) long. *Stem* is often branched; arises from a rooted base. Short zigzag rhizomes lack tubers. *Flowers* are borne in umbels on spikes at end of a long stalk, up to 12 in (30 cm) long, arising from the sheath at leaf base; *bloom* July-September. *Fruit* is pulpy, black; bears a single seed. *Confusing species:* Horned pondweed, *Zannichellia palustris* (p. 165), has opposite, threadlike leaves. Sago pondweed, *Potamogeton pectinatus* (p. 165), has pointed (not rounded) sheaths at leaf base; bushier.

Eelgrass, *Zostera marina* (**b**), grows in moderately brackish to marine waters. *Leaves* are linear and ribbonlike with 3-4 distinct veins; alternate; up to 3 ft (90 cm) long and 1/2 in (12.7 mm) wide. *Stem* is slender, often branched; arises from a rooted base. *Flowers* appear in rows, hidden in a sheath on side of leaf; *bloom* June-August. *Fruit* is a cylindrical seed.

GREEN ALGAE (Chlorophyta), or green seaweeds, are common in the Bay, often found washed up on the shore or growing in the shallows. Seaweeds lack the stem, leaves, and roots of higher plants, but have body parts with similar functions: leaflike *fronds*, or blades, and rootlike *holdfasts*.

Sea lettuce, *Ulva lactuca* (**c**), occurs in brackish and marine waters. At maturity the plant drifts freely in the water, but initially attaches to rock, shell, or pier via holdfast (see p. 168). *Frond* is a bright green sheet; translucent; lobed or wavy at edges. *Size:* up to 3 ft (90 cm).

Enteromorpha, *Enteromorpha* spp., are hollow green seaweeds, of which at least 11 species are found in the Chesapeake Bay. *Frond* is green and tubular; up to 1 ft (30 cm) or more long and 1 in (25 mm) wide. *Common species:* E. *intestinalis* (not shown) has single, unbranched fronds; air bubbles often apparent inside plant. E. *compressa* and others (**d**) have branches near holdfast. *Size:* up to 1 ft (30 cm) long.

AQUATIC INVERTEBRATES of the shallows are most numerous and diverse in the submersed grass communities of the Bay. These rooted aquatic beds provide shelter and food for countless crustaceans, molluscs, worms, and lesser animals such as bryozoans (Bryozoa). Blue crabs come here to molt. However, this is not the only subhabitat of the shallows. Pier pilings, rock jetties, oyster reefs, and the bottom substrate provide various anchoring and burrowing sites for epifaunal and infaunal communities. In the water column, planktonic forms typical of open waters also appear in the shallows (see p. 179). The community members vary according to the salinity of the local waters. In freshwater regions where wild celery thrives, one finds mostly freshwater invertebrates (see p. 64). In moderately brackish zones where redhead pondweed is common, a mixture of estuarine and marine invertebrates reign (p. 84). In highly brackish waters where eelgrass predominates, one finds higher diversity, mostly marine species such as in the scene *below.*

blue crab
(p. 182)

Not to scale.

KT

UNIVALVES (Gastropoda; Mollusca)

Variable bittium, *Diastoma varium* (**1**), uses its *radular teeth* to rasp diatoms and other epiphytes from the surface of eelgrass. Note the raised rib (*varix*) on upper side of shell. *Size:* to $^1/_5$ in (5 mm). *Range:* 10 ppt to marine.

Convex slipper shell, *Crepidula convexa* (**2**), has a distinctive cup-shaped shell with a shelflike platform underneath, covering one-third of aperture. *Size:* to $^1/_3$ in (8 mm) on eelgrass. *Range:* 10 ppt to marine.

CRUSTACEANS (Crustacea; Arthropoda)

Eelgrass isopod, *Paracerceis caudata* (**3**), has a flattened, segmented body and a pair of appendages (*uropods*) at end of abdomen. *Size:* Females to $^1/_2$ in (12 mm); males to $^1/_4$ in (6 mm). *Range:* 10 ppt to marine.

Tube-building amphipod, *Ampithoe longimana* (**4**), builds a weblike tube at base of eelgrass. It has black eyes and long antennae. Amphipods have bodies flattened from side to side. *Size:* to $^1/_2$ in (12 mm). *Range:* 5 to 30 ppt.

Common grass shrimp, *Palaemonetes pugio* (**5**), has a strongly toothed, pointed *rostrum*; only 1 tooth on crest behind eye. Second claw is larger than first. *Size:* to $1^1/_2$ in (3.8 cm). *Range:* 0.5 to 30 ppt. *Related species:* Freshwater grass shrimp, *P. paludosus* (p. 64), has carpus (first joint above claw) on second leg much longer than claw itself; 0 to 5 ppt.

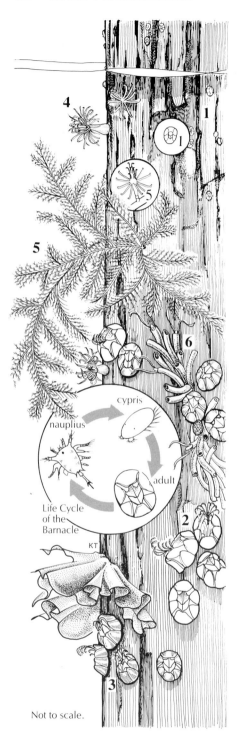

cypris

nauplius

adult

Life Cycle
of the
Barnacle

KT

Not to scale.

BARNACLES (Cirripedia; Crustacea) are perhaps the best-known *epifauna* (i.e., fouling organisms) of pier pilings. Barnacles also adhere to plants, rocks, and shells in intertidal (p. 139) and subtidal (p. 167) habitats. The barnacle shell has a trapdoor opening consisting of 2 plate pairs: the larger plates (*scuta*) overlap the smaller plates (*terga*).

Little gray barnacle, *Chthamalus fragilis* (**1**), is a small, dull white to gray barnacle of the upper intertidal zone. The floor (*basis*) of the barnacle is membranous. *Size:* up to $^3/_8$ in (9 mm). *Range:* 10 ppt to marine.

Ivory barnacle, *Balanus eburneus* (**2**), is a large white barnacle of lower intertidal and subtidal waters. The smooth plates are widely spaced. Scuta are grooved lengthwise. Basis is hard (not membranous). *Size:* up to 1 in (25 mm). Estuarine. *Range:* 5 to 30 ppt.

Bay barnacle, *Balanus improvisus* (**3**), is the most common estuarine barnacle below the intertidal zone. Plates are narrowly spaced. Scuta smooth (not grooved). Basis hard (not membranous). *Size:* up to $^1/_2$ in (12 mm). *Range:* Subtidal; 0.5 to 30 ppt.

OTHER EPIFAUNA of pier pilings include:

Ghost anemone, *Diadumene leucolena* (**4**), a translucent whitish to pinkish white anthozoan (Anthozoa). Typically 40-60 tentacles. *Size:* up to $1^1/_2$ in (3.8 cm) tall; $^1/_2$ in (12 mm) wide. *Range:* Intertidal to subtidal; 5 to 30 ppt.

Feather hydroid, *Halocordyle disticha* (**5**), is a colonial, branching hydrozoan (Hydrozoa). The individual *zooids* on the branches consist of a stem (pedicel) and flowerlike *hydranth* (see enlargement). *Size:* Colony to 6 in (15 cm). *Range:* Intertidal to subtidal; 5 to 30 ppt.

Whip mud worm, *Polydora ligni* (**6**), a sedentary bristle worm (Polychaeta; Annelida), constructs a soft, mud-covered tube from which it extends a pair of long palps for feeding. *Size:* up to 1 in (25 mm). *Range:* Mostly subtidal (including oyster beds); 0.5 ppt to marine.

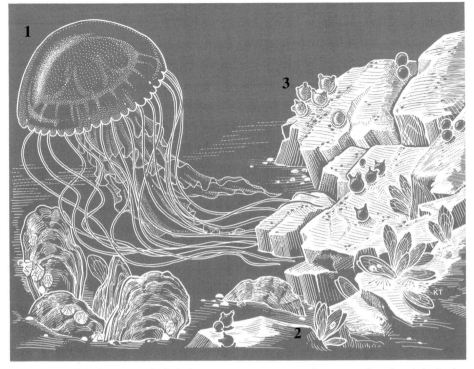

PLANKTON of shallow waters include the same zooplankton and macrozooplankton of deep, open waters (see p. 179). The pelagic larvae (*meroplankton*) of many shallow-water invertebrates, including snails, oysters, worms, barnacles, shrimps, and crabs, are also planktonic at certain times of the year. Among the macrozooplankton, the best known in shallow waters are the notorious jellyfishes (Scyphozoa; Cnidaria).

Sea nettle, *Chrysaora quinquecirrha* (**1**), is the common nemesis of the Bay swimmer. The adult *medusa* has 2 forms: estuarine and marine. The marine form is larger and pinkish with up to 40 tentacles. The estuarine form, appearing in the Chesapeake Bay during May-October, is half as large, milky white, with up to 24 tentacles that originate from marginal clefts in the bell. The stinging cells (*nematocysts*) on tentacles are responsible for painful welts on contact with human skin (see p. 181). *Size:* Estuarine form to 4 in (10 cm) across. *Range:* 5 to 30 ppt.

EPIFAUNA of oyster reefs and rock jetties include many of the subtidal forms that attach to pier pilings. Also see pp. 182-183.

Bent mussel, *Ischadium recurvum* (**2**), is a bivalve (Pelecypoda; Mollusca). Note the flat, hooked shell with many strongly curved, radiating ribs. Mussels spin a *byssus* (threads of protein secreted by the foot) that anchors the shell to hard substrates. Though *sessile*, mussels can move slowly by abandoning an old byssus and casting a new one farther away. *Size:* up to 1½ in (38 mm). *Range:* Intertidal to (mostly) subtidal; 5 ppt to marine. *Confusing species:* Atlantic ribbed mussel, *Geukensia demissa* (p. 140), an intertidal species, has straight ribs; 10 to 30 ppt.

Sea squirt, *Molgula manhattensis* (**3**), or sea grape, a *sessile* tunicate (Ascidiacea; Urochordata), has a globular *test* with 2 siphons. Test is semitransparent, but often covered with encrusting debris. *Size:* to 1⅜ in (3.4 cm). *Range:* Intertidal to subtidal; 10 ppt to marine.

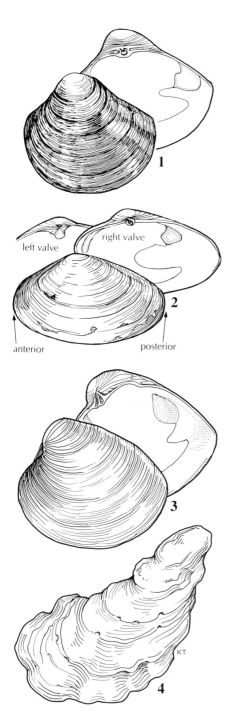

left valve

right valve

anterior

posterior

BIVALVES (Pelecypoda; Mollusca) have 2 valves forming the shell. The valves are kept shut by adductor muscles, the position of which is often marked in empty shells by a purplish scar. The anterior (front) end is where the foot protrudes; the posterior (rear) end is where the siphons extend, marked on an empty shell by a U-shaped *pallial sinus.* Also see p. 155.

Brackish-water clam, *Rangia cuneata*

(**1**), a member of the Mactridae, has a thick shell. Exterior is rough; white with a grayish brown paper-thin covering (*periostracum*). Strong hinge bears an oval pocket (*chondrophore*) which holds a horny pad (*resilium*) that keeps the valve agape. *Size:* to 2 in (5 cm). *Range:* Intertidal to subtidal; 0.5 to 10 ppt. Edible but rarely harvested.

Soft-shelled clam, *Mya arenaria* (**2**), is

distinguished by a leathery tube that encases its extremely long, retractable siphons (p. 155). White shell is elliptical. The left valve (*at far left*) has a spoonlike *chondrophore* and the right valve has a padlike *resilium,* which serves to keep the valves slightly ajar. *Size:* to 3 in (7.5 cm). *Range:* Intertidal to subtidal in sandy mud; 5 to 30 ppt.

Hard clam, *Mercenaria mercenaria* (**3**), has

a thick shell, bearing concentric growth lines on exterior. Heavy tan shell is egg- or heart-shaped. Interior is white with a deep purple stain. Hinge bears 3 white *cardinal teeth. Size:* up to 4 in (10 cm). *Range:* Intertidal to subtidal; 15 ppt to marine.

American oyster, *Crassostrea virginica*

(**4**), is a nonburrowing, edible bivalve (Ostreidae). The rough grayish shells vary greatly in shape depending upon environmental conditions. Upper (right-hand) valve is smaller and flatter than deeply cupped, lower (left) valve. At metamorphosis, oyster larvae cement themselves to rocks and other oysters, thus creating extensive beds or reefs (see p. 183). *Size:* to 4 in (10 cm). *Range:* Intertidal (mostly oceanside) to subtidal (mostly 8 to 35 ft; 2.4 to 10.6 m); 7 ppt to marine.

FISHES of the shallows consist mostly of estuarine and marine species. This habitat, especially when sheltered by SAV, supports huge fish populations. The shallows at the head of the Bay also host *freshwater species* such as the brown bullhead and white catfish (p. 66). At mid-Bay, the shallows of Eastern Bay, Tangier Sound, and other locales are important nursery areas for *marine species*, particularly the drums (p. 186), and *anadromous species* such as the striped bass (p. 85) and herrings and shads (pp. 65 and 185). The young of marine and anadromous species typically have shapes and markings different from those of adult forms patrolling deeper waters. This makes identification of marine juveniles difficult. Here, we look at mostly small estuarine species. Killifishes (Cyprinodontidae), such as the spotfin killifish (*Fundulus luciae*), frequent tidal guts in marshes and may become stranded in pools at low tide. Others, such as the pinfish (*Lagodon rhomboides*), prefer sea grass meadows. In winter, most of the shallow-water inhabitants migrate to channels or burrow into mud.

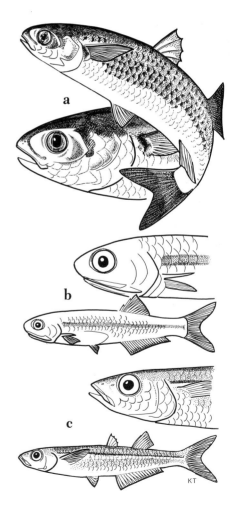

Striped mullet, *Mugil cephalus* (**a**), is a marine species that visits the brackish reaches of the Bay and rivers (down to 17 ppt). Swimming along the shore, schooling mullets leap in unison if disturbed. Dorsal fin has 4 weak spines. Pectoral fins are high on body with blotch at base. Greenish above, silvery body has 5-7 dark stripes. Eye partially covered by *adipose membrane. Size:* to 18 in (46 cm). *Related species:* White mullet, *M. curema*, lacks stripes and *adipose eyelids;* marine to 1 ppt.

Bay anchovy, *Anchoa mitchilli* (**b**), is an estuarine species, spending its entire life within the estuary. A small, translucent fish (4 in; 10 cm), it has a pale silvery body and a faint lateral band that fades after death. Large mouth extends behind rear margin of eye. Note single dorsal fin (like herring but situated farther back, opposite anal fin); tail deeply forked. *Related species:* Striped anchovy, *A. hepsetus*, has dorsal fin at midbody, forward of anal fin; stripe more distinct; estuarine.

Atlantic silverside, *Menidia menidia* (**c**), is estuarine. Two dorsal fins are widely separate. Greenish shading above reaches faint black line bordering a silver stripe. Tail is forked; anal fin edge straight. *Size:* to 5 1/2 in (14 cm). *Related species:* Tidewater silverside, *M. beryllina*, has strongly curved anal fin. Rough silverside, *Membras martinica*, prefers deeper waters; scales rough to the touch. Both estuarine.

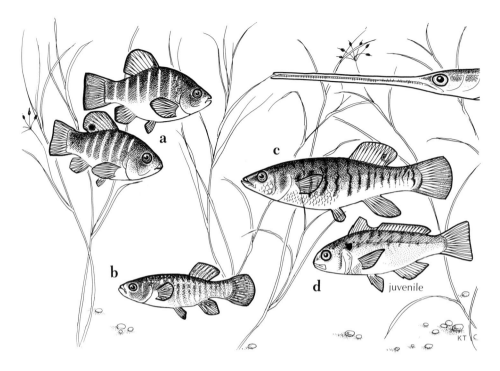

a

b

c

d juvenile

KT C

KILLIFISHES (Cyprinodontidae) are small, schooling fishes that are never far from shore. Also known as bull minnows, these estuarine fishes have robust bodies, a single, spineless dorsal fin, and a rounded or squared-off tail.

Sheepshead minnow, *Cyprinodon variegatus* (**a**),

is stout and deep-bodied; coloration variable with dark bars on sides. Tail has straight edge and, on males, ends in a black bar. Females have spot (ocellus) at rear of dorsal fin. *Size:* to 3 in (7.5 cm). *Range:* 0 to 32 ppt.

Mummichog, *Fundulus heteroclitus* (**b**),

is distinguished by its blunt snout; sides are marked with 13-15 alternating silver and dusky bars. *Size:* to 5 in (12.5 cm).

Striped killifish, *Fundulus majalis* (**c**),

is similar to mummichog but has a longer snout and darker markings. Female has 2-3 black stripes; male (shown) has 15-20 black vertical bars. *Size:* to 7 in (18 cm). *Related freshwater species:* Banded killifish, *F. diaphanus* (p. 68), is more slender; with pointed snout; freshwater to 20 ppt.

JUVENILE FISHES, such as the **spot** (*Leiostomus xanthurus*; **d**; also p. 186), are the dominant species in most shallow-water habitats. Grass beds and mud flats function as nurseries for a variety of immature forms. Estuarine species such as the white perch (p. 85) and hogchoker, *Trinectes maculatus* (p. 189), forage here. Offspring of anadromous river herrings (p. 65), rockfish (p. 85), and shad (p. 185), and young elvers of the catadromous American eel (p. 65) pass through in large schools.

OTHER YOUNG MARINE FISHES of shallow waters:

Sandbar shark, *Carcharhinus plumbeus,* p. 184
Atlantic menhaden, *Brevoortia tyrannus,* p. 185
Black sea bass, *Centropristis striata,* p. 187
Bluefish, *Pomatomus saltatrix,* p. 185
Silver perch, *Bairdiella chrysoura*
Spotted seatrout, *Cynoscion nebulosus,* p. 186
Weakfish, *Cynoscion regalis,* p. 186
Atlantic croaker, *Micropogonias undulatus,* p. 186
Black drum, *Pogonias cromis,* p. 187
Red drum, *Sciaenops ocellatus,* p. 187
Summer flounder, *Paralichthys dentatus,* p. 189

OTHER FORAGERS of the shallows, besides adult carnivores such as striped bass, bluefish, and drums, include the following species that favor grass flats. Also see naked goby, *Gobiosoma bosci* (p. 188).

Atlantic needlefish, *Strongylura marina* (**a**), gets its name from its long, slender jaws, used to catch small fish. Greenish above, the sides are silvery with a narrow lateral band extending to tail. A single dorsal fin is situated far back, near tail and above anal fin. *Range:* Marine to 0 ppt. *Size:* to 2 ft (61 cm). *Confusing species:* Halfbeak, *Hyporhamphus unifasciatus*, has long lower jaw; marine to 12 ppt.

Fourspine stickleback, *Apeltes quadracus* (**b**), is named for its 4 dorsal spines; the first 3 free, the last being attached to the soft dorsal fin. Body mottled with brown. Male builds nest of weeds. *Size:* to 2¹/₂ in (6.3 cm). Estuarine. *Range:* 3 to 26 ppt. *Related species:* Threespine stickleback, *Gasterosteus aculeatus*, has 3 dorsal spines, the first 2 free; anadromous.

Lined seahorse, *Hippocampus erectus* (**c**), a surprising Bay resident—though marine, invades the lower Chesapeake (down to 15 ppt), inhabiting grass flats in summer, deep channels in winter. A member of the pipefish family (Syngnathidae), it has a small mouth at the end of a long snout. Swims upright, as head is perpendicular to body. The tail is prehensile; lacks a caudal fin. Coloring is variable; changes with background. Female deposits eggs in pouch on belly of male, from which juveniles hatch. *Size:* to 5 in (13 cm).

Northern pipefish, *Syngnathus fuscus* (**d**), a relative of the seahorse, is estuarine, occupying the same seasonal habitats in the lower, but also the upper, Bay. Dark, mottled body is long and cylindrical, with a tubular snout (about equal in length to rest of head) and a long fan-shaped tail. Long dorsal fin at midbody. *Size:* to 10 in (25 cm). *Range:* 0 to 30 ppt. *Related species:* Dusky pipefish, *S. floridae*, has a snout longer than rest of head; shorter dorsal fin (set farther back); estuarine; lower Bay, 15 to 30 ppt.

WADERS AND WATER BIRDS of the shallows, like birds of marsh

habitats, can be divided into 2 groups: breeding species and migrants. Because of its position along the Atlantic flyway, the Chesapeake Bay and its shoals host more migrant species than natives. On these 2 pages are illustrated a few of the many transient and nesting birds that wade, swim, dive, or hover over the shallows. Representatives from 6 families are discussed. For detailed accounts of herons and egrets, see pp. 142-143. For other marsh ducks, see p. 110. For diving ducks, many of which feed upon SAV in shallows, see pp. 91-92 and 193-195. For gulls and terns, see pp. 159 and 196. Other shallow-water species include the brant (*Branta bernicla;* p. 192), which feeds upon eelgrass, and, at the mouth of the Bay, the black skimmer, *Rynchops niger,* and brown pelican, *Pelecanus occidentalis,* formerly an endangered species, now recovering with a northwardly expanding range. Cruising overhead throughout the Bay, ospreys (p. 111) hunt for fish.

webbed foot of cormorant for swimming

wading foot of egret (note long, slender toes that minimize sinking into mud, and middle toenail with comblike margin)

KT

Double-crested cormorant, *Phalacrocorax auritus* (**a**), a member of the cormorant family (Phalacrocoracidae), is a common transient of the shallows and open Bay. *Field marks:* A large black water bird with a long, hooktipped bill. Note orangish face and chin pouch. Crests are often not apparent. On pilings, cormorants may stand with wings "spread-eagle." *Size:* Length to 33 in (83 cm); wingspan averages 52 in (132 cm). *Call:* Silent outside breeding territory. *Feeding behavior:* Dives for fish and crustaceans. *Season:* Mostly spring and fall; uncommon in winter and summer. Nonbreeder.

Snowy egret, *Egretta thula* (**b**), a member of the bittern and heron family (Ardeidae), is a transient and summer resident of tidal wetlands and shallows. *Field marks:* A medium-sized, white heron with a slender black bill, black legs, and contrasting yellow feet. When breeding, recurved plumes adorn breast and back. *Size:* Length to 27 in (68 cm); wingspan averages 41 in (104 cm). *Call:* A low croak or, when breeding, a "woola-woola-woola." *Feeding behavior:* Stirs up prey with feet, then stabs into water with bill. *Season:* Spring-fall; very local breeder. Nests colonially in low shrubs or trees near water. Territorial. *Confusing species:* Cattle egret, *Bubulcus ibis,* an immigrant from Africa, has a short yellow bill; yellow legs and feet; smaller; typical of wet pastures, marshes, and fields; range expanding. Great egret, *Casmerodius albus* (p. 142), has yellow bill and black legs and feet; larger; typical of marshes and shallows.

Common tern, *Sterna hirundo* (**a**), a member of the gull and tern family (Laridae), is a common transient and summer resident of shallow bays. *Field marks:* Terns are distinguished from gulls (p. 196) by their pointed bills, forked tails, and feeding technique. Note dark wing tips, which distinguish this species from Forster's tern (p. 144). *Size:* to 16 in (40 cm). *Call:* A piercing "key-urrr." *Feeding behavior:* Terns hover over shallow water and plunge headfirst for fish. *Season:* Spring-fall; rare in winter; very local breeder on Bay islands; locally common nester on Atlantic Coast (Maryland and Virginia).

Pied-billed grebe, *Podilymbus podiceps* (**b**), a member of the grebe family (Podicipedidae), is a transient and winter resident of shallow bays, rivers, and marshes. *Field marks:* A small, brown ducklike bird with a chickenlike bill. Note black ring around bill and black throat (both absent in winter; areas turn white). *Size:* to 13$^1/_2$ in (34 cm). *Call:* A series of whistles: "kuk-kuk-kuk." *Feeding behavior:* Grebes dive after fish and invertebrates. *Season:* Fall-spring; uncommon in summer; rare breeder (status uncertain).

American coot, *Fulica americana* (**c**), a member of the rail family (Rallidae), is a transient and winter resident of shallow rivers, marshes, and bays. *Field marks:* A blackish, ducklike rail with a white bill. Note reddish brown forehead shield and 2 white patches under tail. *Size:* to 16 in (40 cm). *Call:* Short croaks ("kuk-kuk-kuk") and cackles ("ka-ka-ka-ka"). *Feeding behavior:* Dives after SAV, seeds, and invertebrates. *Season:* All year, but mostly spring and fall; less common in winter; rare in summer; local breeder (status uncertain).

American black duck, *Anas rubripes* (**d**), a member of the waterfowl family (Anatidae), is a transient and winter resident of tidal marshes and bays. *Field marks:* Body is dark brown, almost black at distance in contrast to pale brown head. Sexes similar, but female bill is mottled. *Flight:* White wing linings are distinctive. *Size:* Length to 25 in (63 cm); wingspan averages 36 in (92 cm). *Call:* Same as mallard. *Feeding behavior:* Tips up at surface to feed on seeds and SAV. *Season:* All year; less common in summer; local to common breeder. *Note:* Winter population declining along Chesapeake Bay.

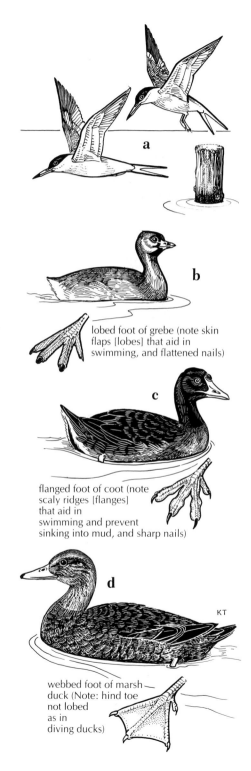

lobed foot of grebe (note skin flaps [lobes] that aid in swimming, and flattened nails)

flanged foot of coot (note scaly ridges [flanges] that aid in swimming and prevent sinking into mud, and sharp nails)

webbed foot of marsh duck (Note: hind toe not lobed as in diving ducks)

Deep, Open Water

THE open Chesapeake is a seasonal habitat: a summer haven for marine fishes and a winter refuge for migratory waterfowl. True estuarine species that remain in the basin year-round, such as the bay anchovies schooling *at left*, retreat to deepwater channels in winter when shallows turn frigid. In spring, they forage along channel edges and serve as prey for visiting bluefish and other large predatory fish that return from their Atlantic winter retreat.

The biannual migrations of marine and anadromous fishes into and out of the Bay are well known to fishermen. In all, 10 anadromous species migrate through the Bay to spawn in freshwater tributaries in early spring. In addition, 152 marine species may visit the estuary in summer as foraging adults or juveniles; most depart by autumn. Six marine species are regular visitors in winter. Only 27 estuarine species (and 2 marine species) are permanent residents.

The open Bay, varying between 4 and 30 miles wide, can be divided into shoal, or shallow, areas and deepwater habitats. Shallows less than 10 ft (3 m) deep hug the shoreline of the Bay and its tributaries. These subtidal shallows are contiguous with the intertidal zone and share many of the same species (see pp. 151-175). Shoulders, less than 30 ft (10 m) deep, are the next step down and border the edges of the main and tributary channels, which run deeper than 60 ft (20 m). The main channel, ancient riverbed of the Susquehanna, is over 100 ft (30 m) deep for much of its length. The deepest point of the Bay, off Bloody Point just south of Kent Island, is 174 ft (53 m). The shoulders, channel edges, channels, and deep holes constitute the deepwater zones of the Chesapeake Bay.

Deepwater habitats may be defined as subtidal waters (and benthos) below a depth of 10 ft (3 m), the approximate limit of colonization by submersed aquatic vegetation (SAV). The delineation between shallow and deep waters, however, is somewhat arbitrary. Typically, at depths between 6 and 10 ft (2-3 m), properties of the shallow-water zone, including superheating in summer, freezing in winter, light penetration, and the lower limit of intertidal species, give way to benthic conditions and communities typical of deeper waters.

Since these open waters are too deep for sunlight to reach the bottom, the only major plant community is phytoplankton, which forms the basis of the direct food chain. Detritus brought in by currents from SAV and emergent wetlands provides another (indirect) source of energy important to benthic organisms. Because of the high input of detritus in summer, benthic populations of a few species are enormous in the Chesapeake Bay.

Besides temperature and seasonal food availability, various other *limiting factors* influence the distribution and abundance of species in deep, open waters. As elsewhere in the wetland-estuarine system, salinity plays a major role. For definitions of salinity zones and seasonal isohalines, see fig. 3 (p. 12).

Two other important factors limiting species distributions in deep waters are oxygen and sediments. Deeper waters, particularly in summer when *thermoclines* retard mixing, may be low in oxygen (hypoxic) or devoid of oxygen (*anoxic*). Deepwater sediments are typically fine clayey silts, which do not support the same diversity of animals as do the coarser sandy muds of channel shoulders, shallow waters, and intertidal zones. Black carbonaceous muds in channel areas may actually be toxic to benthic life. These conditions, coupled with the anoxic overlying waters, account for the virtual absence of important species, such as the American oyster, in deepwater channels. In general, the diversity and numbers of invertebrates and fishes decrease with depth.

Aquatic animals may be divided into 3 major ecological or behavioral groups: *planktonic forms*, which as adults or larvae float passively in estuarine currents; *nektonic forms*, which are strong swimmers in open water (e.g., fishes); and *benthic forms*, which creep upon, burrow into, or are attached to the bottom. Creeping and attached benthos are termed *epifauna* and may crawl upon or anchor to hard surfaces such as rocks or wrecks, which are rare in deep waters, or oyster reefs, which are far more common at middle depths (8-35 ft; 2.4-10.6 m) but may exceed 50 ft (15.2 m). Burrowing organisms (*infauna*), such as tube-building worms (p. 154) and clams (pp. 155 and 170), are mostly limited to channel shoulders (and shallows), where oxygen is available and preferred sandy sediments are more prevalent.

The value of the estuary to commercial fisheries and associated industries exceeds $100 million annually. This provides an economic incentive to keep the Bay healthy. The recent decline of fisheries native to the Chesapeake, particularly the American shad and striped bass, is a warning signal that the estuary itself is in decline. The Bay nursery—haven for juvenile fishes and cradle for molting blue crabs and young oysters—is a fragile ecosystem in need of repair.

BAY PLANKTON AND INVERTEBRATES of open waters com-

prise mostly estuarine and marine forms. *Plankton* are free-floating (nonswimming) organisms and range in size from microscopic plants (*phytoplankton*) and animals (*zooplankton*) to very large (macroscopic) animals such as jellyfish. These larger, more mobile, pelagic invertebrates are called *macrozooplankton*. The planktonic larvae of swimming and sessile invertebrates, such as barnacle nauplii, crab megalopae, and oyster veligers, are collectively called *meroplankton*, which also includes the eggs and larvae of fishes. In addition to these 4 types of plankton, deepwater invertebrates fall into 2 other categories: *nekton*, or swimming (i.e., self-propelled) creatures such as the blue crab, and *benthic invertebrates*, or bottom dwellers, such as the oyster. Epifauna are benthic invertebrates that wander over or attach to hard surfaces. The oyster reef (p. 183) is a complex benthic community with a great deal of epifaunal growth.

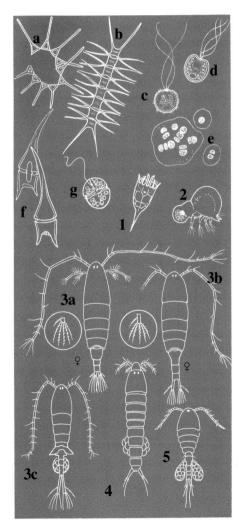

PHYTOPLANKTON (algae) are free-floating single-celled plants. Major groups include: **diatoms** (Bacillariophyceae; Chrysophyta), which consist of 2 types: pennate (Pennales) such as *Asterionella* sp. (**a**), which have rod-shaped (linear) cells (in this case united into chains), and centric (Centrales), such as *Chaetoceros* sp. (**b**), which have circular or elliptical cells; **golden-brown algae** (Chrysophyceae; Chrysophyta), such as *Chrysochromulina* sp. (**c**); **green algae** (Chlorophyta), such as *Carteria* sp. (**d**); **blue-green algae** (Cyanophyta), such as *Anacystis* sp. (**e**); and **dinoflagellates** (Pyrrophyta), which may produce a red tide during heavy blooms and consist of 2 types: armored (Peridiniales) such as *Ceratium* sp. (**f**), which bear plates, and naked (Gymnodiniales) such as *Gymnodinium* sp. (**g**), which have thinner cell walls.

ZOOPLANKTON are minute free-floating multicelled animals. Major groups include the **rotifers** (Rotifera) such as *Keratella* sp. (**1**), and crustaceans (Crustacea), including the ostracods (Ostracoda), **water fleas** (Cladocera) such as *Podon* sp. (**2**), and **copepods** (Copepoda), which can be the most abundant animals in the estuary. The following 5 copepod species make up 95 percent of the biomass: the **calanoids** (Calanoida)—*Acartia tonsa* (**3a**), *A. hudsonica* (formerly *A. clausi*; **3b**), and *Eurytemora affinis* (**3c**); the **harpacticoid** (Harpacticoida)—*Scottolana canadensis* (**4**); and the **cyclopoid** (Cyclopoida)—*Oithona colcarva* (**5**). Females are shown, the latter 3 with characteristic egg sacs, either single or paired.

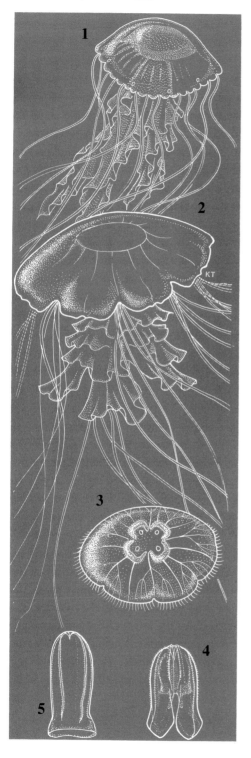

MACROZOOPLANKTON are large, relatively mobile members of the plankton.

True jellyfishes (Scyphozoa; Cnidaria) have tentacles that bear stinging cells (*nematocysts*). All species have alternating polypoid and medusoid generations (see Life Cycle; *opposite page*). Medusae are shown *at left*.

Sea nettle, *Chrysaora quinquecirrha* (**1**), is abundant in the mid- to lower Bay in summer. The bell, or *medusa*, is typically milky white. Up to 24 tentacles arise from marginal clefts in the bell. *Size:* Estuarine form to 4 in (10 cm) wide. *Range* (estuarine form): 5 to 30 ppt.

Winter jellyfish, *Cyanea capillata* (**2**), are not present as medusae during the summer season. This large jellyfish has a broad flattish bell with 8 primary lobes and tentacle clusters. Color is typically orangish brown. *Size:* locally to 8 in (20 cm) wide. *Range:* 5 to 30 ppt. *Note:* Ephyrae typically appear in late November or early December; medusae disappear in May or June.

Moon jellyfish, *Aurelia aurita* (**3**), has 4 pinkish (or white) horseshoe-shaped gonads on top of translucent bell. The short marginal tentacles are fringelike and numerous, up to 30 or more per lobe (octant). *Size:* to 10 in (25 cm) across bell. *Range:* 10 to 30 ppt. *Note:* Seasonal occurrence is similar to the sea nettle.

Comb jellies (Ctenophora) lack nematocysts and sessile polypoid stage. Characterized by 8 rows of ciliary plates, called combs.

Sea walnut, *Mnemiopsis leidyi* (**4**), commonly occurs in huge swarms. The oval body has 2 lobes which exceed main body length. *Size:* to 4 in (10 cm). *Range:* 4 ppt to marine (year-round). *Note:* When disturbed, a green luminescence flashes along combs.

Pink comb jelly, *Beroe ovata* (**5**), has a saclike body; lacks lobes and tentacles. Color is typically pinkish or reddish brown. *Size:* to 4½ in (11.2 cm). *Range:* 10 to 30 ppt (late summer-fall). *Note:* A predator of the sea walnut.

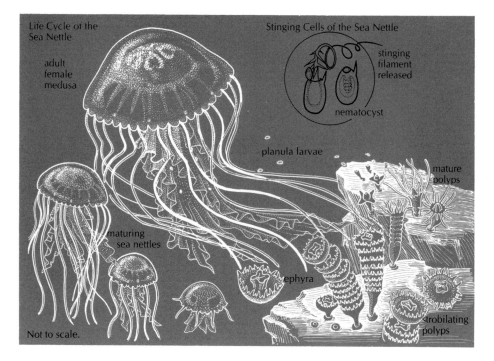

Life Cycle of the Sea Nettle

adult female medusa

maturing sea nettles

planula larvae

ephyra

Not to scale.

Stinging Cells of the Sea Nettle

stinging filament released

nematocyst

mature polyps

strobilating polyps

LIFE CYCLE of the sea nettle

Young sea nettles, called *ephyrae*, appear in the Chesapeake Bay in late April or early May and rapidly mature into adult *medusae*. By midsummer, 4 gonads (shaped like tiny horseshoes) are visible in both sexes through the transparent bell of the adult. Female gonads (shown) are dark olive; male's are mostly pink. Females pump water and sperm (released by the males) into the bell where eggs are fertilized. Tiny ciliated larvae, called *planulae*, are then released into the water. After a few days in the plankton, the planulae attach to a hard surface (e.g., rock or oyster shell) in brackish water (7 to 25 ppt) and develop into *polyps*, up to $5/8$ in (16 mm) tall, which overwinter, sometimes as cysts. In spring, the white or salmon-colored polyps produce tiny saucerlike buds, about $1/16$ in (1.6 mm) wide, which become *ephyrae*. After tripling in size, ephyrae develop tentacles and mature. Medusae usually disappear in September, though may last into November.

STINGING CELLS of the sea nettle

The tentacles of all true jellyfishes are armed with hundreds of stinging cells, called *nematocysts*, which are used to stun and capture prey. These venomous cells contain a coiled barbed tube, which—when triggered—shoots outward, injecting a toxin into the victim.

GLOSSARY OF TERMS (Phylum Cnidaria)

Ephyra (plural ephyrae)—The juvenile stage of true jellyfish; to $3/16$ in (5 mm).

Medusa (plural medusae)—The free-floating sexually reproductive stage of jellyfish.

Nematocyst—The stinging cell of jellyfish and other cnidarians (Cnidaria).

Planula (plural planulae)—The microscopic larvae of cnidarians.

Polyp—The asexual stage of anemones (Anthozoa) and jellyfish (Scyphozoa); a sessile column with a ring of tentacles.

Strobilization, strobilating—The asexual process by which polyps produce ephyrae.

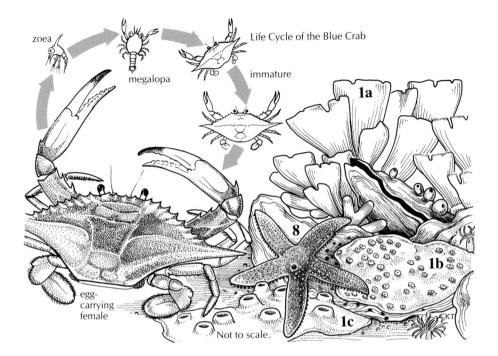

Life Cycle of the Blue Crab

zoea

megalopa

immature

egg-carrying female

Not to scale.

1a

8

1b

1c

KT

NEKTON is the community of large, actively swimming organisms, mostly fishes. The "beautiful swimmer" *Callinectes* feeds primarily in the benthos but migrates within the nekton.

Blue crab, *Callinectes sapidus (above)*, is the best-known crustacean in the Chesapeake Bay. The width of the shell (*carapace*) is characteristically more than twice its length. Note the strong, blue, front claws (tips are red on female) and rear paddle-shaped swimming legs. Behind each eye, 9 marginal teeth end in a strong spine. Typically bluish green or olive above and white below. The male abdomen (apron) is strongly tapered (like an inverted T); adult female apron is broadly rounded; immature female apron is triangular. *Size:* to 9 in (22.5 cm) wide. *Range (adult):* Subtidal, to at least 120 ft (36 m); 0 ppt to marine.

LIFE CYCLE of the blue crab includes 5 major stages: egg, *zoea, megalopa*, immature, and adult (*at upper left*). Adults molt throughout their 3-year lifespan. Females swim to the mouth of the Bay and release up to 2 million zoeae. For migratory pattern, see p. 202.

BENTHIC INVERTEBRATES of oyster beds (bars) range from the primitive sponges (Porifera) to the advanced sea squirts (Ascidiacea; Urochordata; see p. 169).

Redbeard sponge, *Microciona prolifera* (**1a**), varies greatly in color and shape, often bearing branches (as shown). *Size:* to 8 in (20 cm) tall. *Range:* Intertidal to subtidal (also on pier pilings); 10 ppt to marine. *Related species:* **Boring sponge,** *Cliona* sp. (**1b**), bores holes in oysters, leaving "pockmarks" on host; to $^1/_{16}$ in (1.5 mm) tall; subtidal (on shells); 5 ppt to marine. **Volcano sponge,** *Haliclona* sp. (**1c**), has large excurrent pores on raised "chimneys"; to 1 in (25 mm) tall; intertidal to subtidal; 10 ppt to marine.

Bryozoan, *Membranipora tenuis* (**2**), is a *sessile* colonial animal (Bryozoa) that is common on oysters. *Range:* 6 ppt to marine.

Oyster flatworm, *Stylochus ellipticus* (**3**), a nonsegmented worm (Platyhelminthes), preys on oysters and barnacles. *Size:* to 1 in (25 mm). *Range:* 10 ppt to marine.

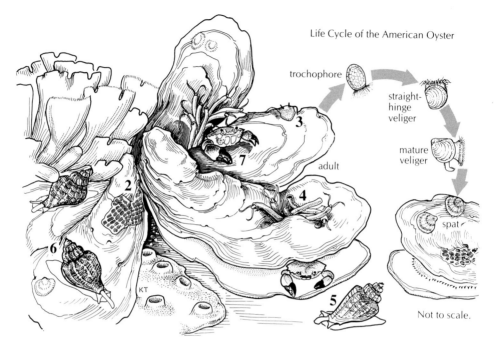

Life Cycle of the American Oyster

trochophore

straight-hinge veliger

mature veliger

adult

spat

Not to scale.

Whip mud worm, *Polydora ligni* (**4**), attaches to the *outside* of oyster shells and pier pilings; see p. 168. *Related species:* Oyster mud worm, *P. websteri,* resides *inside* living oysters; 5 ppt to marine.

Thick-lipped oyster drill, *Eupleura caudata* (**5**), a predatory snail (Purpurinae; Gastropoda), has a narrow, tubular siphonal (anterior) canal where proboscis extends to bore hole in oyster. *Size:* to ³/₄ in (19 mm). *Range:* 20 ppt to marine. *Related species:* **Atlantic oyster drill**, *Urosalpinx cinerea* (**6**), has a flaring (nontubular) anterior canal and a longer, more pointed spire; to 1 in (25 mm); 15 ppt to marine.

Black-fingered mud crab, *Panopeus herbstii* (**7**), is a typical mud crab (Xanthidae). Note large tooth on finger of major black-tipped claw. *Size:* to 1¹/₂ in (3.8 cm). *Range:* Mostly subtidal (on oysters); 5 ppt to marine.

Atlantic starfish, *Asterias forbesi* (**8**), is the only common sea star (Asteriidae; Echinodermata) in the lower Bay. *Size:* to 5 in (12.7 cm). *Range:* 20 ppt to marine.

American oyster, *Crassostrea virginica,* in the Chesapeake Bay colonizes mostly subtidal waters, up to 35 ft (11 m) deep. The live adult oyster (*at upper right*) is feeding, its valves agape, allowing water to be drawn over the gills. Oysters vary greatly in size and shape, depending on depth and substrate. *Range:* 7 ppt to marine. *Note:* In addition to being the object of predation by crabs, starfish, and oyster drills, adult and spat oysters are infected by 2 parasites that cause the diseases MSX and Dermo.

LIFE CYCLE of the American oyster follows the typical stages of most molluscs. The spawning of eggs by the female coincides with the release of free-swimming sperm by the male. The fertilized egg develops into a trochophore larva, which is meroplanktonic. The trochophore develops into a *veliger* stage, in which a straight hinge becomes apparent. The mature pediveliger extends a small foot, which is used to locate a suitable hard substrate. Once attached to an old shell or rock, the juvenile, or *spat,* cements itself to the surface. After 3 years, the adult oyster reaches harvestable size (3 in; 7.5 cm long).

CHESAPEAKE FISHES consist of 4 distinct ecological groups: *freshwater species* (pp. 65-68), such as the channel catfish, limited mostly to tidal fresh and oligohaline (i.e., slightly brackish) waters in the upper Bay and tributaries; *estuarine species* (pp. 85 and 171-173) that live year-round in the estuary, such as the white perch (p. 85); *diadromous species* that spend their adult lives in either fresh or marine waters (catadromous and anadromous species, respectively) and spawn upon migration into the opposite regime, such as the American eel (p. 65) and blueback herring (p. 65); and *marine species*, including most of the fishes discussed here. Marine forms typically spawn in the ocean in spring, then invade the estuary to forage on small fishes and invertebrates. Fish migrations mark the change of seasons (see "Migratory Patterns and Life Cycles," pp. 201-203). The Chesapeake Bay is the most important nursery ground for commercial fisheries on the Atlantic Coast. More than 50 of the Bay's 287 fish species are commercially valuable.

a

b

KT

CARTILAGINOUS FISHES (Elasmobranchiomorphi). Sharks and rays are nonbony fishes that have skeletons made of cartilage. They are primitive, second only to lampreys and other jawless species (Agnatha) in the classification of present-day fishes.

Sandbar shark, *Carcharhinus plumbeus* (**a**), is the most common of several requiem sharks (Carcharhinidae) that frequent the Chesapeake in summer and fall. However, while many other visiting sharks are adults, nearly all sandbars seen here are juveniles; the lower Bay is a nursery for the species. Dark gray above and whitish below. Characterized by a ridge between two dorsal fins. First fin begins at point directly above the inner angle (axil) of pectoral fin. *Size:* Young average 2-3 ft (less than 1 m); adults to 8 ft (2.4 m). *Related species:* Bull shark, *C. leucas*, a summer visitor, lacks mid-dorsal ridge; dorsal fin originates ahead of pectoral axil.

Cownose ray, *Rhinoptera bonasus* (**b**), is one of several rays (Rajiformes) visiting the Bay in summer and fall (see p. 190). Like other eagle rays (Myliobatidae), the cownose "flies" through the water by flapping its long pectoral "wings." Brownish in color, it migrates into the Bay (down to 13 ppt) and into shallow waters to feed on clams and other molluscs. A venomous spine is located at tail base. The squarish snout has 2 lobes. *Size:* to about 3 ft (91 cm) across wings.

BONY FISHES (Osteichthyes). The balance of the fish species other than lampreys, sharks, and rays have well-developed jaws and bone in their skeletons. In open waters anadromous fishes (e.g., shad) migrate through the estuary, along with a variety of marine and estuarine forms.

American shad, *Alosa sapidissima* (**a**), is now drastically reduced in numbers because of dam construction, pollution, and overfishing. Like other herrings (Clupeidae), shad has a strongly compressed body, single dorsal fin (at midbody), deeply forked tail, and sawlike modified scales on belly. Body is bluish above and silvery below. Shoulder has large spot followed by several smaller ones; silvery patch on cheek is deeper than long. *Size:* to 30 in (76 cm). *Related species:* Hickory shad, *A. mediocris,* with mouth closed, has jutting lower jaw.

Atlantic menhaden, *Brevoortia tyrannus* (**b**), is distinguished from other herrings by its large head and pelvic fin that originates ahead of dorsal fin. Bluish green above, silver sides have numerous dark spots behind larger shoulder spot. *Size:* to 14 in (35 cm). Marine. *Note:* Schooling at surface, menhaden may attract gulls and bluefish.

Striped bass, *Morone saxatilis* (**c**), is a valuable sport and commercial species that has declined in recent years. The "rockfish" has two opercular spines and separate dorsal fins. Olive to bluish above, the species is named for the 7-9 stripes along its silvery sides; belly white. *Size:* Grows to 6 ft (1.8 m), but typically 20 in (50 cm) in the Bay. *Related species:* White perch, *Morone americana* (p. 85), lacks stripes; dorsal fins continuous. Estuarine.

Bluefish, *Pomatomus saltatrix* (**d**), is a voracious forager with razor sharp teeth. Built like a torpedo, the bluefish has 2 separate dorsal fins, the second one long, paralleling the anal fin below. Greenish blue above and silvery on sides, it is marked with a black blotch at base of pectoral fin. *Size:* Reaches 45 in (1.1 m). Marine.

Not to scale.

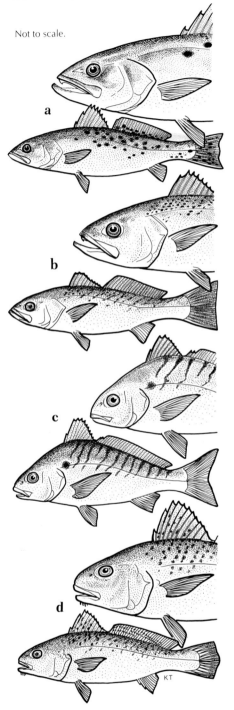

DRUMS (Sciaenidae) are able to make loud croaking or drumming noises by vibrating muscles that surround the air bladder. The next 6 marine species are well-known members of the family, distinguished by 2 separate dorsal fins (sometimes continuous, though deeply notched) and usually a rounded or pointed tail. Anal fin has 2 spines. All migrate offshore and south in winter.

Spotted seatrout, *Cynoscion nebulosus* (**a**), like the other drums shown here, is an important sport and commercial species. It is long and trout-shaped with a protruding lower jaw. Dark gray above and silvery below, the body has numerous black spots on sides, second dorsal fin, and tail. Young have a broad stripe along midbody and, like other drums, use the Bay as a nursery. *Size:* Adults reach 3 ft (91 cm).

Weakfish, *Cynoscion regalis* (**b**), with its pointed snout, resembles the seatrout but has smaller spots arranged in diagonal rows. Dark olive above, the sides are silvery and iridescent; belly silvery white. Like seatrout, it has 2 large canine teeth in upper jaw. *Size:* to 3 ft (91 cm). Name derives from ease with which fisherman's hook tears from mouth.

Spot, *Leiostomus xanthurus* (**c**), a ubiquitous Bay inhabitant, is the only drum in the region with a forked tail. Bluish gray above, the body is brassy and stout with 12-15 narrow diagonal lines on sides. Lower jaw is short (inferior); snout blunt. Named for the distinctive spot on shoulder. Young (p. 172) are elongate; lack fork on tail; mostly under 4 in (10 cm). *Size:* Adults reach 14 in (36 cm).

Atlantic croaker, *Micropogonias undulatus* (**d**), like the black drum, is distinguished by a row of *barbels* on its lower jaw. Bluish gray above and silvery below, the elongate body is marked by dark spots, forming irregular lines on upper sides and 1-3 horizontal rows on second dorsal fin. Second spine on anal fin is less than two-thirds as long as longest ray on fin. Lower jaw is inferior. *Size:* to 20 in (50 cm).

Red drum, *Sciaenops ocellatus* (**a**), also known as channel bass, is our only marine species with a spot (ocellus) at base of tail. Copper or reddish above, the sides are bronze or silvery gray and plain. Mouth large, extending beyond eye; however, lower jaw shorter than (inferior to) upper. Tail is rounded in young, but squared-off in adult. Body is elongate; ventral profile nearly straight. *Size:* to 5 ft (l.5 m). Runs in schools (spring and fall). Juvenile shown.

Black drum, *Pogonias cromis* (**b**), like the next 2 species, is a benthic species, foraging along the bottom on molluscs, crustaceans, and small fishes. The distinctive barbels are longer than those on the croaker (p. 186), as is the second anal spine, which is nearly the length of the longest *anal rays.* Body is deep and brassy (gray after death) with 4-5 broad black bars on sides (absent in older fish); ventral profile almost straight; dorsal profile arched. *Size:* to 4¼ ft (1.3 m). Juvenile shown.

SEA BASSES AND LIZARDFISH are benthic marine species.

Black sea bass, *Centropristis striata* (**c**), is a member of the sea bass family (Serranidae), distinguished from temperate basses (p. 85), by having 3 small, sharp spines on the gill cover and a long, continuous dorsal fin. Anal fin has 3 spines. Dark blue to black above, body is mottled with stripes and dark blotches. Dorsal fin is lined with dark bars and white stripes. Caudal (tail) fin is round or lobed; upper lobe elongate in adults. *Size:* to 2 ft (60 cm); usually half that size. Marine. *Range:* Adults patrol channels in lower Bay (down to 12 ppt).

Inshore lizardfish, *Synodus foetens* (**d**), is known for its sharp, needlelike teeth within its large, pointed jaws. Cylindrical body is olive above and white or yellowish below; marked with 8 diamondlike blotches on sides. Broad pelvic fins are used to "sit" on bottom muds. A small, fleshy *adipose fin* is located behind single dorsal fin. Tail is forked. *Size:* to 16 in (41 cm). Marine. *Range:* In summer and fall, lizardfish invade estuarine waters down to 12 ppt.

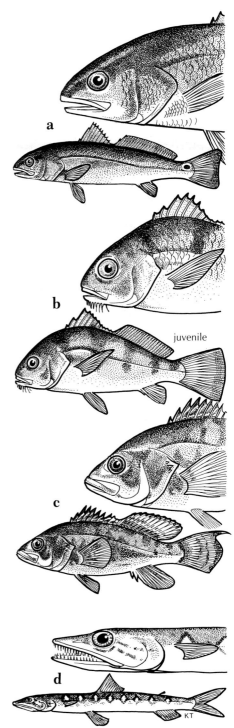

juvenile

KT

BENTHIC FISHES associated with oyster reefs include the next 4 estuarine species. All winter in deep channels.

Oyster toadfish, *Opsanus tau* (**a**), resides on oyster reefs and mud bottoms from spring through fall. The distinctive large head is flattened above; eyes are directed upward. Olivebrown above and pale below, the sides are marked with irregular dark blotches. The tail and pectoral fins are fanlike and streaked with bars; second dorsal and anal fins are long; first dorsal fin has sharp spines (erected when handled). *Size:* to 15 in (38 cm).

Skilletfish, *Gobiesox strumosus* (**b**), clings to oyster shells and other objects by means of a suction disk formed by highly modified pelvic fins (see bottom view *above*). Shaped like a skillet, the head is flattened and distinctly wider than body. Lacks the spiny first dorsal fin found in the larger toadfish, but other fins are similar in shape. Note dark band at base of caudal fin. Head and upper body olive-brown, marked with dark spots. *Size:* to 3 in (7.5 cm).

Striped blenny, *Chasmodes bosquianus* (**c**), is a stout, deep-bodied fish with a pointed snout and long continuous dorsal fin, attached to caudal (tail) fin by membrane on last ray. Anal fin is long but half the size of dorsal. Pelvic fin is reduced to 1 spine and a few soft rays. Brownish above, sides are marked with dark, wavy bands. Breeding male (shown) has blue spot at front of dorsal fin. *Size:* to 4 in (10 cm). *Related species:* Feather blenny, *Hypsoblennius hentzi*, has feathery crest on head.

Naked goby, *Gobiosoma bosci* (**d**), is a small, scaleless fish distinguished by 2 separate dorsal fins and a rounded tail. Prefers weed beds, shallow flats, and oyster reefs, where the males are territorial, guarding the nest. Greenish brown above and pale below, the body has 9-11 evenly spaced, vertical, light brown bars. *Size:* to 2½ in (6 cm). *Related species:* Seaboard goby, *G. ginsburgi*, has more widely spaced, irregular bars. Green goby, *Microgobius thalassinus*, is greenish blue; scales on rear of body.

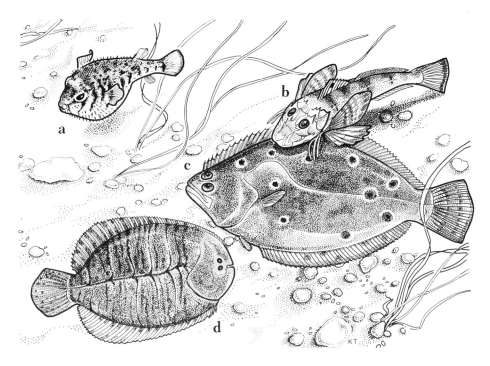

OTHER BENTHIC SPECIES common to deep-water habitats include puffers, searobins, and flounders. Like the black drum, sea bass, and lizardfish (p. 187), the next 3 species are marine and migrate offshore in winter.

Northern puffer, *Sphoeroides maculatus* (a), can rapidly inflate its body with air or water when frightened. Dark brown above and whitish below; yellowish sides are covered with short prickles and marked with tiny black spots and 6-8 vertical black bars; lacks pelvic and spinous dorsal fins. Not toxic like other puffers. *Size:* to 10 in (25 cm). *Confusing species:* Striped burrfish, *Chilomycterus schoepfi*, has rigid spines.

Northern searobin, *Prionotus carolinus* (b), is easily recognized by its broad, flat head, winglike pectoral fins (with 3 rays free—used for "walking" on bottom), and tapering body. The triangular, spinous dorsal fin has a black spot near edge. Body is mottled. *Size:* to 15 in (38 cm). *Related species:* Striped searobin, *P. evolans*, has 2 black stripes along body.

Summer flounder, *Paralichthys dentatus* (c), is a left-eyed flatfish (Bothidae)—both eyes appear on the left side of the head. Body is brown and variable, changing with color of substrate; white underneath. Various large spots present, but 5 always arranged in an X at rear of body, the middle one on *lateral line*, which is strongly arched toward head. Dorsal fin is long and continuous, beginning over eyes. *Size:* to 30 in (76 cm). *Confusing species:* Windowpane, *Scophthalmus aquosus*, has many smaller spots; front of dorsal fin forms crest. Winter flounder, *Pseudopleuronectes americanus* (Pleuronectidae), is right-eyed; *lateral line* straight.

Hogchoker, *Trinectes maculatus* (d), is a sole (Soleidae)—differing from flounders in having a rounded head and no pectoral fin; it is right-eyed. An estuarine species, the hogchoker is a year-round resident in rivers, shallows, and deep water. Eyes and mouth are small. Color is variable, with 6-8 dark bars crossing the straight lateral line. *Size:* to 6 in (15 cm).

OTHER FAIRLY COMMON marine and estuarine fishes of the open Bay:

Note: Many of the marine forms listed below only visit the highly brackish (polyhaline) lower Bay and do not penetrate into the moderately brackish (mesohaline) river mouths. Ecological regime, range, and seasonal occurrence are given in parentheses. *Key:* sp = spring, su = summer, f = fall, w = winter. After Wass *et al.* 1972

Sand tiger, *Odontaspis taurus* (marine; lower Bay; su/f)

Smooth dogfish, *Mustelus canis* (marine; lower Bay; su/f)

Spiny dogfish, *Squalus acanthias* (marine; lower Bay; f/w/sp)

Clearnose skate, *Raja eglanteria* (marine; lower Bay; su/f)

Southern stingray, *Dasyatis americana* (marine; lower Bay; su)

Atlantic stingray, *Dasyatis sabina* (marine; lower Bay; su/f)

Bluntnose stingray, *Dasyatis sayi* (marine; lower Bay; su/f)

Smooth butterfly ray, *Gymnura micrura* (marine; lower Bay; su/f)

Striped anchovy, *Anchoa hepsetus* (marine; mid/lower Bay; sp/su/f), p. 171

Bay anchovy, *Anchoa mitchilli* (estuarine; entire Bay), p. 171

Silver hake, *Merluccius bilinearis* (marine; lower Bay; f/w/sp)

Red hake, *Urophycis chuss* (marine; lower Bay; w/sp)

Spotted hake, *Urophycis regia* (marine; mid/lower Bay; w/sp)

Halfbeak, *Hyporhamphus unifasciatus* (marine; mid/lower Bay; su/f), p. 173

Atlantic needlefish, *Strongylura marina* (marine; entire Bay; su/f), p. 173

Rough silverside, *Membras martinica* (estuarine; entire Bay), p. 171

Tidewater silverside, *Menidia beryllina* (estuarine; entire Bay), p. 171

Atlantic silverside, *Menidia menidia* (estuarine; entire Bay), p. 171

Cobia, *Rachycentron canadum* (marine; lower Bay; su)

Blue runner, *Caranx crysos* (marine; lower Bay; su/f)

Crevalle jack, *Caranx hippos* (marine; lower Bay; su/f)

Bigeye scad, *Selar crumenophthalmus* (marine; lower Bay; su/f)

Atlantic moonfish, *Selene setapinnis* (marine; lower Bay; su/f)

Lookdown, *Selene vomer* (marine; mid/lower Bay; su/f)

Florida pompano, *Trachinotus carolinus* (marine; lower Bay; su/f)

Pigfish, *Orthopristis chrysoptera* (marine; lower Bay; sp/su/f)

Sheepshead, *Archosargus probatocephalus* (marine; lower Bay; su)

Scup, *Stenotomus chrysops* (marine; lower Bay; sp/su/f)

Silver perch, *Bairdiella chrysoura* (marine; entire Bay; sp/su/f)

Southern kingfish, *Menticirrhus americanus* (marine; lower Bay; su/f)

Northern kingfish, *Menticirrhus saxatilis* (marine; lower Bay; su/f)

Atlantic spadefish, *Chaetodipterus faber* (marine; lower Bay; su/f)

Tautog, *Tautoga onitis* (marine; lower Bay; f/w/sp)

Striped mullet, *Mugil cephalus* (marine; mid/lower Bay; su/f), p. 171

White mullet, *Mugil cerema* (marine; mid/lower Bay; su/f), p. 171

Northern stargazer, *Astroscopus guttatus* (marine; mid/lower Bay; all year)

Atlantic cutlassfish, *Trichiurus lepturus* (marine; mid/lower Bay; sp/su/f)

Little tunny, *Euthynnus alletteratus* (marine; mid/lower Bay; sp/su/f)

Atlantic bonito, *Sarda sarda* (marine; mid/lower Bay; sp/su/f)

Atlantic mackerel, *Scomber scombrus* (marine; lower Bay; f/w/sp)

King mackerel, *Scomberomorus cavalla (marine; mid/lower Bay; sp/su/f)*

Spanish mackerel, *Scomberomorus maculatus* (marine; lower Bay; sp/su/f)

Harvestfish, *Peprilus alepidotus* (marine; mid/lower Bay; su/f)

Butterfish, *Peprilus triacanthus* (marine; mid/lower Bay; sp/su/f)

Smallmouth flounder, *Etropus microstomus* (marine; lower Bay; all year)

Blackcheek tonguefish, *Symphurus plagiusa* (marine; mid/lower Bay; all year)

Orange filefish, *Aluterus schoepfi* (marine; mid/lower Bay; su)

Planehead filefish, *Monacanthus hispidus* (marine; lower Bay; su/f)

WATER BIRDS of the open Bay

WATER BIRDS of the open Bay are, for the most part, migrants from the far north. These include loons, grebes, and cormorants, and waterfowl that breed in Canada and the Great Lakes region, then depart, following the Atlantic flyway to winter along the Chesapeake Bay. Meanwhile, in summer the most common and widespread open-water species are perhaps the osprey (p. 146) and the laughing gull, which leave the Bay in autumn to winter farther south. In the estuary, more birds are found in sheltered bays and shallows than in open water. Diving ducks, while often "rafting" offshore, feed in shallows upon SAV, molluscs, and other invertebrates of rooted aquatic beds (see p. 161-167). Marsh ducks (p. 110), such as mallards and black ducks, typically swim and feed close to shore. Most oceanic (i.e., pelagic) birds wander far off the Atlantic Coast; however, some sea-going birds, such as Wilson's storm-petrel, *Oceanites oceanicus*, and the northern gannet, *Sula bassanus*, may be sighted at the mouth of the Bay.

PRIMITIVE DUCKLIKE BIRDS dive for food, mostly fish. All are silent in winter.

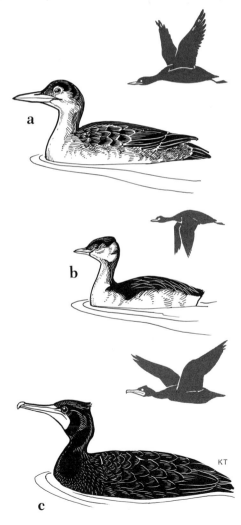

Common loon, *Gavia immer* (**a**), a member of the loon family (Gaviidae), is a common transient and winter resident of open bays and rivers. *Field marks:* A very large swimming bird with a long daggerlike bill. In winter plumage, this loon is distinctly dark above and whitish below. *Flight:* Head held lower than body; webbed feet trail. *Size:* Length to 36 in (90 cm); wingspan averages 58 in (147 cm). *Season:* Fall-spring; rare summer visitor. Nonbreeder.

Horned grebe, *Podiceps auritus* (**b**), a member of the grebe family (Podicipedidae), is a common transient and winter resident of lower rivers and open bays. *Field marks:* A small ducklike bird. In winter plumage, black cap and back contrast with white chin, throat, and belly. Note thin straight bill. *Flight:* Grebes fly with a sagging neck. *Size:* Length to 15 in (38 cm); wingspan averages 24 in (60 cm). *Season:* Fall-spring; rare summer visitor. Nonbreeder.

Double-crested cormorant, *Phalacrocorax auritus* (**c**), a member of the cormorant family (Phalacrocoracidae), is a common transient of the Bay and Atlantic Coast. *Field marks:* A large black water bird. Distinctive hooked bill is tilted upward while swimming. Note orange chin patch. *Flight:* Kink in neck is distinctive. *Size:* Length to 33 in (83 cm); wingspan averages 52 in (132 cm). *Season:* Mostly spring and fall, uncommon and local winter resident and summer visitor. Nonbreeder.

KT

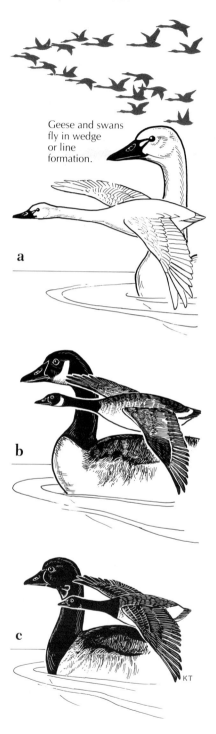

Geese and swans fly in wedge or line formation.

a

b

c

KT

WATERFOWL (Anatidae) include swans, geese, and ducks. Most (except the mergansers) differ from loons and grebes in having flattened bills that act as strainers.

Swans and Geese (Anserinae) are the largest waterfowl. Swans (Tribe Cygnini) are huge and have longer necks than geese (Tribe Anserini). On takeoff, swans and geese patter along the water surface. Swans "tip up" to feed on seeds and aquatic plants; geese primarily graze in fields. In flight, geese and swans form lines or wedges. Sexes are alike.

Tundra swan, *Cygnus columbianus* (**a**), is a transient and winter resident of open bays, rivers, and harvested fields. *Field marks:* Plumage is entirely white; black bill has a yellow basal spot. When swimming, holds neck straight and bill level. *Flight:* Look for white wings and extremely long neck. *Size:* Length to 53 in (133 cm); wingspan averages 80 in (203 cm). *Call:* High whooping or cooing: "woo-hoo, woo-hoo, woo-hoo." *Season:* Mostly spring and fall; less common in winter; rare summer visitor. Nonbreeder. *Related species:* Mute swan, *C. olor,* holds neck in an S-curve while swimming; orange bill with a black knob at base. Introduced.

Canada goose, *Branta canadensis* (**b**), is a common transient and winter resident of tidal rivers, fields, and open bays. *Field marks:* Plumage is dark brown with a white belly. Note long black neck and head, white "chin strap," and white U-shaped rump band. *Flight:* Look for long black neck and contrasting white chest in noisy flocks. *Size:* Length (variable) to 45 in (114 cm); wingspan averages (variable) to 68 in (173 cm). *Call:* Loud honking heard in flight. *Season:* Abundant spring and fall; common in winter; uncommon and local summer breeder. *Related species:* **Brant,** *B. bernicla* (**c**), more typical of highly brackish shallow water where it consumes eelgrass, is a transient and winter resident of the lower Chesapeake Bay. Field marks include solid black chest, head, and neck. Note white flecking on neck (adults only). A smaller, stockier goose. Size: Length to 26 in (65 cm); wingspan 46 in (117 cm) on average. Call: A soft "ronk." Irregular flocks. Nonbreeder.

Bay Ducks (Tribe Aythyini; Anatinae) differ from marsh ducks (p. 110) in that they dive for their food, mostly submersed aquatic vegetation, and patter along the surface when taking wing. Bay and sea ducks "raft" offshore in large congregations (see p. 195).

Canvasback, *Aythya valisineria* (**a**), formerly more common, is now a locally common transient and winter resident of brackish rivers and bays. *Field marks:* Note the long, sloping head profile of both sexes. Male (drake) head and neck are chestnut red. In the water, the canvas white body is bordered by black breast and tail. Female (hen) is a dull gray-brown. *Flight:* Look for drake (shown) with distinctive long profile, white back and belly, and black chest. *Size:* Length to 24 in (60 cm); wingspan averages 34 in (86 cm). *Call:* Drakes croak; hens quack. *Season:* Mostly spring and fall; less common in winter; rare summer visitor. Nonbreeder. *Note:* In the 1950s, approximately 250,000 canvasbacks wintered on the Bay, attracted in large part by the wild celery (SAV) beds at Susquehanna Flats (now diminished); currently, less than 70,000 overwinter, though sometimes in large rafts.

Redhead, *Aythya americana* (**b**), also formerly common, is a transient and uncommon winter resident on tidal rivers and bays. *Field marks:* Drake has a distinctive round (not sloping) reddish head; body is smoky gray; chest and tail black. Hen is brown. Bluish bill has white band next to black tip. *Flight:* Drake (shown) has gray wing stripe, gray back, and black chest. *Size:* Length to 23 in (58 cm); wingspan averages 33 in (84 cm). *Call:* Drakes have a deep purr or meow; hens have a loud "squak." *Season:* Mostly spring and fall; less common in winter; rare summer visitor. Nonbreeder.

Greater scaup, *Aythya marila* (**c**), is a transient and winter resident of brackish bays. *Field marks:* Note white midbody and black breast and tail "bookends." Drake has rounded head glossed with dark green. Brown female has white patch at base of bill. *Flight:* Look for long white wing stripe on male (shown). *Size:* Length to 20 in (50 cm); wingspan averages 31 in (79 cm). *Call:* Drakes whistle or call "scaup-scaup." *Season:* Spring and fall; less common in winter; rare in summer. Nonbreeder. *Related species:* Lesser scaup, *A. affinis* (p. 91).

Mergansers and Allies (Tribe Mergini) include the fish-eating mergansers and the diving sea ducks *below* and *opposite*. Sea ducks dive deeper than bay ducks, foraging mostly on molluscs and invertebrates.

Red-breasted merganser, *Mergus serrator* (**a**), is a common transient and winter resident of open bays. *Field marks:* Note the long, narrow bill adapted for seizing fish. Male has a crested, greenish black head and reddish brown breast, separated by a wide white "collar." Female has a crested rusty head and gray body. *Flight:* Note horizontal axis of body. Male (shown) has dark chest and white wing patches. *Size:* Length to 26 in (65 cm); wingspan averages 26 in (66 cm). *Call:* Silent. *Season:* Fall-spring; rare summer visitor. Nonbreeder. *Related species:* Common merganser, *M. merganser* (male), is entirely white below.

Oldsquaw, *Clangula hyemalis* (**b**), is a common transient and winter resident of open bays and lower tidal rivers. *Field marks:* The only sea duck with a white body and solid dark wings. Breeding and winter plumages are different. In winter plumage, male has white head with dark cheek patch; black chest; long needlelike tail. Female in winter has dark wings, white face, and gray breast. *Flight:* Look for white head and solid dark wings. *Size:* Length (male) to 22 in (56 cm), female to 16 in (41 cm); wingspan averages 30 in (76 cm). *Call:* Yodeling "oh-owdle-oh." *Season:* Fall-spring; rare summer visitor. Nonbreeder.

White-winged scoter, *Melanitta fusca* (**c**), is a common transient and winter resident of open bays and shores of the Chesapeake Bay. *Field marks:* Scoters are stocky black sea ducks. Male has a white "teardrop" below eye; orange bill with a black basal knob. Female has 2 light face patches (fading in older hens). *Flight:* Look for distinctive white wing patches; body black. *Size:* Length to 21 in (53 cm); wingspan averages 38 in (97 cm). *Call:* Typically silent. The whistling in flight emanates from wings. *Season:* Fall-spring; rare summer visitor. Nonbreeder. *Related species:* Black scoter, *M. nigra* (male), is entirely black. Surf scoter, *M. perspicillata* (male), has 1 or 2 white patches on forehead and nape.

Common goldeneye, *Bucephala clangula* (**a**), is a transient and winter resident of tidal rivers and bays. *Field marks:* Male has round white spot on face. Body plumage is white; dark head is glossed with green. Female has gray body and brown head, separated by white "collar"; dark bill with yellow tip. *Flight:* Note square white wing patches (male shown), large on both sexes. Wings make whistling sound. *Size:* Length to 20 in (50 cm); wingspan averages 31 in (79 cm). *Call:* Drakes have piercing "spear-spear"; hens a low quack. *Season:* Fall-spring; rare summer visitor. Nonbreeder.

Bufflehead, *Bucephala albeola* (**b**), is a small transient and winter resident of tidal rivers and bays. *Field marks:* Male has distinctive white "bonnet." Back is black; white underneath. Gray female has white spot behind eye. *Flight:* Smaller than goldeneye. Look for black-and-white body pattern and white wing patch (male shown); female wing patch is smaller. *Size:* Length to 15 in (38 cm); wingspan averages 24 in (60 cm). *Call:* Drakes squeak; hens quack weakly. *Season:* Fall-spring. Nonbreeder.

Stiff-tailed Ducks (Tribe Oxyurini) are small diving ducks with short necks like sea ducks. If alarmed, they dive (rather than fly), using tail as a rudder.

Ruddy duck, *Oxyura jamaicensis* (**c**), is a common transient and winter resident of tidal rivers and bays. *Field marks:* Male has white cheek patch; body is dull brown in fall. In winter, body of male is gray like female. Female has dark stripe on cheek. *Flight:* Look for dark wings and dark chest. On male (shown) look for white cheek patch. *Size:* Length to 16 in (40 cm); wingspan averages 23 in (58 cm). *Call:* Silent in winter. *Food:* Dives for insects, crustaceans, and aquatic plants. *Season:* Fall-spring; rare summer visitor. Nonbreeder.

Note: Most mergansers, sea ducks, and bay ducks run and patter on takeoff. Exceptions are the hooded merganser (p. 92) and bufflehead (*above*), which leap suddenly into the air like marsh ducks. All "raft" offshore in large winter flocks.

Diving ducks (bay and sea ducks) "raft" on water

. . . run and patter when taking wing.

KT

GULLS (Laridae) are long-winged swimming birds. Immatures are confusing. Sexes similar. *Feeding behavior:* Mostly scavengers, gulls alight on water to feed. Terns, members of the same family, dive for fish. Caspian tern (p. 93) is an open-water bird. Others are typically found close to shore (see p. 159).

Laughing gull, *Larus atricilla* (**a**), is a common summer resident and transient of open water and shallow bays. *Field marks:* Adult is a small black-hooded gull in summer. In winter plumage, white head is smudged with gray. *Flight:* Look for dark wings with black tips; white edge on rear of wing. *Size:* Length to 17 in (43 cm); wingspan averages 40 in (102 cm). *Call:* A laughing ha-ha-ha. *Season:* Spring-fall; rare in winter; breeds in salt marshes; postbreeding flocks move up tidal rivers.

Bonaparte's gull, *Larus philadelphia* (**b**), is a common transient near the coast and along lower tidal rivers and bays. *Field marks:* A petite, tern-sized gull. In winter plumage, adults have white head (black hood disappearing) and a black ear spot. Bill is small and black. *Flight:* Look for flashing white wedges on each wing tip. *Size:* Length to 13½ in (34 cm); wingspan averages 33 in (84 cm). *Call:* A nasal "cheer." *Season:* Mostly spring; less common in fall; uncommon in winter; rare in summer. Nonbreeder.

Herring gull, *Larus argentatus* (**c**), is a common permanent resident of beaches, open water, rivers, and bays. *Field marks:* Our commonest gull. Note gray mantle and black wing tips. Heavy yellow bill has red spot. In winter, head and body streaked with brown. *Flight:* Look for white spots on black wing tips. *Size:* Length to 26 in (65 cm); wingspan averages 58 in (147 cm). *Call:* Often a "ga-ga-ga." *Season:* All year; less common in summer than fall-spring.

Great black-backed gull, *Larus marinus* (**d**), is a common transient and winter resident of beaches and bays. *Field marks:* A large black-winged gull. Head and underparts are snowy white. *Flight:* Note black wings with trailing white edge. *Size:* Length to 31 in (78 cm); wingspan averages 65 in (165 cm). *Call:* A low, deep "cow-cow-cow." *Season:* All year; less common in summer.

Glossary

Achene A small dry, hard, 1-seeded nutlet.

Adipose eyelid A thick, transparent membrane covering part of the eye in some fishes.

Adipose fin A fleshy fin (without rays) between the dorsal and caudal fins in some fishes.

Alternate leaves Not opposite each other on branch or stem.

Amphipod A small crustacean belonging to the phylum Arthropoda, with a body compressed from side to side.

Anadromous Migrating from the ocean to breed in fresh water.

Anal fin The median, ventral fin between the pelvic and caudal fins.

Anal plate The scale covering the anus in snakes, which may be divided or single according to species.

Anal ray One of the soft supporting elements in an anal fin.

Annual plant: Its full life cycle is completed in one year or season; typically propagates by seeds.

Anoxic Lacking oxygen; also hypoxic.

Anterior Toward the front.

Anterior temporal scales On snakes, the first scale (or scales) behind the row of postocular scales behind the eye.

Associated species Organisms that sparsely inhabit a community which is typified by other, more dominant species.

Barbel A fleshy projection of the skin near the mouth (or chin) on some fishes (and turtles).

Basal leaves Arising directly from the roots.

Basis The floor of the igloolike structure of the barnacle which may be hard (calcified) or membranous.

Benthos, benthic The life associated with the bottom of a water basin.

Bivalve A mollusc with 2 valves, or shells (e.g., clam).

Brackish Water with a salinity of 0.5 to 30 ppt (see fig. 3; p. 12).

Bracts Modified leaves associated with the flower.

Bryozoan A sessile, colonial animal of the phylum Bryozoa.

Byssus, byssal In molluscs, a clump of threadlike fibers that anchor the shell to the substrate.

Calcareous Composed of calcium carbonate.

Carapace A shieldlike covering (or upper shell) in many crustaceans (and turtles).

Cardinal teeth In bivalves, the largest teeth present on inner shell surface, near the hinge.

Catadromous Migrating from fresh water to the ocean to breed.

Caudal Part of, or positioned on, the tail (e.g., caudal spot or fin).

Chitin, chitinous The skeletal substance of the shell or skin of arthropods made of the carbohydrate glucosamine.

Chondrophore In bivalves, a spoonlike pit in the shell hinge holding the padlike resilium.

Ciliate A member of the protozoan class Ciliatea, characterized by tiny hairlike cilia used for motility.

Cirrus (plural cirri) An elongate, fleshy appendage.

Community A group of plant and animal species living together in a habitat.

Compound leaf Composed of separate smaller leaflets.

Copepod A member of the order Copepoda in the arthropod class Crustacea.

Coriolis effect The deflection of air or water, relative to the solid earth beneath, as a result of the earth's eastward rotation. North of the equator this results in a deflection to the right.

Critical salinity A salinity of 5 to 8 ppt that marks a minimum of species diversity in an estuarine system.

Crustacean A member of the arthropod class Crustacea, including copepods, isopods, amphipods, barnacles, shrimp, and crabs.

Cypris The second larval, free-swimming stage of a barnacle.

Decomposer An organism, such as a bacterium, that breaks down organic matter, thereby freeing compounds for use by other organisms.

Decurved Curved downward.

Deposit feeder An animal that feeds on organic materials (e.g., detritus) deposited on a substrate.

Detritovore A detritus feeder.

Detritus, detrital Fragments of dead plants or animals in the process of decay; a major food source for many animals.

Dextral Right-handed, opposite of **sinistral**.

Diadromous Living in one salinity regime as an adult but migrating to another to spawn.

Diatom A microscopic plant; a single-celled alga.

Dihedral Posture of wings held above horizontal.

Dioecious Individuals of a species having distinct sexes; having two types of flowers (male and female) borne on separate plants.

Diversity, species The number of distinct species in a community or ecosystem.

Dorsal fin The median fin, situated along the midline of the back, supported by rays and often notched or divided.

Dorsolateral Neither directly down the center of the back (dorsal) nor at the side (lateral) of the body, but in between.

Ecology The study of the various relationships between organisms and their environment.

Ecosystem An assemblage of communities that exchange components and are, therefore, dependent on one another; an ecological unit.

Ecotone A transitional area between two communities.

Emergent species Herbaceous, nonwoody plant standing erect; appearing above the water surface.

Endemic species Confined to a specific habitat or region.

Energy flow Movement of energy through a food web, beginning with the solar energy fixed by green plants during photosynthesis.

Entrainment velocity The speed of water (e.g., seawater) drawn into another area (e.g., surface layer) vacated by outflowing water.

Ephyra (plural ephyrae) The tiny 8-armed stage of young jellyfish which matures into a medusa.

Epifauna, epifaunal Benthic animals that live on or move over the substrate.

Epiphyte, epiphytic A plant that is attached to another plant but is not parasitic.

Estuarine species An organism

that spends all or most of its life cycle in the estuary; a resident.

Estuary A semi-enclosed coastal body of water that has a measurable salinity gradient from its freshwater drainage to its ocean entrance.

Euryhaline Able to tolerate a wide range, or wide fluctuations, in salinity.

Fall line The boundary between the piedmont and the coastal plain where waterfalls often occur and where coastal cities (e.g., Baltimore, Washington, and Richmond) are sometimes located.

Faunal break A transition area where species diversity decreases rapidly or is at a minimum. Our estuary has 2: near the mouth of the Bay (25-30 ppt) and at the critical salinity (5-8 ppt).

Filter feeder An animal that filters or screens water flowing through or around its body to capture suspended food; a suspension feeder.

Floating-leaved plant A nonemergent aquatic species with leaves typically floating at the surface.

Flowering scale A modified leaf encasing a minute flower; typical of sedges, in which overlapping scales may resemble a bud.

Food chain The flow of organic material via feeding relationships from lower to higher trophic levels.

Food web A network of food chains depicting the feeding interactions among species in a given area.

Freshwater species An organism that typically lives in water with a salinity less than 0.5 ppt.

Frond In seaweeds, a leaflike form that lacks the vascular structure of true leaves in higher plants.

Gastropod A mollusc with only one shell (e.g., snail).

Gill cover Collectively, the various bones which cover the gills.

Habitat The native environment of an animal or plant.

Halophyte A salt-tolerant plant.

Herb, herbaceous Fleshy, nonwoody plant.

High marsh The elevated, irregularly flooded area of a marsh above MHT.

Holdfast In seaweeds, the anchoring structure at the base of the plant.

Hydranth In hydroids, the structure bearing the mouth and tentacles.

Hydroid The sessile polypoid stage of hydrozoans (Hydrozoa; Cnidaria); the medusoid stage is called the hydromedusa.

Infauna, infaunal Benthic animals that live within, or burrow through, bottom sediments.

Intertidal The area of a shoreline or tidal wetland between mean high and mean low tides.

Introduced species Not native; released locally either accidentally or purposely by man.

Isohaline A line that joins points of equal salinity concentration.

Isopod A member of the order Isopoda in the arthropod class Crustacea, with a body flattened from top to bottom.

Lateral line On the side of a fish, the series of pored scales associated with the sensory system that usually extends from behind the gill to the base of (or onto) the tail.

Limiting factor A condition, substance, or influence that in excess (or absence) limits the population growth or distribution of an organism.

Local species A species limited to a relatively small area or isolated locales within a given range.

Low marsh The regularly flooded zone of a tidal marsh below MHT.

Macrozooplankton The large, relatively mobile zooplankters easily seen with the naked eye; also macroplankton.

Marine species An organism that resides all or most of the time (and typically breeds) in the ocean where salinities exceed 30 ppt.

Median fins The unpaired, vertical fins: dorsal, anal, and caudal.

Medusa (plural medusae) The sexually reproductive stage of jellyfish; a free-floating form.

Megalopa (plural megalopae) The last larval stage of a crab (Decapoda) before metamorphosis into a juvenile.

Meroplankton Organisms that spend only part of their life cycle in the plankton state; planktonic larval stages.

Mesohaline Pertaining to moderately brackish water with a salinity of 5-18 ppt (see fig. 3; p. 12). The upper mesohaline is 10-18 ppt; the lower mesohaline is 5-10 ppt.

MHT Mean high tide.

Migrant A regular, seasonal visitor; a transient.

MLT Mean low tide.

Nauplius (plural nauplii) The earliest larval stage of crustaceans such as copepods and barnacles.

Neap tide The minimal high and low tides that occur in association with the second (or waxing, first quarter) and fourth (or waning, last quarter) phases of the moon; opposite of maximal **spring tides**.

Nekton Free-swimming aquatic organisms, such as fish.

Nematocyst The stinging cell of jellyfish and other cnidarians (Cnidaria).

Niche The functional role of an organism within a community or ecosystem, including its distribution, trophic level, and habitat.

Niche expansion The spread of a species into alternative habitats or feeding modes, in the absence of competition or due to a decrease in predation pressure.

Nursery grounds Areas utilized by larval and juvenile fishes; in the estuary, the oligohaline and lower mesohaline sections are the most productive.

Nutrients Compounds or elements required by organisms for growth and reproduction (C, O, N, P, etc.).

Oligohaline Pertaining to slightly brackish water with a salinity of 0.5 to 5 ppt (see fig. 3; p. 12).

Omnivore An organism that feeds on both animals and plants.

Operculum A lid or flap, such as the horny or limy plate attached at the foot of many gastropods, used to seal the shell opening (aperture).

Opposite leaves Occurring in pairs, with one leaf on either side of branch or stem.

Organic Any compound containing carbon (C).

Overenrichment The excessive loading of nutrients (e.g., N or P) in a body of water that results in algal blooms and associated turbid and anoxic conditions; eutrophication.

Ovipositor The egg-laying apparatus of certain insects.

Pallial sinus In bivalves, an indentation in the interior scar (pallial line), indicating where the siphon-retracting muscles are attached.

Palps In polychaete worms, one of several types of sensory appendages on the head.

Panicle An elongated, compound (branched) flower cluster.

Pannes Depressions in irregularly flooded salt marshes.

Parapodium (plural parapodia) In polychaete worms, one of the lateral footlike appendages.

Parotoid gland One of a pair of external wartlike glands on the shoulder, neck, or behind the eye in toads.

Pectoral fins The paired fins attached to the shoulder girdle, typically near the gills.

Pectoral scute The third scute on a turtle's plastron.

Peduncle The primary stalk of a flower or flower cluster.

Pelagic Living in open water (usually oceanic); opposite of **benthic**.

Pelvic fins The paired fins on the lower front part of the body.

Perennial plant One that lives for three years or more, typically supported by underground rhizomes, tubers, or bulbs.

Perigynium The inflated sac enclosing the seed of some sedges.

Periostracum In shelled molluscs, a skinlike outer covering on the shell.

Petiole The leafstalk.

Phytoplankton Planktonic plants (e.g., algae).

Plankton, planktonic Organisms that float at or near the surface of open water; some are capable of vertical migration.

Planula (plural planulae) The microscopic larvae of cnidarians.

Plastron The lower shell of a turtle (*see also* **Carapace**).

Polyhaline Pertaining to highly brackish water with a salinity of 18-30 ppt (see fig. 3; p. 12).

Polyp The asexual, sessile stage of anemones and jellyfish; column with a ring of tentacles.

Posterior Toward the rear; situated away from the anterior (front) part of the body; toward the "tail."

ppt (parts per thousand) Used in describing the concentration of salt in brackish and marine waters; refers to the number of parts (grams) of salt per thousand parts (grams) of water.

Precocial Having advanced development at birth; in mammals, born with eyes open and body furred.

Primary feathers (or primaries) The longest, outer flight feathers of the wing.

Primary productivity The net amount or rate of organic material produced by plants during photosynthesis.

Proboscis A snout or trunk; typically adapted for smelling, tasting, or feeding.

Protozoan A single-celled member of the phylum Protozoa.

Pulmonate snail An air-breathing snail that lacks gills.

Radular teeth In gastropod molluscs, a rasplike organ used in feeding.

Resilium A triangular ligament structure or pad along the inner hinge margin of a bivalve that causes the shell to spring open when the muscle relaxes.

Retention time The duration over which a volume of water cycles completely through a given basin.

Rhizome In perennial plants, an underground stem, usually horizontal, that produces aerial shoots.

Rootstalk A short erect or horizontal underground stem; a **rhizome** or rootstock.

Rostrum In shrimps, the bladelike projection between the eyes.

Saline Pertaining to seawater (over 30 ppt salinity); marine.

Salinity The measurement of dissolved salts in water; the number of grams (parts) of dissolved salts in 1,000 grams (parts) of water, usually expressed in parts per thousand (ppt).

Salinity gradient A change in salinity, either vertically or over the length of an estuary (horizontally), the latter shown by isohalines.

Scute A modified scale, often large and shieldlike.

Sessile (1) Permanently attached to substrate; stationary. (2) In plants, without a stalk (e.g., a sessile flower).

Seta (plural setae) A bristle; a hairlike extension especially in annelid worms.

Sinistral Left-handed; opposite of **dextral**.

Spadix A fleshy spike of flowers, sometimes enclosed by a spathe.

Spat Juvenile, newly attached oysters.

Spathe A large hoodlike bract or pair of bracts enclosing a spadix.

Spawn To release eggs and/or sperm into water.

Species (sp.; plural spp.) A distinct taxonomic group of interbreeding organisms.

Speculum In marsh ducks, the colorful band of secondary feathers on the wing.

Spire On a snail, the upper whorls of the shell from the apex to (but excluding) the body whorl.

Spring tide The maximal high and low monthly tides, which occur in conjunction with the first and third (new and full) phases of the moon; opposite of **neap tide**.

Submersed aquatic vegetation (SAV) Underwater aquatic plants.

Subspecies (ssp.) A taxonomic subgroup of interbreeding organisms that inhabit a geographic subdivision of the range of a given species.

Substrate The bottom surface of a body of water on/in which benthic organisms dwell (e.g., sand, mud, oyster shell).

Subtidal The zone of the shoreline and water basin below low tide, always covered by water.

Supratidal The zone of the shoreline above high tide.

Suspension feeder *See* **Filter feeder**

Test A hardened outer shell or covering.

Thermocline A depth zone in the water column where temperature changes dramatically; a density barrier.

Tidal current The horizontal movement of water masses coincident with the vertical tide.

Transient *See* **Migrant**

Trochophore A microscopic early larval stage of some segmented worms and molluscs.

Trophic level A food-producing or feeding level along a food chain (e.g., producer [plant], herbivore, carnivore, etc.).

Tubercle A small bump or wartlike projection.

Tunicate A member of the subphylum Urochordata, commonly called a sea squirt.

Turbidity Cloudiness in water derived from algae, suspended silt, or other impurities.

Tympanum The external eardrum visible on some frogs.

Uropods In crustaceans, the terminal pair of abdominal appendages.

Varix Prominent, raised axial rib (ridge) on the surface of a snail shell made during a major growth stoppage.

Veliger A molluscan larval stage which has ciliated bands and often an embryonic shell showing the hinge or beak (umbo).

Ventral The lower (bottom) side; opposite of **dorsal**.

Ventrolateral At the junction of side and bottom.

Wetlands Low areas (e.g., swamps, marshes, and tidal flats) that retain soil and moisture.

Whorl (1) Three or more leaves radiating from a single node. (2) A single turn in the spiral coil of a snail's shell.

Zoea (plural zoeae) An early larval stage of crabs and shrimp.

Zonation The distribution of plant and animal species into zones in response to environmental conditions such as salinity, soil type, elevation (or depth), and tides.

Zooid In colonial animals such as hydrozoans (Hydrozoa), one of the individuals of the colony.

Zooplankton Small planktonic animals (e.g., copepods).

Migratory Patterns and Life Cycles

NEARLY 300 species of fish frequent the Chesapeake and its tidal tributaries. Of these, most are visitors—migratory species that enter the Bay for a few months to forage or breed. Permanent residents are few, including the small killifishes, anchovies, and silversides that provide food for larger, transient species. *Freshwater fishes* that visit the estuary are of 2 types: *foragers* such as catfish that descend into the brackish regions of major rivers, and *catadromous species*, like the American eel, that traverse the estuary to spawn in the sea. At the other extreme, *marine fishes* visiting the Bay can be placed in 3 categories: *anadromous species*, *adult foragers*, and *nursery stocks*. Anadromous species such as the American shad (*below*) cross the estuary in spring to spawn in freshwater streams. Making a shorter journey, semi-anadromous species like the white perch (p. 203, *top*) are typically *estuarine* and migrate from the main Bay into freshwater areas to spawn. Of the foragers, adult bluefish (p. 202, *top*) breed in the ocean and invade the estuary only to feed. Some foragers like the Atlantic croaker (p. 202, *bottom*) spawn in the Atlantic Ocean near the mouth of the Bay, and their larvae are transported into the Chesapeake nursery. Here, they develop into juveniles and adults. In a similar fashion, the female blue crab (p. 203, *bottom*), after mating in the estuary, moves seaward and releases zoeae near the ocean. Afterwards, megalopae are carried by deepwater currents into the Bay, where the life cycle continues.

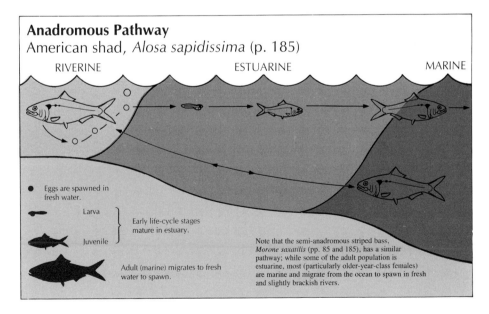

Anadromous Pathway
American shad, *Alosa sapidissima* (p. 185)

RIVERINE   ESTUARINE   MARINE

Eggs are spawned in fresh water.

Larva

Early life-cycle stages mature in estuary.

Juvenile

Adult (marine) migrates to fresh water to spawn.

Note that the semi-anadromous striped bass, *Morone saxatilis* (pp. 85 and 185), has a similar pathway; while some of the adult population is estuarine, most (particularly older-year-class females) are marine and migrate from the ocean to spawn in fresh and slightly brackish rivers.

Plates on pp. 201-203 adapted from Cronin and Mansueti 1971.

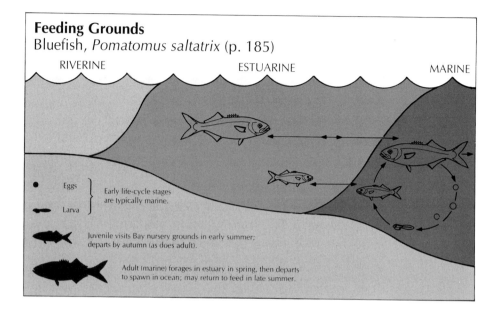

Feeding Grounds
Bluefish, *Pomatomus saltatrix* (p. 185)

RIVERINE   ESTUARINE   MARINE

● Eggs }
━ Larva } Early life-cycle stages are typically marine.

Juvenile visits Bay nursery grounds in early summer; departs by autumn (as does adult).

Adult (marine) forages in estuary in spring, then departs to spawn in ocean; may return to feed in late summer.

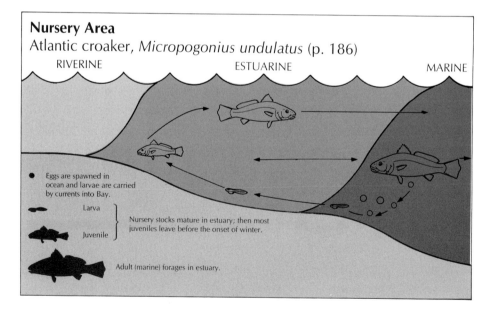

Nursery Area
Atlantic croaker, *Micropogonius undulatus* (p. 186)

RIVERINE   ESTUARINE   MARINE

● Eggs are spawned in ocean and larvae are carried by currents into Bay.

━ Larva }
Juvenile } Nursery stocks mature in estuary; then most juveniles leave before the onset of winter.

Adult (marine) forages in estuary.

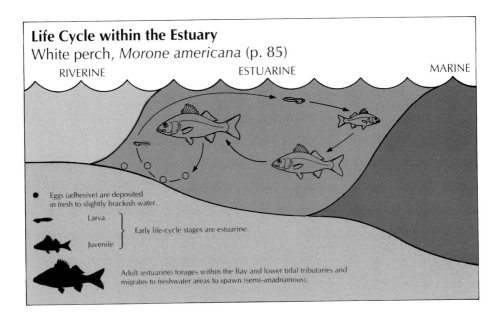

Life Cycle within the Estuary
White perch, *Morone americana* (p. 85)

RIVERINE   ESTUARINE   MARINE

● Eggs (adhesive) are deposited
in fresh to slightly brackish water.

Larva

Juvenile

} Early life-cycle stages are estuarine.

Adult (estuarine) forages within the Bay and lower tidal tributaries and
migrates to freshwater areas to spawn (semi-anadromous).

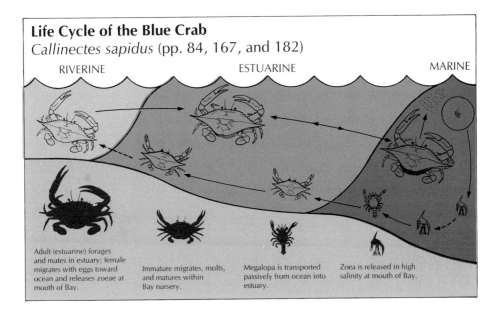

Life Cycle of the Blue Crab
Callinectes sapidus (pp. 84, 167, and 182)

RIVERINE   ESTUARINE   MARINE

Adult (estuarine) forages
and mates in estuary; female
migrates with eggs toward
ocean and releases zoeae at
mouth of Bay.

Immature migrates, molts,
and matures within
Bay nursery.

Megalopa is transported
passively from ocean into
estuary.

Zoea is released in high
salinity at mouth of Bay.

Selected References

American Ornithologists' Union. 1983. *Check-list of North American birds.* 6th ed. Washington: American Ornithologists' Union.

Army Corps of Engineers. 1977. *Wetlands plants of the eastern United States.* NADP 200-1-1. New York: U.S. Army Corps of Engineers.

Barnes, R. D. 1974. *Invertebrate zoology.* 3rd ed. Philadelphia: W. B. Saunders Co.

Borror, D. J., and R. E. White. 1970. *A field guide to the insects of America north of Mexico.* Boston: Houghton Mifflin Co.

Boschung, H. T., Jr., J. D. Williams, D. W. Gotshall, D. K. Caldwell, and M. C. Caldwell. 1983. *The Audubon Society field guide to North American fishes, whales, and dolphins.* New York: Alfred A. Knopf.

Burke, D. G., H. Groman, T. Henderson, J. A. Kusler, and E. J. Meyers, eds. 1985. *Wetlands of the Chesapeake: proceedings of the conference.* Washington: Environmental Law Institute.

Burt, W. H., and R. P. Grossenheider. 1976. *A field guide to the mammals.* 3rd ed. Boston: Houghton Mifflin Co.

Carter, V., P. T. Gammon, and N. C. Bartow. 1983. *Submersed aquatic plants of the tidal Potomac River.* Geological Survey Bulletin no. 1543. Washington: U.S. Department of the Interior.

Collins, J. T., R. Conant, R. E. Huheey, J. L. Knight, E. M. Rundquist, and H. M. Smith. 1982. *Standard common and current scientific names for North American amphibians and reptiles.* 2d ed. Athens: Society for the Study of Amphibians and Reptiles, Department of Zoology, Ohio University.

Conant, R. 1975. *A field guide to reptiles and amphibians of eastern and central North America.* 2d ed. Boston: Houghton Mifflin Co.

Cowardin, L. M., V. Carter, F. C. Golet, and E. T. LaRoe. 1979. *Classification of wetlands and deepwater habitats of the United States.* FWS/OBS-79/31. Washington: Office of Biological Ser-

vices, U.S. Fish and Wildlife Service.

Cronin, L. E. 1987. "The Bounty of the Bay: 1584-2034." In *Maryland our Maryland,* ed. V. Geiger, 39-68. New York: University Press of America.

Cronin, L. E., and A. J. Mansueti. 1971. The biology of the estuary. In *A symposium of the biological significance of estuaries.* Washington: Sport Fishing Institute.

Department of Agriculture. 1982. *National list of scientific plant names.* 2 vols. SCS-TP-159. Washington: Soil Conservation Service.

Environmental Protection Agency. 1982. *Chesapeake Bay: introduction to an ecosystem.* Washington: U.S. Environmental Protection Agency.

Farrand, J., Jr., ed. 1983. *The Audubon Society master guide to birding.* 3 vols. New York: Alfred A. Knopf.

Fassett, N. C. 1957. *A manual of aquatic plants.* Madison: University of Wisconsin Press.

Fernald, M. L. 1950. *Gray's manual of botany.* 8th ed. New York: American Book Co.

Godfrey, R. K., and J. W. Wooten. 1979 and 1981. *Aquatic and wetlands plants of the southeastern United States.* 2 vols. Athens: University of Georgia Press.

Gosner, K. L. 1971. *Guide to identification of marine and estuarine invertebrates.* New York: John Wiley and Sons.

———. 1979. *A field guide to the Atlantic seashore: from the Bay of Fundy to Cape Hatteras.* Boston: Houghton Mifflin Co.

Greeson, P. E., J. R. Clark, and J. E. Clark, eds. 1979. *Wetland functions and values: the state of our understanding.* Proceedings of the National Symposium on Wetlands, 1978. Bethesda, Md.: American Water Resources Association.

Hall, E. R. 1981. *The mammals of North America.* 2d ed. New York: John Wiley and Sons.

Halstead, B. W., M.D. 1980. *Dangerous marine animals.* Centreville, Md.: Cornell Maritime Press.

Harris, H. S., Jr. 1975. Distributional survey (Amphibia/Reptilia): Maryland and the District of Columbia. *Bulletin of the Maryland Herpetological Society* 11, no. 3: 73-170.

Hedeen, R. A. 1982. *Naturalist on the Nanticoke.* Centreville, Md.: Tidewater Publishers.

Hildebrand, S. F., and W. C. Schroeder. [1928] 1972. *Fishes of Chesapeake Bay.* Reprint. Washington: Smithsonian Institution Press.

Horton, T. 1987. *Bay country.* Baltimore: Johns Hopkins University Press.

Hotchkiss, N. 1972. *Common marsh, underwater, and floating-leaved plants of the United States and Canada.* New York: Dover Publications.

Jones, J. K., Jr., D. C. Carter, H. H. Genoways, R. S. Hoffman, and D. W. Rice. 1982. *Revised checklist of North American mammals north of Mexico, 1982.* Occasional Papers no. 80. Lubbock: The Museum, Texas Tech University.

Klingel, G. C. 1951. *The bay: a naturalist discovers a universe of life above and below the Chesapeake.* New York: Dodd, Mead and Co.

Larner, Y. R. 1979. *Virginia's birdlife: an annotated checklist.* Virginia Avifauna no. 2. Lynchburg: Virginia Society of Ornithology.

Lawrence, S. 1984. *The Audubon Society field guide to the natural places of the mid-Atlantic states: coastal.* New York: Random House, Pantheon Books.

Lee, D. S., C. R. Gilbert, C. H. Hocutt, R. E. Jenkins, D. E. McAllister, and J. R. Stauffer, Jr. 1980. *Atlas of North American freshwater fishes.* Publication no. 1980-12. Raleigh: North Carolina Biological Survey, North Carolina Museum of Natural History.

Lippson, A. J., ed. 1973. *The Chesapeake Bay in Maryland: an atlas of natural resources.* Baltimore: Johns Hopkins University Press.

Lippson, A. J., and R. L. Lippson. 1984. *Life in the Chesapeake Bay: an illustrated guide to fishes, invertebrates, and plants of bays and inlets from Cape Cod to Cape Hatteras.* Baltimore: Johns Hop-

kins University Press.

Lippson, A. J., et al., eds. 1981. *Environmental atlas of the Potomac estuary.* Baltimore: Johns Hopkins University Press.

Magee, D. W. 1981. *Freshwater wetlands: a guide to common indicator plants of the Northeast.* Amherst: University of Massachusetts Press.

Manooch, C. S., III, and D. Raver, Jr. 1984. *Fisherman's guide to the fishes of the southeastern United States.* Raleigh: North Carolina State Museum of Natural History.

Martin, A. C., H. S. Zim, and A. L. Nelson. 1951. *American wildlife and plants: a guide to wildlife food habits.* New York: Dover Publications.

McClane, A. J. 1978a. *Field guide to freshwater fishes of North America.* New York: Holt, Rinehart and Winston.

———. 1978b. *Field guide to saltwater fishes of North America.* New York: Holt, Rinehart and Winston.

McCormick, J., and H. A. Somes. 1982. *The coastal wetlands of Maryland.* Annapolis: Maryland Department of Natural Resources.

McLusky, D. S. 1971. *Ecology of estuaries.* London: Heinemann Educational Books.

Meanley, B. 1972. *Swamps, river bottoms and canebrakes.* Barre, Mass.: Barre Publishers.

———. 1975. *Birds and marshes of the Chesapeake Bay country.* Centreville, Md.: Tidewater Publishers.

———. 1978. *Blackwater.* Centreville, Md.: Tidewater Publishers.

———. 1982. *Waterfowl of the Chesapeake Bay country.* Centreville, Md.: Tidewater Publishers.

Metzgar, R. G. 1973. *Wetlands in Maryland.* Maryland Department of State Planning Publication no. 157. Annapolis: Maryland Department of Natural Resources.

Niering, W. A. 1966. *The life of the marsh: the North American wetlands.* New York: McGraw-Hill Book Co.

———. 1985. *Wetlands.* The Audubon Society Nature Guides. New York: Alfred A. Knopf.

Nybakken, J. W. 1982. *Marine biology: an ecological approach.* New York: Harper and Row.

Perkins, E. J. 1974. *The biology of estuaries*

and coastal waters. New York: Academic Press.

Perry, B. 1985. *A Sierra Club naturalist's guide to the middle Atlantic coast.* San Francisco: Sierra Club Books.

Peterson, R. T. 1980. *A field guide to the birds east of the Rockies.* 4th ed. Boston: Houghton Mifflin Co.

Peterson, R. T., and M. McKenny. 1968. *A field guide to wildflowers of northeastern and north-central North America.* Boston: Houghton Mifflin Co.

Petrides, G. A. 1972. *A field guide to trees and shrubs.* 2d ed. Boston: Houghton Mifflin Co.

Pomeroy, L. R., and R. G. Wiegert, eds. 1981. *The ecology of a salt marsh.* New York: Springer-Verlag.

Reid, G. K., and R. D. Wood. 1976. *Ecology of inland waters and estuaries.* 2d ed. New York: Van Nostrand Reinhold Co.

Reiger, G. 1983. *Wanderer on my native shore.* New York: Simon and Schuster.

Robbins, C. S., and D. Bystrak. 1977. *Field list of the birds of Maryland.* Maryland Avifauna no. 2. Baltimore: Maryland Ornithological Society.

Robbins, C. S., B. Bruun, and H. S. Zim. 1983. *Birds of North America: a guide to field identification.* 2d ed. New York: Golden Press.

Robins, C. R., and G. C. Ray. 1986. *A field guide to Atlantic coast fishes of North America.* Boston: Houghton Mifflin Co.

Robins, C. R., R. M. Bailey, C. E. Bond, J. R. Brooker, E. A. Lachner, R. N. Lea, and W. B. Scott. 1980. *A list of common and scientific names of fishes from the United States and Canada.* 4th ed. Special Publication no. 12. Bethesda, Md.: American Fisheries Society.

Schubel, J. R. 1981. *The living Chesapeake.* Baltimore: Johns Hopkins University Press.

———. 1986. *The life and death of the Chesapeake Bay.* College Park: University of Maryland Sea Grant College.

Schubel, J. R., and D. W. Pritchard. 1987. "A brief description of the Chesapeake Bay." In *Containment problems and management of living Chesapeake Bay resources.* S. K. Majumdar, L. W. Hall, Jr., and H. M. Austin, eds. Easton: Pennsylvania Academy of Science.

Silberhorn, G. M. 1982. *Common plants of the mid-Atlantic coast: a field guide.* Baltimore: Johns Hopkins University Press.

Smith, H. M., and E. D. Brodie, Jr. 1982. *Reptiles of North America: a guide to field identification.* New York: Golden Press.

Smith, H. M., and S. Barlowe. 1978. *Amphibians of North America: a guide to field identification.* New York: Golden Press.

Teal, J., and M. Teal. 1969. *Life and death of the salt marsh.* New York: Random House, Ballantine Books.

Thomas, B. 1976. *The swamp.* New York: W. W. Norton and Co.

Tiner, R. W., Jr. 1987. *A field guide to coastal wetland plants of the northeastern United States.* Amherst: University of Massachusetts Press.

Tobey, F. J. 1985. *Virginia's amphibians and reptiles: a distributional survey.* Purcellville: Virginia Herpetological Survey.

Virginia Marine Resources Commission. 1982. *Wetlands guidelines.* Newport News: Virginia Marine Resources Commission.

Warner, W. W. 1976. *Beautiful swimmers: watermen, crabs and the Chesapeake Bay.* Boston: Little, Brown and Co., Atlantic Monthly Press Book.

Wass, M. L., and T. D. Wright. 1969. *Coastal wetlands of Virginia.* Special Report no. 10. Gloucester Point: Virginia Institute of Marine Science.

Wass, M. L., et al., eds. 1972. *A check list of the biota of lower Chesapeake Bay.* Special Publication no. 65. Gloucester Point: Virginia Institute of Marine Science.

White, C. P. 1982. *Endangered and threatened wildlife of the Chesapeake Bay region: Delaware, Maryland, and Virginia.* Centreville, Md.: Tidewater Publishers.

Index to Illustrated Species

SCIENTIFIC NAMES

COMMON NAMES